SIMI
SINCE 1876

SONOMA

CONTENTS 770 ml (26. Fl. OZ)

LABOURÉ-ROI
MAISON FONDÉE EN 1832

PRODUCE OF FRANCE

PULIGNY-MONTRACHET
1er CRU LES FOL...
APPELLATION PULIGNY-MONTRACHET

MIS EN BOUTEILLE PAR
LABOURÉ-ROI, NÉGOCIANT-ÉLEVEUR A NUITS-S...

WHITE BURGUNDY
TABLE WINE

FONDÉE   EN 1859

...JADOT
...CONTROLÉE

...PAR
...INE · COTE-D'OR · FRANCE

3/4 ...

BRUT IMPÉRIAL
1971
Maison fondée en 1743

MOËT & CHANDON
CHAMPAGNE
ÉPERNAY-FRANCE

PRODUCE OF FRANCE   N.M. 3.342.272

ALCOHOL 12,6% BY VOLUME

RIDGE
CALIFORNIA
ZINFANDEL
LYTTON SPRINGS
1976

ELLIS SON & VIDLER L...
LONDON   HAST...

1977
Royal Silver Jubilee
MADEIRA
Bual
Vintage
1952

SPECIMEN ✚

CHÂTEAU
LA MISSION HAUT BRION
APPELLATION GRAVES CONTRÔLÉE
Grand Cru classé
1970

FREEMARK ABBEY

TIO PEPE
REGISTERED TRADE MARK

TRY CHILLED

GONZALEZ, BYASS
JEREZ

70 cl.e

...ez, Byass Ltd., 91 Park St., London. W.1

SANDEMAN.

BY APPOINTMENT
TO HER MAJESTY
QUEEN ELIZABETH II

WINE MERCHANTS
GEO. G. SANDEMAN
SONS & CO. LIMITED

CREAM
SHERRY

Fine Rich

SANDEMAN
BROS. & CO.   EST. 1...
Proprietors: The House of...
PRODUCE O...

17.8% vol.

KENWOO...

SOCIÉTÉ CIVILE DES DOMAINES
PROPRIÉTAIRE

BORDEAUX
FRANCE

SONOMA COU...
Gamay Beau...
PRIME 1976 VINT...

1974
Cabernet Sauvignon
Napa Valley
Stag's Leap Vineyards
Cask 23

STAG'S LEAP WINE CELL...

Produced & bottled by Stag's Leap Wine Cellars, Napa, Calif. · Alcohol 13% ...

1977
Chateau St. Jean

PAVILLON BLANC
1970
CHÂTEAU MARGAUX
APPELLATION BORDEAUX CONTROLÉE
GRAND VIN BLANC SEC DE BORDEAUX
SOCIÉTÉ CIVILE DU CHATEAU MARGAUX
PROPRIÉTAIRE A MARGAUX (GIRONDE)
PRODUCE OF FRANCE

MIS EN BOUTEILLE AU CHÂTEAU
DÉPOSÉ   FRANCE

WINDSOR VINEYARDS

PRODUCED AND BOTTLED BY WINDSOR VINEYARDS
WINDSOR, SONOMA COUNTY, CALIFORNIA. ALCOHOL 12% BY VOLUME.

MADEIRA

Mea... Rich

IMPORTED BY
COSSART GORDON & Co. Ltd
LONDON SW1

Schramsberg
FOUNDED 1862

CRÉMANT

NAPA VALLEY
CHAMPAGNE   DEMI-SEC

VILLA BANF...

Dry Red Wine
Chianti Classico
DENOMINAZIONE DI ORIGINE CONTROLLATA
Riserva
The noble red wine of Tuscany.

THE
DOUBLEDAY
WINE COMPANION
1983

A vineyard in the Lombardy region of Italy, which is noted for producing particularly fine red wines.

THE DOUBLEDAY WINE COMPANION 1983

James Wagenvoord

Doubleday & Company, Inc.
Garden City, New York

Library of Congress Cataloging in Publication Data

Wagenvoord, James.
    The Doubleday wine companion, 1983.
    Bibliography: p.
    Includes index.
    1. Wine and wine making.   I. Doubleday and
Company, inc.   II. Title
TP548.W27   641.2122

ISBN 0-385-18516-2

Library of Congress Catalog Card Number 81-43751

Firestone Vineyard, Santa Barbara, California.

A James Wagenvoord Studio, Inc. Book

Author-Editor—James Wagenvoord

Associate Editors—Fiona St. Aubyn, Patricia Coen

Researcher-Writers—Fiona St. Aubyn, Patricia Coen, Glynn O'Donnell, Howard Smallowitz

Research Assistant—Tracy Tang

Copy Editor—Cyrus Rogers

Photography—James Wagenvoord

Index—Maro Riofrancos

Design—Ginger Legato

Acknowledgments

I am grateful to the many people who generously gave me their time and insight during the creation of *The Doubleday Wine Companion 1983*.

The following people and organizations deserve particular credit—*Villa Banfi*—Lucio Sorre, Carmel Tintle; *Heublein, Inc.* Alexander McNally, Tom Cockrill, Erik Pierce, Ann Marie Kall, John Cox; *Pedro Domecq*—Michael Domecq, Marlene Sandground; *German Wine Information Bureau*—Lamar Elmore, Alan Olson; *Buckingham Corporation*—Chris Avent; *Lauber Imports*—Ed Lauber; *French Government Tourist Office*—Françoise Le Tondeaux; *Browne Vintners Company*—George Scheppler; *Sherry Institute of Spain*—Dan Langdon, Irving Smith Kogan; *Christian Brothers*—Brother Timothy, Peg Pavia; *Benmarl Wine Company*—Mark Miller; *San Francisco Wine Museum*—Ernest Mittelberger, Mary Rodgers; *Christie's*—Jacqueline Quillen; *John Harvey & Sons Ltd. (UK)*—Michael McWatters, John Mostyn, Michael Hobbs; *All Souls College, Oxford University (UK)*—Dr. Bryan Wilson; *Cossart Gordon & Company Ltd. (UK)*—David Cossart; *The Cafe Royal (UK)*—Percy Smith, George Robertson; *Croft & Company Ltd. (UK)*—Ben Howkins; *Ellis' Son & Vidler Ltd. (UK)*—Major Bruce Shand, Brian Steedman, Michael Card; *Government Hospitality (UK)*—Brigadier Cowan, Jack Brearley, Colin Taylor; *The Guild of Sommeliers (UK)*—Geoffrey Hasler; *Gonzalez*

Cottages and a vineyard in Alsace, France.

Byass, Ltd. (UK)–Geoffrey Hawkings-Byass, Anita Craig; *Malmaison Wine Club (UK)*–Elizabeth Morcom; *British Transport Hotels, Ltd. (UK)*–Clive Coates; *George G. Sandeman Sons & Company, Ltd. (UK)*–Timothy Sandeman, David Sandeman; Christopher Selmes (UK)–David and Vivian Reigelman; *U.S. Lithograph*–Joanne Blackwelder, Colleen Neff; Kevin Shannon.

A special thanks must also go to–Robert Travers; Bernard Portet; Joseph Heitz; Ben Snyder; James Prevett (UK); Commander R. D. Ross, RN (UK); David Palengat (UK); JBS Associates, Ltd. (UK); Peter Lewis (UK); Ann Polya-Ramsey; Elizabeth Shaw; David Milligan; Catherine Bardy; Uta Hoffmann; David Brokaw; Frank De Falco; Lucio Caputo; Maria Woodley; Bel & Stanton; John Grisanti; Charles Mara, Robert Dulong; Byron Tosi, Dana Abrams; Elizabeth Grant; François Zilliox; John Loder, Margaret Kerns; Roger Bowlin; Ron Fonte; Arthur and Glorya Hale, Shirley Knudson; Sam Aaron; Edwin Oppenheimer.

Lastly I am grateful for the help that was given to me by the following people–Oliver and Gloria Jessel (UK); Mireille Giuliano; Stephanie Steffansen; Frank Passanante; Leslie Sharpe; Brian Roberts; Octavio Abarca Castelli; Louikainos Karonis; Ioannis Cambas; Gerald Keller; The Embassy of Spain; Marjorie Dundas; Carleen Beard; Harvey Possert, Susan French; Sotheby's New York and

7

These rolling hills, well-kept vineyard and distant patches of oak trees are typical of California's coastal wine region.

London; Mary Caroline St. Aubyn, UK; Rupert Carington, UK; Joseph Sarig; Portuguese Government Trade Office; Ron Barnes, Sakowitz Department Stores; Rosamond Kaufman; Lois Leal; Jan Wells; Ely Callaway, Bev Ashbrook; Janet Trefethen; Richard Strousse; Marsha Palanci; Brian Abott; Jean Ficklin; Gerald Vitek; Carolyn Wente; John Taddeucci; Myron Redford; Lolly Mitchell; Bob Wollersheim; Lucille Canepa; Fay Tucker; Holli Tanana; Angela Seracini; Betty Ann Held; Walter S. Taylor, Lorraine Donley; Judith Braun; Scott Phillips; Robert Deford; Denise Deyette Taylor; Marianne Eddins; Connie Johnson; James Powell; J. Renier Van Tuyn; Debbie Fields; Dan Soloman; Michaela Rodeno; Carol Parden; Barry Miller; Kathleen Welch; Arthur Gerold; Speed-Graphics; Mary Lyons; Pamela Magginetti; Eden Lee-Murray; Corey Romao; Elizabeth St. John; Richard Kankaris; William Rice; Denman Moody, Jr.; Kenneth Bradley; Steven R. Truter; Robert Parker, Jr; Lewis Martin; Bill Davis; Humbert Travel; The World of Oz; Hanns Ebensten Travel Inc; Barbara Glunz; Lou Iacucci, Bill Singer.

PICTURE CREDITS

Bordeaux Wine Information Bureau; The Wine Spectrum; Guild

Wineries and Distilleries; Schenley Industries, Inc.; Sakonnet Vineyard; Christian Brothers Winery; The Christian Brothers Collection at The Wine Museum of San Francisco; German Information Center; The Buckingham Corporation; Beringer Vineyards; Benmarl Vineyards; Italian Wine Center; Sogge Studio; Wiederkehr Wine Cellars; United Vintners; Beaulieu Vineyards; Chateau St. Jean; Wollersheim Winery; Joseph Garneau Company; Bouchard Père et Fils, Beaune, France; John W. Ray, Mobile, Alabama; The Wine Museum of San Francisco; Almaden Vineyards; Trefethen Vineyards; Julius Wile Sons & Co., Inc.; Joseph E. Seagrams & Sons, Inc.; Wente Brothers; Banholzer Wine Cellars; Moet & Chandon, Epernay, France; Bronte Champagne & Wines Co., Inc.; The Taylor Wine Company; White Mountain Vineyards; Ficklin Vineyards; Stone Hill Wine Co., Inc.; German Wine Information Bureau; The French Embassy; Paul Masson Vineyards; Bully Hill Wine Company. The Franz W. Sichel Glass Collection at the Wine Museum of San Francisco; Jennifer Young; Philippe Cottin; WNET New York; House of Sandeman; Sherry Institute of Spain; Pedro Domecq; Charles Mara; John Loder; Terrence McCarthy; John Grisanti; Christie's; Heublein, Inc; California Wine Institute; French Government Tourist Office.

Contents

The Wine Year

 It was a planning session for another wine-tasting. This tasting would be shorter than most (less than ten minutes). But the projected attendance (over 70,000), the location (Denver's Mile High Stadium), and the moment (half-time of a Denver Broncos' football game just a few weeks after the completion of a wine harvest) gave the idea the scope of a Woodstock of wine-sipping. That such an event could even be seriously considered by a wineshop (it's now tentatively scheduled for the fall of 1983) is testimony that Wine with a capital W is settling in as a fixed element of the American leisure culture.

This attitude is relatively recent within the United States. For years, wine was accepted as a beverage for special occasions, as part of a ritual. In effect, wine overwhelmed the individual. Wine producers, by treating wine as fashion, were themselves largely responsible for the state of the art. And many wine drinkers, rather than trusting their own experience, accepted the dogma that only certain wines were to be drunk only on certain occasions and only by certain people.

But finally the barriers are down and few people in the wine world take exception to the thought that wine has but a single purpose—to give pleasure to a drinker.

Living, as we do, in an era where last season's failed television programs immediately become questions in nostalgia quizzes, to look back, even to the mid-seventies, the period when wine began to actually become a broadly based consumer subject, is to look back a full generation. Consider a few numbers. In 1975, slightly over 200,000,000 gallons of wine were shipped into trade channels in the United States. In the year 1981 the total was in excess of 350,000,000 gallons. Perhaps the most significant trend of the period was the growth of still (non-sparkling) white wine as a cocktail and as a table wine. In 1975, thirteen times as much red wine as white was consumed. By 1982, consumption had shifted radically and white wine was outselling red at a ratio of 3 to 1. And in 1981, a landmark was reached when, for the first time, table wine overtook hard liquor in United States beverage consumption. Other early '80s industry media headlines tell other parts of the story. For instance, more tourists now visit the Napa Valley winemakers than visit Disneyland. More than fifty wine magazines and journals reach millions of subscribers. The number of wine bars in the United States grew sevenfold between 1975 and 1982. Half of the nation's daily newspapers with circulations in excess of 100,000 offer regularly scheduled wine columns. And in 1982, over 1,000,000 people enrolled in wine appreciation courses. Behind the statistics on where we've been and projections as to where we're going are people who drink wine as a cocktail or apéritif, and as a complement and accompaniment to food. It all comes down to a glassful of wine.

A Problem of Riches

The problem that faces the wine buyer is positive in nature. It's that there are an incredible number of specific wines available on the nation's wine shelves. And no one, not a single self-styled or popularly acclaimed "expert," can keep up with all of the action that occurs in the wine marketplace. This fact, however, should not be intimidating, for it is possible to be an intelligent wine drinker and get the most out of the money that you want to spend. It only requires some interest, and a willingness to ask a few questions and to experiment, to try out some of the products of the vineyards of the world. The position of the United States as a relatively new but unquestionably important market for the world's wine producers is the best thing going for an American wine drinker. Throughout the country, the consumer indeed possesses a tremendous amount of clout and control in the marketplace.

Magnum —
1.5 liters (2 bottles)
Double Magnum —
3.0 liters (4 bottles)
Jeroboam —
4.5 liters (6 bottles)
A jeroboam of sparkling wine is equal to 3 liters.
Imperial —
6.0 liters (8 bottles)
Salmanazar —
9.0 liters (12 bottles)

For example, when French wine prices go up, you can switch to other wines. When German wines or California wines go up in price, switch back to France or Italy or try the wines of Argentina, Chile, or Spain. As a wine drinker with three to five dollars in your hand, you can literally shop the world and have a choice of twenty-five to thirty different wines. The variety is phenomenal, and your power—as you determine what you like—is enormous.

WINEMAKING BASICS

The making of still table wine begins in the vineyards with the selection and planting of grape varieties, a result of carefully considering the grape types that can be best produced from a particular soil and within a particular climate.

The spring to fall growing cycle ends when the mature grape possesses what a winemaker considers to be a proper balance of sugar and acidity. The actual moment of harvest is determined, as a rule, through a combination of scientific testing of the grape's sugar levels and the individual judgment as to whether the grape will continue to improve if left for additional time on the vine. The primary steps in the processing of wine include crushing, pressing, fermentation, racking, and bottling.

A modern press, capable of extracting juice from crushed grapes without breaking the seeds.

Crushing

The grapes are crushed (lightly pressed) as soon as possible after picking. The mass of the juice and the grape solids that accumulate as a result of the crush, termed the "must," is then treated with sulfur dioxide, a sterilizing agent that kills potentially harmful microorganisms without diminishing the natural wine yeasts that have already formed on the grapes.

Pressing

This is, in effect, a second crush, which separates the juice from the solid grape residues (skins, stems, and seeds). The quality of the extracted juice is in inverse relation to the degree that the must is pressed. Some premium wines are made from free-run juice, which can be drawn from relatively unpressed must. Juice from must pressed two or three times in order to extract all the juice that is available is used for blending lesser wines. White wines, which are often made from red-skinned grapes, are made from grapes that are pressed promptly after crushing and before the juice begins to pick up the tannins and the pigments of the skins and stems. Red wines, on the other hand, are left "on the must" for a time. This juice is separated later during a stage of the fermentation process.

Fermentation

Following the pressing, the juice is transferred to a fermentation tank, where it is innoculated with a small dose of carefully bred and purified wine yeast that supplements the natural yeasts that form on the grape skins. Fermentation is a process in which the yeasts convert the natural sugars in the grape juice into alcohol. The actual fermentation, which begins within several hours of the transfer of the juice to the tanks, continues until one of two things happen naturally, or a third artificial act is performed: 1. all the sugars are consumed, 2. the alcohol content of the new wine reaches the level at which the yeasts are neutralized, or 3. alcohol is added to the mixture, killing the yeast and halting the fermentation process.

Refrigerated stainless steel fermentation tanks.

One of the most important, relatively recent, improvements in the winemaker's art has been the development and use of a technique called cold fermentation. Fermentation, the tumultuous action of yeasts on the sugar and the conversion of sugar to alcohol, generates considerable heat. The first three or four days the fermenting juices bubble, as if they were boiling. And if fermentation is not checked, it will extract the natural sugar, resulting in high alcohol content. The wine will then require a longer time to develop—more time in the cask and in the bottle. If, however, fermentation is controlled, using a coolant system of coils wrapped around the fermenting vat, whenever the temperature reaches a specific level (seldom in excess of 60°F.), the coils are activated, the temperature is dropped, and the fermenting juice is cooled. By holding down the heat in the sealed, oxygen-tight fermentation vats, the pace of fermentation is slowed and can be controlled by the winemaker. The result is a wine that is fruitier, fresher-tasting, and, depending on the winemaker's goal, a wine with a predetermined degree of sweetness. Cold fermentation was introduced as an American winemaking technique during the late 1960s and early 1970s. Since the mid-1970s this system has been adopted in many of the world's major wine-producing areas.

Racking

Following fermentation, the new wine is transferred to other tanks where the process known as clarification begins. The wine is allowed to stand quietly until most of the residue suspended in the liquid settles to the bottom of the tank. Once the residue, known as the lees, has fallen, the nearly clear wine is transferred—pumped off from the top—into other vats. The transfer, called racking, is carried out as soon as possible after fermentation in order to lessen the chance of disagreeable characteristics being picked up and retained by the wine. Every few months thereafter the wine is

The following facts were gathered by the Virginia Department of Agriculture and Commerce: One ton of grapes makes 200 gallons of juice. 200 gallons of juice makes 180 gallons of wine. 180 gallons of wine is equal to 900 bottles. Four tons of grapes per acre equals 3,600 bottles.

—The Wine Spectator

drained off into clean containers, leaving the lees behind. The racking process is repeated several times before a wine is ready for final treatment and bottling. Red wines and some whites go directly into wooden casks for aging following their first racking. The casks, usually made of oak or redwood, impart some of the wood flavor to the wine and allow the wine to breathe slowly. During the aging period, other filtering and clarifying processes will be carried out.

Wines such as the many white wines, and most light red wines, which are not aged in wood, undergo their own final clarification processes following a second racking. This is followed by other finishing operations. Blending, if any, is done, and bottling, and then a final treatment with sulfur dioxide, or a last microfiltering, which sterilizes any bacteria bottled. Once a wine is bottled and corked, it will still continue to develop and age, each at its own particular pace.

There are two reasons for drinking wine: one is, when you are thirsty, to cure it; the other, when you are not thirsty, to prevent it . . . Prevention is always better than cure.
— *Thomas Love Peacock*

VINTAGE

The word gives rise to countless perceptions. Wine growers live or die by it. Experts violently debate it. And many self-styled wine insiders loudly misuse it.

Vintage is simply the word used to designate the year in which a given wine's grapes were harvested. The vintage, or vintage year, is the year of the harvest. Nothing more than that. If a bottle states on its label "Vintage 1974," for example, that's the year in which the grapes used to make that particular wine were harvested.

That's simple, but *nothing* about wine is quite that simple, nor should it be, perhaps, for a subject that has so deliciously fascinated mankind for millennia.

A "vintage wine" means a wine that carries a vintage designation on its label because that wine is made exclusively from grapes harvested in a single year. Only a very small percentage of wines carry such a vintage designation, for most wines are made from grapes harvested during several different years. But it's not just ordinary wine which doesn't tell you its exact beginnings. Several of the world's best wines are also non-vintage. Sherry is just one example of a fine wine lacking a specific vintage, or date of birth.

Surprisingly, a non-vintage version of a specific wine type may, in certain cases, be better than its prouder vintage cousin. The basic difference between the vintage and non-vintage version of the same good wine is that the non-vintage version will be a pleasant, drinkable, and enjoyable wine, consistent from year to year, but it will never have great characteristics. However, in a poor or barely average year, the vintage wine will not be as good as the less heralded non-vintage version.

The confusion and controversy over vintage occurs when experts debate the quality of a certain vintage and when would-be connoisseurs mistake a bad wine produced in a good year for a good wine. The two are far from synonymous. The experts make their very subjective judgments by continually comparing different vintages. But not all wines in a great year are necessarily even good, and some wines from a poor vintage year will be excellent.

The reason for this apparent paradox is that the elements that add up to a great vintage—perfect wine-growing weather capped by a bountiful crop harvested at the optimum moment—simply do not occur uniformly and universally within a wine-growing region. One cannot say, for example, that any vintage appraisal in Germany is universally true. Within Germany there are eleven distinct wine regions. Within each of those regions there are hundreds and hundreds of vineyards, each with its own unique microclimate. Rather than one absolute vintage, it's really like a huge smorgasbord of vintages. Thus, what was a gruesome growing year in nearly all of France, for example, may not really have been very bad at all for Monsieur Saoul's tiny vineyard.

As a result, blindly following vintage charts—those miniature cards furtively glanced at by shoppers in the aisles of major liquor stores—is not that valid an idea. To be sure, the growing year and the harvest conditions are significant factors in understanding wine, but it isn't possible to reduce a nation's or even a region's wine taste, style, and quality to numerical simplicity.

The years 1963, 1965, and 1968, for example, are frequently referred to as really bad numbers. These are the worst of the bad years for French wines. The weather was so awful that in those years some French vineyards didn't even produce a single grape. And many wine beginners go around mouthing 63-65-68 as if this were the secret formula to warding off the evil eye. Yet, a number of people have written about some quite good '65 and '68 Bordeaux, especially the great growths. And many of these falsely generalized "bad year" Bordeaux are excellent and still available in wine-shops at *very* low prices.

Which brings up an undeniable point: vintage does affect price. When the growing period is nearly complete, and wine merchants begin to suspect that it will be a good year, the prices for that year's still unharvested crop already start to creep up. Once harvested and bottled, and once the experts have their palates on it, and a year has been designated as "great"—then the sky's the limit. National wine councils and artful wine promoters do the rest: the year is called *sensational*. The prices surely will be,

The wine cellar of Kloster Eberbach, headquarters of the German Wine Academy.

but not all the wines. Even France's legendary great 1961, or Germany's 1971, for example, produced some disappointing wines. But those wines come from a great vintage year—and greatest of all are their prices!

To taste and, from that taste, to be able to identify a specific vintage from a particular wine is a great art, but one that with patience and practice any serious wine person can learn. First, you must carefully construct a wine memory on your palate. Start with a wine you particularly like. Taste different vintages of that wine and keep detailed notes. Choose one vintage as your own standard by which you will measure and remember all others. Keep going back to that standard until your palate recognizes each vintage as measured against it. Even if you should never become truly proficient at easily identifying a specific year, you will establish your own personal standards for rating a particular wine's vintage—personal and independent from any widely circulated vintage charts.

And while the vintage designation may be an indicator of general quality for that year, its greater significance is in indicating when a wine is ready for drinking. That's the moment when your personal preference—and palate—far outweighs any numbers on a wine bottle's label.

PAYING UP

The price you pay for a bottle of wine is the product of a complex mix of closely connected variables. Taste—the result of the winemaker's skill and the weather—is but one of a number of factors that establish a wine's retail price. Supply, demand, and reputation also play integral parts in the setting of a wine's price. When added to "experts'" determination of quality, these elements become the basis of the price assigned to a wine released into general distribution.

A rich meal without wine is like an expensive automobile equipped with hard rubber tires.

—Roy Louis Alciatore, Proprietor of Antoine's, New Orleans

Getting to the Shelves

The business of distribution and the language used in the business of moving wine from wineries to wineshops can give rise to a confusion both in reading a label and shopping a wine for drinking. And it is the framework of the pricing structure that dictates the final price you pay for an individual bottle of wine. It begins, of course, for either the domestic or imported wines, with the winemaker who either grows and processes his own grapes or buys grapes from individual grape farmers and processes the grapes into his particular labeled wines. The French example can be considered reasonably typical of the imported wine system. The sequence flows from the grower or winemaker, to the French *négociant*/shipper, to the U.S. importer, then to a statewide or local distributor, and finally to the retailer.

The Négociant/Shipper

In most instances it is the shipper who will choose and assemble estate-bottled château wines from different vineyards or, as happens frequently, maintain and use his own facilities for master blending, finishing, and aging wines prior to moving them in the direction of wine drinkers. Although modern winemaking technology can rescue a relatively poor harvest from doom, it is nature that continues to rule the quality potential of the crop. Experts' evaluations of that quality represent the initial step in determining what a wine from a particular harvest will cost. In effect, and justifiably, many of the leading French shippers—Joseph Drouhin, Louis Jadot, Alexis Lichine, and B & G, to name only a few of the leading *négociant*/shippers—have become accepted as brand names representing consistent standards of quality. The U.S. importer buys from the shipper when the wine is moved from its source into the American wine trade.

Sherry butts in the main patio of the House of Sandeman in Jerez.

The Importer

The importer, federally licensed to bring wine into the country and allowed to ship wines across state lines, sells to distributors. Only in some states, such as New York State, can an importer also function as a distributor. As a result, many do sell directly to retailers at, at least theoretically, more competitive prices.

With wines produced and distributed within the United States, the distributor, instead of being supplied by an importer, works directly with a wine producer. It is the wine producer who, whether he grows his own grapes or produces wine from individual grape growers, is basically in control of the sequence and represents the first tier of the domestic "three-tier system" (producer, distributor, retailer).

The Distributor

Licensed by the individual states, a distributor is the traditional link with the retailer. Legally licensed to sell statewide, the majority of independent distributors specialize in specific geographic areas within a state. They sell directly to retail outlets, i.e., liquor stores, wine specialty shops, and, in the states that have wine sales controlled by state governments, the distributor works directly with state buying agencies. They are also the suppliers to what is referred to as on-premise sellers, the restaurants, bars, caterers, and vendors who sell and serve wine for drinking on the spot.

Pricing A Bottle

The step in the wine pricing process when a finished wine enters the distributor network is crucial in determining the ultimate retail price. For in the case of a foreign wine importer—or with domestic wine, the distributor—the decisions made in determining the wine's purchase price are vital to their organization's economic welfare and to the final retail price of the wine. What they pay is reflected directly in the wholesale prices they set. It is at this point that the skill and insight of the importer or distributor is demonstrated. For an importer or distributor to buy well requires consideration of several factors: the wine's traditional reputation or standing, the quantities available, the potential consumer demand, a knowledge of the competition, current taste trends and consumer patterns, and a personal understanding and sense of the marketplace.

How do restaurants mark up their wines? Basically, any way they want to. Restaurateurs buy wines at the same price as does a retail store owner. The retail guy, however, marks his wines up between 5% and 50%, depending on competition, state laws, and other variables, but the usual mark-up is closer to 40% or 50%. The restaurateur, on the other hand, might take a mark-up of 200% to 300%—which is becoming the norm—on the exact same wine.

The best way to gauge how much a restaurant is charging is to check the price of a wine one knows the store price of.

—John Mariani, The Wine Spectator,

The situation is the same whether it involves an importer negotiating for a foreign wine with a *négociant*/shipper, or a distributor determining prices with a producer of domestic wines. The producer wants the highest possible price. The importer or distributor wants to buy at the lowest price. And the result, which will vary from day to day, is usually somewhere in between the two extremes. No producer sells all of his wine at the same time or at the same price. Because of this, wholesale prices shift. There are also other reasons that retail prices vary greatly from time to time. Volume buyers can often offer lower prices. Importers and distributors periodically run promotional sales and inventory closeouts. And eventually the lowered wholesale pricing to the retailer may be, and frequently is, offered to you.

If the traditional markups are included throughout the three-tiered system, a bottle of imported wine for which an importer pays a shipper $3 will cost you approximately $7.50 at your wine store. The importer adds 25 percent as his share and will sell the bottle to a distributor for $3.75. The distributor, in turn, will sell the bottle to a retailer for $5 (the "markup" is approximately 33 ⅓ percent of the cost). The retailer then adds 50 percent to his bottle cost and marks the selling price to you at $7.50. This example, of course, doesn't allow for vagaries within state laws, but represents approximate guidelines.

An additional factor in the cost of imported wine is the value of the U.S. dollar at any given time within the world's money system. During 1979 and 1980, as the U.S. dollar dropped in value in relation to most major overseas currencies, a given bottle of imported wine, particularly the higher quality wines, cost more dollars first at the importer level and ultimately to the wine drinker. When the dollar not only ended its dip but increased significantly in value in relation to foreign currencies in late 1980 through 1981, many expected an added buying power to be reflected in lowered imported wine prices. It didn't happen immediately. The increase in the dollar versus France's franc, Germany's deutschmark, and Italy's lira was more than offset by inflation rates, particularly throughout Europe's wine-producing countries. This was due, in part, to the continuing increases in the dollar cost of petroleum— priced not in terms of local currencies but in dollars worldwide.

But in 1982 the picture began to change in favor of wine drinkers in the United States. A combination of an increasingly strong dollar and lower world-wide petroleum prices have made it practical for overseas wine producers to "lower" or at least hold their prices. Wine price levels should stabilize or diminish slightly throughout 1983 and into 1984.

PRODUCTS OF THE TIMES

America is shaping up! Vigorous health— *Time* magazine calls it the Fitness Craze—is certainly one of the most universal themes of life in the 1980s. Attendant to the jogging, swimming, weight training, and aerobics is an underlying weight consciousness. And now joining ever-present diet foods, diet soft drinks, and diet beer is "diet" wine. It's not quite "diet" of course, but the new light white wines are significantly lower in caloric content than wines made in the traditional manner.

The Wine Drinker's Waistline

It was only recently suggested, even within the wine trade itself, that although wine isn't particularly fattening, more people would enjoy more wine if a way could be found to reduce the caloric content. However, nothing was really possible on a serious scale until 1979, when a change in California state law permitted a much broader legal definition of wine. Under the new law, California winemakers can now produce and distribute a fermented grape beverage containing less than 10% alcohol and still label it wine. Now 7% is the minimum alcohol level required nationwide, setting the stage for the introduction of "light," or low-calorie, wine. The first wines promoted under the low-calorie umbrella were introduced in 1981 by major American producers, Beringer Vineyards, Taylor California Cellars, Sebastiani Vineyards, Paul Masson, Los Hermanos, Delicato and St. Julian. And in late 1982, Franzia introduced a "light champagne" with less than 8% alcohol.

Producing Light Wine

The calories in wine come from only two sources: the residual sugar and/or the alcohol itself. Wine simply cannot be "lightened," or reduced in calories, without reducing either the sugar or the alcohol content or both. To do so requires a major change in the winemaking process. The grapes must be harvested at what has long been considered an immature stage in the ripening process; when the natural sugar concentration is lower than that termed ideal for producing regular table wine. Fermenting a wine at this "premature" low-sugar level results in a wine that contains 20 to 30 percent fewer calories. Early harvesting is the basis for light wines produced by Taylor California Cellars and Beringer Vineyards, while Sebastiani Vineyards and Paul Masson produce light wines from fully matured grapes. Rather than retaining the natural sugar level of the grape, the sugars and alcohol in the Sebastiani and Masson light wines are dissipated during the fermenting process. During a normal fermentation process the sugar level is reduced in the conversion to alcohol. Fermenting wines at extremely low temperatures causes the sugar to be automatically deposited out.

A wine produced with low sugar, however, tends to be high in acidity. In order to balance out this acidity, the winemakers will blend in other wines characteristically low in acidity. The result is a blended wine with few marked, natural characteristics and a diminished individual wine style.

Dry white wines, rosés and champagnes are the products that are being moved onto store shelves, since for the moment no commercial winemaker has evolved a system that can create an effective, excellent tasting lower-calorie red wine.

Soft Versus Light

Hillside terraces in Trentino, one of the renowned wine-producing regions in Northern Italy.

As the word "light" is rapidly becoming synonymous with fewer calories and, on a secondary level, less alcohol, the word "soft" has over the years become identified with wine that is on the low end of the wine alcohol levels. Italy's Lambrusco wines, e.g., Riunite, have been widely accepted as refreshing, low-alcohol wines that are incidentally low in calories. Since the mid-1970s California's San Martin Winery has been producing soft wines. Basically, soft wines are produced through an arrested fermentation process. To restore flavor, which is diminished during the extended cold fermentation, juice is added back into the wine, and with it calories are raised slightly toward the norm. These wines tend to be fruitier than "light" wines. Some domestic soft wines are slightly carbonated in order to challenge the Italian Lambrusco market.

BOTTLES & BOXES & CANS

Last year's wine bottles and corks may well turn up as next year's collectibles. As more table wine is consumed, more containers must be produced, sealed, and shipped. And tomorrow's bottles and corks are going to be different. These changes in packaging will, however, not alter the presentation of the most expensive premium wines, which need time to develop in the bottle. Tradition will always be available at a price. The change is coming primarily in the lower- and middle-priced wines. It is a product of the wine producers' need to keep down the final costs of a wine. Since the late 1970s, for example, as the supplies of top-quality cork in both Europe and the United States have been diminishing, corks have become relatively expensive. As a result, alternative methods of sealing a wine bottle are being explored. More and more wines are going to be seen with closures other than cork—this is a certainty. Whether this will mean aluminum caps, such as those already on certain less expensive wines, or plastic stoppers, such as those currently in use on many of the imported European jug wines, will be determined by the mid-1980s. There is also a great deal of research currently underway to develop an artificial cork-style closure that, although manmade, will have the same breathing characteristics of the traditional corks. The products of this research, when ready, will be found on the wines slightly below the top rank, those which are ready to drink at or near the time of their commercial release.

A man who was fond of wine was offered some grapes at dessert after dinner. "Much obliged," he said, pushing the plate to one side. "I am not accustomed to taking my wine in pills."
—Brillat Savarin

A Loaf of Bread, A Can of Wine

Perhaps the most dramatic potential change in wine packaging is the introduction of wine in cans. "Pick up a six-pack of chablis" will, if industry seers are correct, soon be a reasonable statement. On hindsight, the proliferation of wine in cans could have been anticipated in the United States when Coca-Cola, through its wholly owned subsidiary The Wine Spectrum, entered the wine industry on a broad scale. It was only logical that their sophisticated beverage canning technology and cost efficiency would be translated to wine. In 1980, they were the first to test the consumer acceptability of wine in cans with an initial tasting of canned Taylor California Cellars wine on Delta Airlines. They have since contracted to serve Chablis and Burgundy wine in cans throughout the Delta system. The final decision of whether or not wine in cans becomes taken for granted is, of course, going to be up to the consumer. If a wine drinker insists upon wine from a glass container and is willing to accept the cost, ultimately the wine is going to be in a glass container. The initial reaction to the airline tests did not look particularly promising. However, when it was explained to the passengers that the wine was in cans rather than bottles because of weight and the need for fuel efficiency, the reception markedly improved. The aluminum cans themselves, developed for The

Wine Spectrum by Reynolds, contain a special interior coating that keeps the wine free of any metallic taste. The most significant Reynolds breakthrough was in making it possible for a still liquid to give the individual aluminum cans sufficient strength to be stacked heavily upon one another. Soft drinks and beer offer this storage strength because of their carbonation, which creates an outward expanding pressure. Reynolds' system is based on the injection of a small dose of liquid nitrogen just prior to sealing the container. This substance has the same expanding characteristics of carbonation and results in satisfactory can strength. The pressure of the liquid nitrogen, which forces oxygen out of the can's "headspace," also serves to maintain the flavor and lengthen the storage life of the wine. Of the wines initially available in cans, Taylor California Cellars White and Red are being offered in a 6.3-ounce (1½ serving) container. Geyser Peak Summit wines are also being packaged in the 6.3-ounce cans, as are California's Villa Bianchi's Red Lite and White Lite carbonated wine "coolers."

Pass The Wine Box

No one seems certain where the idea for wine-in-a-box originated, but regardless of the creative sources, boxes of generic wines have been popular in Australia, South Africa, and Canada since the mid-1970s. In Australia, 40% of all wine consumed in 1980 was served up from boxes. Now it's the United States' turn. Functionally, the wine is in a bag within a box. The cardboard container gives the package rigidity and handling ease. The internal copolymer and foil bag, which contains the wine, does not affect the flavor or taste. Because air is excluded during packaging and use (the bag collapses during use in much the same manner as a baby's pouch-lined formula bottle), oxidation is prevented. The wine is drawn off through a spigot at the bottom of the box. Boxed wines, because their pouches are basically free of oxygen, can be kept for up to ten to twelve months after opening the sealed cap. And when pre-chilled prior to serving, the foil bag can keep the wine cold for up to four hours. To date, most boxed wines have come in large sizes (equivalent to two cases of wine) and are being used in restaurants as carafe-served house wines. But during the years to come, box-packaged wines in one- to four-liter sizes will be increasingly available in wine stores and supermarkets. The use of boxes is becoming important primarily with the inexpensive wines traditionally bottled in jugs. It's a question of cost, and as glass and shipping costs increase (wine-in-a-box weighs less than the equivalent amount of bottled wine), the availability and use of inexpensively packaged lower-range wines will grow rapidly.

A cluster of ripe California Zinfandel grapes, ready for the harvest.

THE UNITED STATES

For a few days in September, it looked to the winemakers of California, and to the worldwide wine industry, as though 1982 would be remembered as the year without a significant California harvest. Rains deluged the vineyards twice within a 12-day period just as the harvest was being readied. But in late September a combination of the benevolent winds and sunshine that California wine producers are accustomed to dried the vineyards and grapes, and, although there were serious losses, the harvest did indeed take place. Products of the '82 California harvest will be available for judging in '84. In the years to come consumer prices will not be adversely affected, due to major financial losses taken by the winemakers. Wine prices, because of a combination of factors, should be more favorable to wine drinkers throughout 1983 than in recent years. The continuing strength of the dollar versus overseas currencies has affected the prices of imported wines, either holding these prices at recent levels or in many cases resulting in a slight reduction. This, in turn, has put pressure on domestic producers and wine dealers to keep the prices of American wines in line with the imports. This pressure plus abundant American wine harvests in recent years of the wines that are now making their way onto the shelves should favor the wine drinker's pocketbook.

Excellent wines are being produced throughout the United States. California, of course, sets the standards for quality and the price levels of all American wines. This is as it should be, for 70 percent of the wines sold and consumed within the United States are grown, processed, and shipped from California. Trends begin there, and innovations tend to spring from California's classrooms, laboratories, and wineries. There are a number of premium wines to look for and experience throughout 1983 and into 1984:

Cabernet . With these lusty, full-bodied reds of California, it is still a toss-up as to whether '74, '78, or '80 will prove to be the best of the period. Within the tasting rooms, the '78 available in reasonable quantities is considered to be on a par with the '74s, but it is doubtful that anyone has seen harvest conditions and the general wine quality on a level with the 1980s. The '80s will begin to be released during the year and should probably be laid down for a considerable period. The '75 vintage is considered by many experts to be a somewhat underrated vintage, and some can still be found in wineshops. The '79s are also thought of as good buys.

Chardonnay. These wines continue to grow in favor. The average price of the highest quality '81 Chardonnay will continue to be over $10. The '79s (some are still available) and the '81s

"Buying a winery here is like buying a piece of fine art," says Bob Dwyer of the Napa Valley Growers'Association. *"It's like purchasing a Rembrandt or Picasso."*

The Wine Spectator

*Callaway Vineyard, Teme-
cula, California.*

represent excellent harvests, and by tasting selectively a wine
drinker should be able to determine a favorite.

Sauvignon Blanc. The '81s, with their drier, fruitier styles,
will offer some excellent wines. The '82s should be tasted selectively.

Zinfandel. In 1980, Amador County in the Sierra foothills,
the king of the Zinfandel regions, produced a wine fruitier and
lighter than its predecessors, one that offers a nice style, good
flavor, and is not overripe in character. The excellent 1980 vintages
began to be released onto the market in late 1982.

Pinot Noir. The '81s that will be available during the year are
considered to be very good buys. They represent a lighter vintage
with slightly less color than in the past, but wine drinkers should
like their more delicate style. The '80s, which tend to be block-
busters, are also beautiful wines. The '81s are considered to offer
a bit more finesse and should turn out to be of excellent quality.
This is a comparison well worth experiencing.

FRANCE

*France is the vineyard
of the earth. Her fer-
tile soil, gentle acclivi-
ties, clear sunny skies,
and fine summer tem-
perature, place her, in
conjunction with her
experience and the ad-
vantages of science ap-
plied to vinification,
the foremost in the art
of extracting the juice
which so gladdens the
human heart.*

—A History and
Description of
Modern Wines
*Cyrus Reddling
London, 1871*

Although wines from each region of France should, as a rule, be
considered individually because the weather conditions vary from
region to region, the harvests of 1981 and 1982 are the exceptions.
These wines are described as "very good to excellent" throughout
all of France. These wines will begin to be available in late 1983 or
early 1984, and will continue to enter the marketplace throughout
1985. And, through a combination of large quantity harvests and
the significant devaluation of the franc from the equivalent of 25½
cents to 14 cents, all the wines of France, including Champagne,
should be available within the American marketplace at either
stabilized or reduced prices.

There are also excellent, reasonably priced French wines available from earlier vintages.

Bordeaux: Although 1975 was an abysmal year for most of
France, in Bordeaux that hot, dry summer produced truly rich,
full, and intense wines that, because they are quite tannic, will take
a long time to mature. The 1976s are better buys for current
consumption, as are the somewhat light and thin 1977s. 1978
produced elegant wines that require some development. The 1979s,
very pretty wines, are available now, and the 1980s, a year considered disappointing by many winemakers, will be widely available
at excellent prices throughout 1983.

Burgundy: The 1976 vintage was very good, and some are
still available. It's just right for laying down. Don't bother with

most of the 1977s, but the 1978s are better . With a good shipper and a wine that's made in the old style, they are definitely for putting away. The 1979s, on the other hand, are wines for much more current consumption. The 1980 vintage was extremely spotty. In this case, you must find the right wine or the right shipper. The 1981 vintage is infinitely better and is just becoming available, although Burgundies from the major estates won't be on the market until late 1983. The white 1981 Burgundies are on the market now, and they're considered quite good, especially Pouilly-Fuissé. First reports concerning the 1982s that will be on the market throughout 1983 are good.

Rhône: This region offers some of the best values for any of the French red wine producing areas, as it has not suffered the vagaries of weather and the resulting spotty vintages that other French wine regions have had to endure. Year after year, from 1976 to the present, the Rhônes have produced tremendous vintages. The quantity and quality have been excellent. The prices have stayed down. And among the many exceptional Rhônes the 1978s stand out above all the rest. A truly extraordinary year.

Alsace: 1976 and 1978 were some of the best Alsatian wines produced in a long time. 1979 was a decent commercial vintage, but 1980 was an absolutely disastrous year for this lovely region of lush green fields and tiny villages on the German border.

A vineyard in the St. Emilion district of Bordeaux.

GERMANY

Wines from Germany's last great harvest, in 1976, are still on the market and will continue to be available through 1983. The wines produced since 1976 are considered, in the wine trade, to be of average (meaning very good) quality. Because of weather problems, however, the quantities have been limited. For example, frost conditions in the spring of 1981 severely damaged the Mosel valley wine crop, the source of much of the German wine that is favored by American wine drinkers. The German Wine Information Bureau in the United States has for eleven years been educating American wine drinkers to Germany's excellent wines by cutting through the elaborate and thorough wine labeling system (p. 55) and offering an effective way to experience the wines. It's a simple method of region and color. They advise you to start with the Mosel wines made of the Riesling grape (in green bottles). These wines offer a light, brisk nature and character. And once one has tasted and become familiar with the wines of the Mosel, the Rhine wines (in brown bottles) can be better understood. The

Rheingau's hillside vineyards serve as a backdrop for Die Pfalz, a castle on the Rhine River. Constructed in 1326 as a toll station, the fortress is open to tourists.

Rhine wines, also predominantly Riesling, currently available offer a slightly more developed body than the Mosels. These wines are a bit more upscale in price, ranging from less than three dollars to over $100 for the Trockenbeerenauslese. Germany's most famous wine district, the Rheingau, the area of areas, has contained some of the finest vineyards in the world since the days of Charlemagne, who took a personal interest in the development of the vineyards. The '79, '80 and '81 Mosels and Rhine wines currently available are the products of relatively small yet excellent general quality harvest. The 1981 harvest yielded only about half the number of grapes gathered in a normal harvest and produced good Kabinett wines— wines that might have made it to Spätlese quality but had to be picked before that point because of early rains. At the end of 1982, wine supplies in German cellars were low, but price increases that might have resulted from the scarcity have been offset by the devaluation of the deutschmark against the dollar—the same situation as in France. You should shop carefully, as some retailers or wholesalers may be hesitant to pass the savings along to the consumer.

The 1982 vintage, which produced wines that will begin to appear on the market in 1984, was of good quantity and quality.

ITALY

The Italian wine category continues to be dominated by the Lambruscos, perhaps the most phenomenally successful imported wines available in the United States. There is no indication that this will diminish, but it seems certain that throughout the mid-1980s the American wine drinker will also be tasting and enjoying more of the premium Chiantis, Valpolicellas, Bardolinos, Soaves, and wines of the Piedmont region. The fact that 1981 wine crops suffered from heavy spring rains in the south and severe frosts in the north during the time of budding and flowering, and then received heavy rain throughout a large portion of the growing season will not have an immediate effect on American wine drinkers. The wines in distribution throughout 1983 are the products of excellent growing seasons. The '78 wines of the Piedmont, the Veneto, and Tuscany are the result of perhaps the finest general growing year since 1947. The Barolo and Barbaresco wines produced in 1978 are considered to be suitable for laying down and aging positively for five to ten years without problem. Both 1979 and 1980 were outstanding growing years. In both years production was high and the general quality regarded as excellent. The

Barolos and Barbarescos, two differently styled wines of the Nebbiolo grape, have understandably become increasingly popular throughout the U.S. The Barbarescos are lighter, more feminine, and more elegant than the rich, full-bodied Barolos, and are ready for drinking earlier.

The Chiantis currently available are significantly different from those that were widely sold in the U.S. in the late 1950s and throughout the 1960s. Fuller bodied, they offer more of a Bordeaux style than that of a Burgundy. Excellent bottles of aged Chianti, the *classicos* and *riservas*, are available for five and six dollars. There are excellent Italian wines often available at extremely practical prices.

SPAIN

The red wines of Spain's Rioja region have become respected as among the best values in the wine world. In recent years the Rioja region, basically an area of Basque farmers, has been to some degree invaded by what can be termed multi-national winemakers. As a result, the style of the wines has been changing. The general quality standards have improved tremendously since the early '70s as technology and science have been applied to everything from the vineyard to the cellar. Many excellent wines are being shipped into the U.S., but keep in mind that you should be somewhat wary of general vintage markings. As a rule, it makes sense to shop the producer as opposed to a specific vintage marking. The regulations, tightened somewhat as Spain readied itself for entry into the European Economic Community, still lack the teeth to completely protect a consumer from dishonest or misleading labeling. For example, if a wine says 1976, it technically might have only 10% of '76 grapes in it, and the winemaker will not be penalized. It becomes almost a matter of looking at whom you feel has the most to lose by not being totally honest with you. Most important, of course, is the actual tasting of the wines. The good Riojas produced and distributed by the important producers are remarkable values. In terms of growing grapes of wines that are currently available in stores, 1976 is considered to represent the highest standard. 1977 was a difficult year for nearly all growers, and 1978 represented a good general wine year. Wines from the '78 harvest will be increasingly seen on the shelves throughout 1983 and after a bad '79, the 1980 harvest and the 1981 harvest represent a return to the good years.

Workers harvesting grapes.

The Art
of Mouton

 A recent development in the complex business of marketing American wine is the "artist" label, whereby a fine artist is commissioned to design a wine label for a particular wine vintage. It is an idea gleaned from France. Since 1945, distinguished artists such as Cocteau, Laurencin, Dali, Moore, Miró, Chagall, Picasso, Motherwell, and Warhol have created art for the Mouton-Rothschild wine labels.

To exchange the product of a winemaker's craft with that of a painter's was the inspiration of Baron Philippe de Rothschild. Each year a different artist is asked by the Baron to compose and execute an illustration. Traditionally, the artists are given an advance of five cases of excellent vintage wines, delivered when the new label is firmly affixed to the vintage for which it was created and the wine released into the marketplace. To date, more than thirty outstanding artists have been represented on these labels, and in 1981 a retrospective exhibition of the original artwork was mounted for the first time for showing in Bordeaux and Montreal.

The labels are characteristic of the Baron's sense of style and lifelong interest in the arts. "My cousins' *raison d'être* is banking,"

30

he once said, referring to his rivals, the Rothschild owners of Château Lafite. "On my tombstone I should like to have engraved the word 'poet.' " He is a translator of Elizabethan poetry, and his own poetry has won several literary awards. In the 1930s Philippe de Rothschild produced one of the first international French "talkies." In addition, the Baron is an art collector, and with his American-born late wife, Pauline, he assembled a fascinating wine museum at Mouton.

Mouton had long been renowned for its wine when, in 1922, the twenty-year-old Philippe de Rothschild took over management from his father Baron Henri. He was the fourth Rothschild to inherit Mouton, but the first actually to live there and play an active part in producing and promoting its wine. The Baron's daughter and only child, Philippine Seyres de Rothschild, is co-proprietor of Château Mouton-Rothschild. Her eldest son, Philippe, was legally adopted by his grandfather so that the Baron's title and the Rothschild name would continue. His many innovations have proved enormously successful. One of his current ventures is joining forces with the Robert Mondavi winery in California, where a single wine is being produced that will, it is hoped, embody the characteristics of both the Mouton and Robert Mondavi wine styles. The wine is due to be released in late 1983 or early 1984, under a proprietary name and label to be decided by the two families.

Baron Philippe de Rothschild holds a jeroboam of the 1977 vintage, whose label commemorates the visit of England's Queen Elizabeth, the Queen Mother, to Château Mouton-Rothschild.

In the past, many of the Baron's artist friends illustrated the labels for Mouton-Rothschild. The requests were impromptu and informal—there was Braque's spur-of-the-moment sketch for the 1955 label and Salvador Dali's ram, drawn in ink for the 1958 label.

Within the last decade the artists have been commissioned in a more conventional manner, and there has been a conscious effort to have a representative selection of fine artists from different parts of the world. Jean Paul Riopelle, a Canadian painter, submitted two pieces of art for consideration for the 1978 label. Unable to decide which one he preferred, the Baron chose both illustrations, and each case has been packed with a random selection of the two labels. The latest artwork for the Mouton-Rothschild series was designed by the Austrian artist Hartung for the 1980 vintage. Because of the three years between the grape harvest and the wine's availability, Mouton-Rothschild 1980 will be released in late 1983.

It wasn't until 1921 that the family name was added to Mouton and the wine became known as Mouton-Rothschild; previous labels were simply inscribed with the word Mouton and, in smaller lettering, date, appellation, and Rothschild ownership. The first ornamental label is dated 1924, and it was one of the first French wine labels to designate château bottling. The label bore a cubist design by Jacques Carlu that was incorporated within the Mouton-Rothschild emblem in 1925. However, it is so small that it is scarcely visible on the shield, which is upheld by two Mouton rams and surmounted by a coronet.

In 1934 another trend was set when each bottle was numbered and the label stated how many bottles the vintage had produced. But until 1945 the only design was the Mouton-Rothschild emblem introduced on the 1925 label. The designs were not considered notable until Philippe Julian designed the "Year of Victory" label to celebrate the end of World War II—and, as it turned out, the vintage of 1945, one of the great years for claret. The layout of his design, which runs about an inch deep across the top strip of the label, has been used ever since.

Inevitably much nonsense is talked about wine and its virtues, but surely it is undeniable that the ability to detect quality, so vital in the tasting of wine, holds a message applicable to the study of art.
—Denys Sutton, editor of Apollo, *an English art magazine*

However abstract the design, each illustration relates to the subject of wine or portrays an important occasion at Mouton, as on the labels for 1953, 1973, and 1977. The centenary year, 1953, was celebrated on the label with a cartouche of Baron Philippe's great-grandfather Nathaniel.

The label for 1973 is a bacchanale by Picasso, chosen as a tribute to the artist, who died in that year, and to celebrate the year that Mouton-Rothschild was elevated from second to first growth—

Here are 22 examples of the art of Mouton-Rothschild, ranging from the simple 1887 label to the work of Austrian artist Hartung for the 1980 vintage (released in 1983). In between are the works of some of the most famous artists of the 20th century.

(Top to bottom; left) 1887 label; 1928 Jacques Carlu—introduction of Mouton emblem; (Top to bottom; right) 1945 Philippe Jullian-Year of Victory label; 1947 Jean Cocteau

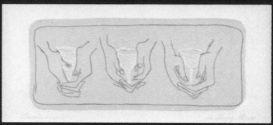

(Top to bottom; left) 1955 Georges Braque; 1959 Richard Lippold; 1960 Jacques Villon; (Top to bottom; right) 1962 Sebastien Antonio Matta; 1964 Henry Moore; 1965 Dorothea Tanning

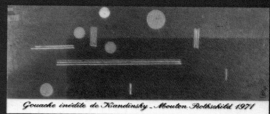

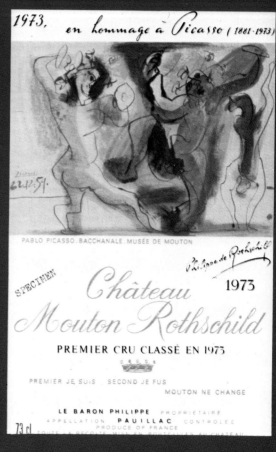

(Top to bottom; left) 1966 Alechinsky; 1968 Bona; 1969 Joan Miró; (Top to bottom; right) 1970 Chagall; 1971 Wassily Kandinsky; 1973 Pablo Picasso

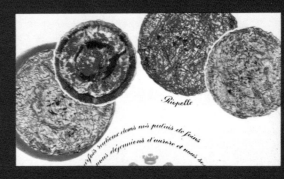

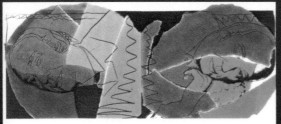

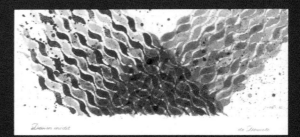

(Top to bottom; left) 1974 Robert Motherwell; 1975 Andy Warhol; 1976 Pierre Soulages; (Top to bottom; right) 1978 Jean-Paul Riopelle; 1979 Domoto; 1980 Hartung

for which the Baron had long campaigned. Until the reclassification, he had adopted the motto *" Premier ne puis, second ne daigne, Mouton suis."* (First, I cannot be, second I scorn to be; I am Mouton.) So to proclaim the first reclassified vintage, the 1973 label was inscribed *"Premier je suis, second je fus, Mouton ne change."* (First I am, second I was, Mouton does not change.)

In 1977 England's Queen Mother stayed at Mouton and a label was designed to commemorate the event. The Mouton label for that year is decorated with the British royal coat of arms.

In recent years, labels signed by artists have become valuable collector's items. At an auction in Ulster County, New York, in 1981, a single label autographed by Marc Chagall fetched $700. A jeroboam and a case of newly released wine signed and numbered by the artist have become a major feature at the annual New York City Public Broadcasting fund-raising art and antique auction. In 1977 a jeroboam and a case of wine signed and numbered by Robert Motherwell sold for $1,275. The following year a jeroboam and a case of wine signed and numbered by Andy Warhol went for $2,550. In 1981 a case signed and numbered by Jean Paul Riopelle sold for $2,750.

The most expensive lot was for a jeroboam and a case of the 1977 vintage, which fetched $4,150 in 1980. Although the vintage wasn't one of the finest, the expense was justified. The labels were personally signed by the man who started it all more than fifty years ago, Baron Philippe de Rothschild.

The Baron (r.) and artist Pierre Soulages.

Laws and Labels

A sign in the window of nearly every wine store in the United States could read, "English, French, German, Italian, Spanish, Portuguese, Hungarian, Greek, Hebrew, Serbo-Croatian—and a lot of regional dialects—spoken here," for the language of the wine marketplace is as international as the grape. Consider, the next time you visit a wine retailer, that the products of vineyards from around the world are on the racks and shelves. Wines from distant countries, bottled months, years, and in some instances decades earlier, wait there to be selected, uncorked, and enjoyed. You are shopping the world's vineyards at a single location, and you are doing it primarily in your own language.

In the late nineteenth century, Polish futurist Dr. L. L. Zamenhof believed that, as increased trade between nations in effect made the world smaller, a common language would be needed. He developed Esperanto, an amalgam of the most common words in the chief European languages, and began a lifelong campaign to standardize the world's speech. Whether he was right or wrong is yet to be judged. The fact is, his personal efforts went unrewarded.

While individuals are often resistant to change, trades and industries are frequently quick to adapt and assimilate to suit the times. The wine industry is an outstanding example of this trait.

Within the wine trade, national standards of terminology and quality have been adopted as international standards, which then affect the internal standards of other nations, and so on. This process is largely responsible for the development of legal production standards, labeling practices and the vocabularies of wine consumers.

Actually, wine laws are almost as old as wine itself. Stone tablets bearing wine regulations dating back centuries before the birth of Christ still exist, and massive bureaucracies have evolved since then to write new controls covering different aspects of the industry. Many of today's quality-control and labeling laws are rooted in France's *Appellation d'Origine Contrôlée* (AOC) system, enacted in the mid-1930s. For centuries in France, cheap wines had been sold under the labels of rare and expensive French varieties. Since few people had actually tasted a rare French Burgundy, for instance, almost nobody knew that they had been duped when they purchased a cheap imitation. However, the producers of first-rate wines knew, and they also knew that each time a consumer had a bad experience with a bottle of counterfeit wine, their reputations (not to mention their profits) were being threatened. In a move that would seem surprising today, industry leaders lobbied the government and insisted that the trade be regulated.

The results of that lobby, our current wine laws, do more than ensure that the wine trade generates tax revenues. A standard part of most control laws is the chemical analysis—testing that the wines are fit for human consumption. The laws also ensure that the buyer is provided with answers to basic questions about specific wines. The label is the grape's calling card, and as you are confronted with wines from many nations, it is the label that stands between you and confusion. With some slight variations among countries, the label will tell you whether the wine is red or white, dry or sweet, who made it and where, how old it is, and whether it is a common table variety or a high-quality wine.

"This year the wine IS wine . . . Hurry up and buy some . . . I can't guarantee that it will always stay that way." Lithograph by Honoré Daumier (French, 1808–1879), from Le Charivari, *1858. From The Christian Brothers Collection at The Wine Museum of San Francisco.*

UNITED STATES

The United States was the site of perhaps the most drastic, all-encompassing wine control legislation ever passed—Prohibition. Effective January 16, 1920, the 18th Amendment to the Constitution brought the commercial production of wine in America to a standstill.

The impact of the temperance movement of the 1920s can still be seen in the U.S. wine industry of the 1980s. The poor wines that were rushed onto the market after the repeal of the amendment in 1933 inspired at least the basis for today's quality-control legislation. Current laws regulate all wines distributed within the country, both imported and domestic. All must meet minimum standards of quality, labeling, and distribution set by the federal and state governments.

The Government

A wine label is like a person's face. It should tell you what you want to know about him.
—Walter S. Taylor, Bully Hill Vineyards

On the federal level, the administration of wine regulations in the United States is shared by the Bureau of Alcohol, Tobacco and Firearms (BATF) and the Food and Drug Administration (FDA). The BATF regulates every aspect of the industry from wine production to wine destruction (a wine producer must request and receive government permission before any wine can be destroyed). The FDA becomes involved in wine regulations only in cases in which a wine contains less than 7 percent alcohol by volume, because a wine under that percentage would not be covered by the Federal Alcohol Administration Act. In most cases, the BATF is responsible for making sure that all wines are safe for human consumption.

In addition, many states, notably California (see "California Laws and Labels"), impose additional regulations on their wine industries. Although attempts are made to decide what is best for the consumer, other interests lobby to keep the regulations in favor of the wine manufacturers. For example, U.S. labeling laws help domestic wineries sell more wine by permitting them to call their products by the names of great foreign wines with a minimum of restrictions, and this may mislead the consumer. The BATF classifies the wines sold under foreign designations as "semi-generics."

Semi-generics

These are wines sold under names generally recognized in this country as broad categories of wine, often the same names that are regarded as appellations in Europe. They include Port, Chianti, Angelica, Burgundy, Chablis, Champagne, Claret, Madeira, Málaga, Marsala, Rhine Wine or Hock, Sauterne (note the exclusion of the French "s"), Haut Sauterne, Sherry, and Tokay. While elsewhere in the world wines with these names would probably be subject to stringent qualifications regarding place of origin and method of production, U.S. laws require only that the wines have the generally accepted taste and characteristics of the wines bearing the name to be used, and that they contain varying minimum percentages of alcohol by volume.

Wine producers justify this system by claiming that the names have come to be associated with and identify *types* of wine and not *specific* wines. When you buy United States Chablis, for instance, you can be absolutely certain of only one thing—the wine you purchase will be white.

The only restriction attached to the use of a semi-generic name is that it must include an appellation of origin. The broadest appellation permitted by law is "American." Others are the names of two or three adjoining states; a single state or county; a combination of counties within the same state, or a viticultural area that has been recognized by the director of the BATF, such as Napa Valley. The wine must be 85 percent from grapes grown in a viticultural area in order to use that place name, but only 75 percent from any of the other appellations. However, if a wine is from two or more states or counties, all of the grapes used must have been grown in those states or counties indicated, and the percentage of wine from each must be listed on the label.

Proprietary Wines

These are wines that have been given brand names by their producers in an attempt to develop brand distinction and customer loyalty. Proprietary wines are blended and aged to make one batch consistent with the next. Proprietary wines range from the popular Mateus, Blue Nun, and Almadén varieties to the inexpensive Night Train Express and Thunderbird.

Under the Treasury Department's *Regulations Under the Federal Alcohol Administration Act, Title 27*, the brand name may convey "no erroneous impressions as to the age, origin, identity, or other characteristics of the product."

Varietals

These are wines named after the grapes from which they are made. Under regulations implemented in January 1983, 75 percent of a wine must be made from a specific grape for it to be called a varietal. For example, a bottle labeled "Chardonnay" must derive 75 percent of its volume from Chardonnay grapes that must have been grown in the label's appellation-of-origin area. There is an excep-

For value, the best buys are California and New York wines, but many uninformed sophisticates view them with contempt because they can understand the labels. I have solved this problem with a supply of empty French wine bottles and a funnel.

—Russell Baker

tion to that rule. The *Vitis labrusca* grape would be undrinkable at a 75 percent concentration, so the regulation allows wines labeled "Labrusca" to be only 51 percent derived from that grape. A Labrusca wine must bear on its label the phrase "contains not less than 51 percent" of the specific grape.

America's best red varietals are generally considered to be Cabernet Sauvignon, Pinot Noir, Zinfandel, and Gamay Beaujolais. The best white varietals include Pinot Chardonnay, Johannisberg Riesling, Pinot Blanc, and Chenin Blanc.

Labeling the Wine

Other information must also appear on all wine bottles, regardless of classification. The bottler's name and address must be listed, along with the alcohol content and net contents. In the case of a wine containing 14 percent or less alcohol by volume, the designation "table wine" or "light wine" may be used in place of the specific alcoholic content. Some wines have their net contents etched into the bottle itself; in these cases that figure need not be printed on the label. A vintage date may be listed only if 95 percent of the wine is derived from grapes grown in that year.

New York Laws and Labels

Cross a delicate *Vitis vinifera* of Europe with sturdy native American grapes and what do you have? A strain of vine commonly known as the French-American hybrid—a vine capable of surviving the harsh winters of the Northeast and producing a palatable wine. Such hybrids as Baco Noir, Foch, Chelois, de Chaunac, and natives Labrusca, Catawba, Concord, and Isabella grapes have made New York the second-largest wine producing state in the nation.

Because New York is not blessed with the abundant sunshine or long growing season of California, the nation's largest wine producer, New York's grapes do not ripen as quickly or develop as much sugar as those grown on California vines. Because of this, it

1—The producer.
2—The generic name.
3—The name and address of the producer, blender, and bottler.
4—Alcohol content (this may be omitted if the information is etched on the bottle).

1 —— HUDSON VALLEY *White Burgundy* —— 2

A smooth balanced New York State table wine of unusual versatility. Served well chilled, it is the perfect white wine for any occasion. Produced, blended and bottled by Hudson Valley Wine Co., Highland, N.Y. —— 3

Alcohol 12% by volume. —— 4

is often necessary to add sugar to the grapes' juice to ensure that after fermentation the wine will have a sufficiently high alcohol content. Federal law requires that 65 percent of the sugar used in the production of any wine has to come naturally from its grapes. Also, state law requires that 75 percent of the volume of the wine in each bottle is derived from New York grapes.

A typical New York State wine label will probably (but not necessarily) include a varietal, generic, semi-generic or proprietary name; a vintage date; and an appellation of origin. It is not uncommon for top wineries to include additional information voluntarily, so a careful look at all the labels on the bottle can provide valuable information about the quality of the wine.

California Laws and Labels

The grapes from this state's fertile valleys and hillsides produce wines that rival the finest in the world. Despite their ability to grow excellent grapes and produce first-rate varietals, some California winemakers cling to the practice of labeling their wines with the names of renowned European wine regions. However, California burgundies, sherries, and chablis are quite different from their European namesakes. Fortunately, many of the state's better wines are now taking varietal names, and a classic style of labeling for these wines is developing. A typical label contains the generic, semi-generic, varietal, and/or proprietary name, the net contents and alcohol content, the bottler's name and address; a vintage date; and the particular plot of land (providing it is an approved viticultural area) on which the wine's grapes were grown. California law requires that any wine carrying a California appellation be 100 percent from that state.

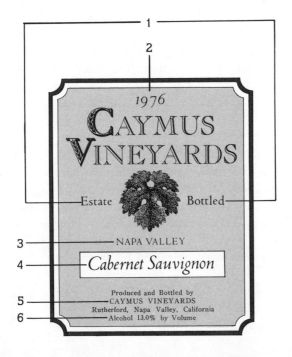

1–The wine was bottled where it was made.
2–Vintage.
3–The area where the wine was produced.
4–The varietal name.
5–Name and location of the producer and bottler.
6–Alcohol content.

EUROPEAN ECONOMIC COMMUNITY

Half of the world's wines—including most of its finest—are produced within the member nations of the European Economic Community (the Common Market). In order to attain common quality standards, avert fraud, and promote equalized treatment for EEC wine producers, a European wine market organization was established on April 28, 1970. This organization has subsequently been restructured and enlarged to form the European law governing the production and international trade in wine for the ten EEC member countries.

Regulations begin in the halls of the EEC's headquarters in Brussels. There, a body known as the Commission administers the EEC. It formulates policy and implements what is approved. The European Parliament, 434 elected officials who represent their home countries, consider the Commission's proposals. Parliament's decisions are "influential" but not binding on the European Community's Council of Ministers, the EEC's principal decision-making body. On all agricultural matters, including wine, the agricultural ministers of the member countries of the EEC enact major legislation. A Court of Justice, with one representative from each member state, is the final arbiter in legal disputes arising from EEC laws. In 1980 the EEC's Market Organization for Wine implemented a five-year program to promote quality and reduce wine surpluses by restricting wine production to only the most suitable areas.

Member States of the EEC

Belgium
Denmark
France
Germany
Greece
Ireland
Italy
Luxembourg
The Netherlands
The United Kingdom

Since European wine regions vary markedly, regulations useful in one area might not be suitable for the wine production in another. To accommodate the viticultural variations in each of the member countries, the EEC carved the territory up into a series of wine-producing zones and set quality and production standards for each. Most countries have their own system of regulations in addition to the EEC's.

The EEC's map of wine-producing Europe consists of three zones. The regulations for each region differ, but all have some standards governing the use of preservatives, alcohol enrichment acidification, deacidification, and the use of sweetening agents in table wines.

Zone A: includes all of the wine-producing regions of Germany (except Baden), Luxembourg, Holland, the United Kingdom, and Belgium. Wines must have a minimum natural alcohol content of 5 percent, and the total alcohol level may be raised by from 3.5 to 4.5 percent. Partial removal of acid is permitted.

Zone B: covers Baden and the northern vineyards of France. A minimum of 6 percent alcohol must be in the wine, and the total alcohol content may be raised by from 2.5 to 3.5 percent.

The Berlaymont Building in Brussels where the EEC's Council of Ministers meets.

Addition or removal of acid from these wines is allowed within prescribed limits.

Zone C: which is divided into five subzones, includes Greece, Italy, and the rest of France. Depending on the subzone, wine must contain a minimum of between 7.5 and 10 percent natural alcohol; the total alcohol level may be increased by 2 percent. The addition of 1.5 grams of acid per liter is permitted. Table wines can be sweetened only with grape juice, grape juice concentrate, grape must, or concentrated grape must.

Table wine: one of the three general types of wine recognized by the EEC, is subject to less stringent production constraints than are the quality wines. If a table wine is a blend of wines from more than one EEC country (a relatively new addition to the European wine inventory), it must be labeled "wine from different EEC countries" in the language of the country in which it will be sold. Wine produced in one EEC country and bottled in another will be labeled "Table wine of the EEC."

The second category of wine defined by the EEC is quality wine produced in specified regions within the wine-producing member countries. Individual countries have been left with the power to control the production of these wines, and as long as they respect EEC laws on labeling and quality control, Member states may enforce their own supplementary regulations.

The third type of wine defined by the EEC can be summed up as wine not produced within the EEC. These wines must conform to the EEC's definition of "wine" and the word "wine" must appear on the label. Their importation into the European Community is controlled by a complex system of import levies, licenses, and quotas.

The EEC's wine regulations aim to maintain stable prices and high quality, and are supplemented by a system of indirect price supports and restrictions on the planting of new vineyards. Above all else, however, the production and prices of good wines ultimately depend upon the weather, so the wine regulations are geared to adjust to the fluctuations in the balance between demand and supply.

FRANCE

A wine's home determines its character. The best wines frequently come from the best environments. Poor wines, on the other hand, might be described as the victims of a poor environment. Along with the vine types and production methods, the soil, climate, and local vegetation play critical roles in the development of grapes. The French Government tries to bring order to the wide range of wine personalities by carefully regulating all phases of the country's winemaking industry through a process that divides France's wine into three categories.

Appellation d'Origine Contrôlée (AOC Wines)

The most exceptional French wines receive this classification. AOC wines carry a government guarantee that the place of origin and method of production cited on the label are accurate and authentic. The French Agricultural Ministry's Institut National des Appellations d'Origine (INAO) formulates rules for the growing of grapes and the production of wine, and controls place names. If a grower is found to be in violation of the law, he may be fined or his wine listed as a lower grade.

The standards governing the AOC wines are the highest, since it is the most exclusive class of wine. Regulations designate which grapes may be legally used, how they must be cared for, how many kilos of grapes each acre can yield, and how the wine must be produced. Authorities subject the wine to a barrage of chemical analyses, then to taste tests by panels of representatives from the wine industry, the government, and the scientific community. If they accept the wine, it will be granted the right to be called by a particular place name or appellation. If the panel feels the wine is not of sufficient quality, but has the potential to improve with age, it may reserve judgment and review the wine another day. However, if the wine is poor or violates the region's standards, it may be denied an appellation and sold as a table wine. It should be noted that not every country honors the AOC place names—they are protected and observed only by the member nations of the European Economic Community (EEC) and by the nations who subscribe to the 1933 "Madrid Pact." The United States is not among them. Within France, the law puts strict controls on what a wine may be called. Winegrowers feature on their labels the most respected name for which a wine can qualify. For instance, any wine produced within the region of Burgundy has the right to call itself a Burgundy, but if a wine is produced in a particularly renowned district of Burgundy, such as the Côtes de Nuit, it will probably list "Côtes de Nuit" on its label, rather than simply "Burgundy." Furthermore, if it comes from a region within the Côtes de Nuit district that may be considered superior, such as the Gevry-Chambertin commune, it will undoubtedly be labeled "Gevry-Chambertin." Since the Chambertin Vineyard within that commune is considered one of the best in the world, a wine grown there will probably not bear the name of the commune but will simply be called "Chambertin." Even the name of an individual grower (there are thirteen, for example, within the Chambertin Vineyard) can accompany the name of the wine as an indication of how well it was produced.

Vins Délimités de Qualité Supérieure (VDQS)

"Delimited Wines of Superior Quality" is the next category of French wines. This category is composed of usually good wines that must remain in the shadow of AOC wines. The production methods of VDQS wines are controlled by the French Government and are allowed to meet slightly lower standards than AOC wines.

Table Wines

The third class of French wines, table wine, is composed of two categories: *vin de pays* and *vin ordinaire*.

Vins de Pays

"Wines of the country," is the higher classification of the two types of table wine. In 1976 *Office National Interprofessional de Vins de Table* (ONIVIT), which oversees the production of table wines, established seventy-five regions qualified to produce *vins de pays*. ONIVIT also counsels producers and buys surpluses of wine in accordance with the EEC's market stabilization program. The quantity of grapes that can be harvested and the alcohol, acid, and preservative levels are regulated by the Agricultural Ministry. Regional wines are also subject to taste tests by local commissions.

Blanc—*White.*
Blanc de blanc—*White wine made from white grapes.*
Blanc de noirs—*White wine made from dark grapes.*
Brut—*Very dry.*
Cave—*Cellar.*
Crémant—*Half sparkling.*
Cuvé, Cuvée—*A blend of wines.*
Demi-sec—*Semi-sweet.*
Doux—*Very sweet.*
Extra Sec—*Dry.*
Mis en bouteille (bouteilles) au château (or domaine)—*Estate-bottled.*
Mousseux—*Sparkling wine.*
Négociant—*Shipper or wine marketer.*
Propriétaire—*Owner.*
Récolte—*Vintage.*
Rosé—*Wine that is a rosy pink in color.*
Rouge—*Red.*
Sec—*Fairly sweet.*
Vin—*Wine.*

If the wines fail to meet their region's standards, they will be labeled as *vin ordinaire*.

Vin Ordinaire, also called *vin de consommation courante* (VCC), *vin de table*, and, if exported, *vin de France*, is ordinary table wine. This designation does not mean that the wines are of poor quality or taste; some are quite good, but they lack the pedigree of higher classified wines. Some are AOC, VDQS, and *vin de pays* wines that have not passed the required taste tests. The *vin de table* designation guarantees only that certain standards of hygiene and alcohol content have been met, along with the EEC's most basic laws. *Vin ordinaire* is control-tasted by its producers and, if necessary, checked by the Repression of Fraud bureau to make sure that it is of at least minimum quality.

THE REGIONS

These regulations, not quite fifty years old, could not be expected to change the customs French winegrowers have followed for centuries. The regulations governing each region were designed to conform to traditional notions of what works best, so labeling, quality, and production practices may vary from place to place.

Bordeaux

Regions may bestow their own honors upon their vineyards. In 1855 the wine brokers of Bordeaux, one of the world's most important wine regions, located in southwestern France, rated their region's best vineyards. Sixty Médoc vineyards and one from Graves were selected as *Grand Cru Classé*, or classed growths deemed worthy of special merit. This list was then divided into five subclasses. The highest, *Premier Grand Cru*, or first growth, contained only four names (later expanded to five, to include Château Mouton-Rothschild, in the list's only revision). Vineyards in the remaining four categories usually label their wines as *Grand Cru Classé* rather than revealing that they were designated second, third, fourth, or fifth under the rating system. Below the *Grand Cru Classé* wines, there are over 250 wines of the *Cru Exceptionel*, *Cru Bourgeois*, and *Cru Artisan* classes.

However, the system is now dated. In the years since it was devised, the quality of most wines has changed for better or worse. Wines from châteaux that were designated *Premier Cru* over 125 years ago may today be rivaled by lesser growths. When Bordeaux's St.-Emilion district was classified a hundred years later, provisions were made to revise the list every decade. *Premier Grand Cru Classé A* is the first class, considered to be the best, followed by *Premier Grand Cru Classé B*. Below the *Premier Grand Cru* wines are dozens of wines that are lesser known but of a high quality, designated *Grand Cru Classé*. In 1953 and 1959 the Graves district classified their wines as well (although one, Haut-Brion of Pessac, had been included in the 1855 Médoc classification). All the wines of merit were put into one of two equal classes—*Cru Classé* red or *Cru Classé* white.

Another Bordeaux tradition is the practice of château bottling. Since only a small amount of authentic Bordeaux wines are released into the world market, lesser wines being represented as Bordeaux have always been a problem. Some profiteers have tried to extend the supply by mixing cheap wines with authentic Bordeaux. To ensure that their wines are not tampered with, many Bordeaux producers bottle their wines themselves—a practice that is spreading throughout Europe as mobile bottling plants make estate bottling economically feasible. The words *"Mis en bouteilles au château"* are a guarantee of authenticity. (The phrases *Mis*—or *Mise*—*du domaine, Mis au bouteilles au domaine, Mis du propriétaire, Mis en bouteilles par le propriétaire,* and *Mis à la propriété* may also be used.)

While the practice of château- or estate-bottling has cut down on one type of fraud, another is on the rise. The words *Mis en bouteilles dans mes caves*, meaning "bottled in my caves or cellars," is becoming an impressive way to say nothing. All wines are bottled by someone, somewhere, and if it is not the cellars of the wine's maker, then there is no guarantee that the wine has not been tampered with.

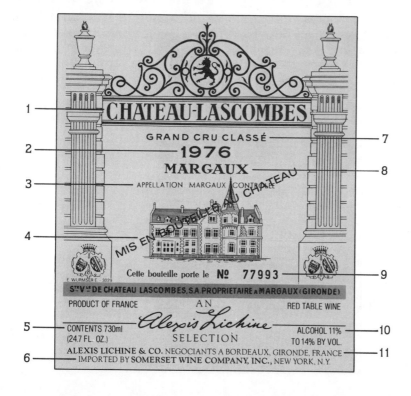

1—Château or wine estate.
2—Vintage.
3—Indicates that this is an AOC wine.
4—Estate-bottled.
5—Net contents.
6—Importer.
7—Indicates that the wine is a product of one of the sixty châteaux designated as a "great classed growth" in the Bordeaux classification of 1855.
8—Location of the château.
9—The serial number. Some better wines are individually numbered.
10—Alcohol content.
11—The shipper.

Burgundy

The wines of Burgundy have to be good. A wine drinker has to go through so much trouble in order to fully understand the region's labeling practices that anything less than a great wine in return for the effort would seem a cruel joke.

Like those of Bordeaux, the wines of the Burgundy region, in east central France, have been classified. Only thirty-one have received the highest classification, *Grand Cru*. A *Grand Cru* wine is usually identified by the name of its vineyard—Montrachet, for example. *Premier Cru* is the second category of Burgundy, ranked just slightly below *Grand Cru*. The label usually carries the village or commune name, then the name of the vineyard.

Other Burgundies can be described as simply "village wines." These are named, logically enough, after the village in which they were made. Often, the village name is combined with the name of the most famous vineyard in the area. Montrachet, for example, is a small *Grand Cru* vineyard producing some of the most delicious, most expensive, wines in the world.

By adding a hyphen, four surrounding vineyards and two communes have attached the Montrachet name to their own less-acclaimed appellation. For instance, the commune that used to be called "Chassagne" is now referred to as "Chassagne-Montrachet." But keep in mind that the more specific the appellation, the more exacting the standards the wine must meet.

The wine's producer may be as important as the place it was made. Many distinguished vineyards are owned and operated by more than one person. The vineyards surrounding the Clos de Vougeot, for example, are owned by more than sixty different people. Some have been blessed with better pieces of land to tend. But they all have the right to call their wine a Clos de Vougeot.

1—Net contents.
2—Region; only wines from a specific area on Burgundy's Mâcon slope are permitted to display the Pouilly-Fuissé appellation on their labels.
3—The bottler and shipper.
4—Alcohol content.
5—Vintage.
6—Indicates that this is an AOC wine.
7—Location of the bottler and shipper.

Rhône

Côte du Rhône is the name given to wines produced in the Rhône River Valley, between Lyons and Avignon. If a wine is from one of fourteen superior villages and meets higher standards, it may call itself *Côte du Rhône-Villages*. However, unlike the practice in most other regions of France, the mention of a specific place of origin does not automatically mean that the wine has met higher standards or is of better quality. The standards for Côte du Rhône-Drôme, for example, are more lenient than those for a Côte du Rhône.

Alsace

Until recently this entire region was encompassed by just one appellation: *Vin d'Alsace*. The method that the winemakers of Alsace use to distinguish one wine from the next is unique in the French wine industry. Other regions label their wine with the place in which it was raised—"Champagne," for instance. In Alsace, if the wine is made from one kind of grape, the name of that grape is listed. The grapes that can go into a bottle of Alsace wine are controlled by law, but wines can be blended. Zwicker is a blend including common grapes; Edelzwicker is a blend of wine from noble, or high-quality, grapes. Blends often appear under brand names. Wines with at least 11 percent alcohol may further distinguish themselves with the term *Grand Cru* or *Grand Vin*.

The name of the shipper will also be on the label. He is often the winegrower as well, and may buy grapes or juice to add to his own. His name may be the only clue to the quality of the wine.

The trademark of Alsace wine is the tall, slim, tapered green bottle in which all the region's wines must be packaged. The bottle is protected by law; no other region of France can use it. The wines of Alsace cannot be sold in any other container, not even by the cask.

1—Appellation.
2—Net contents.
3—Importer.
4—Indicates that this is an AOC wine.
5—"Cuvée Particulière" means that this wine's producer has deemed it one of his best. There are few regulations surrounding the use of this term, so the wine's marketer stakes his reputation on the fact that it is used only on the most deserving wines.
6—Shipper.
7—Varietal name. Unique among the French, Alsace wine is named for the grape from which it was made and not for its appellation of origin.
8—Vintage.
9—Alcohol content.
10—This tells whom the wine was bottled for. The same firm may have also grown, vinted, or blended the wine.

Champagne

All that bubbles is not Champagne. While sparkling wines are produced throughout France and round the world, only those wines produced a few miles northeast of Paris, in the Champagne region, can rightfully bear that name, although many sparkling wines carry the word "champagne" on their labels.

Perhaps the most famous of all wines, authentic Champagne is also the most strictly regulated.

Like all other AOC wines, Champagne must be made on a precisely designated patch of land, in a carefully defined way. Sparkling wine made in any wine district not in Champagne is called *vin mousseux*. Still wines made in the Champagne region are called *coteaux champenois*.

Authentic Champagne must be made by the *méthode champenoise*. The wine is first fermented in bulk, like other wine, but then it is blended, bottled, and fermented again in the bottle. This time carbon dioxide, a normal by-product of fermentation, is trapped in the bottle and dissolves in the wine, giving it its sparkle. The bottle is opened once more to remove any sediment, and some liqueur is added for sweetness.

In the best years Champagnes are declared vintages by a local commission. Although all Champagnes are blends of wine, vintage Champagnes are blends of wine from the same harvest and are entitled to bear that year on their label.

1—Net contents.

2—Region.

3—Producer's location. The ancient city of Reims is one of the major centers of the Champagne trade.

4—Alcohol content.

5—Indication of the wine's sweetness level.

6—Producer.

7—The identification number of the *négociant/ manipulant*. The NM produces wine from grapes purchased from a grower. If the identification number contains the letters RM, for *récoltant manipulant*, it means that the wine was produced by the grower himself. Wine made by a cooperative manipulant, from the grapes of an entire town, will bear an identification number with the letters CM.

GERMANY

In Germany, in contrast to most other wine-producing countries, a wine's rank is not determined solely by its place of origin. Instead, German wines are quality graded according to the ripeness of the grapes at harvest time. A German wine produced in any of the country's eleven specified wine-growing regions can attain a top classification if it meets the appropriate standards. Similarly, even the most renowned vineyards produce wines in lesser categories in off years.

Germany's weather conditions are often precarious, and for that reason, most of its vineyards are cultivated on the slopes and banks near such major rivers as the Rhine and the Mosel, allowing the grapes to benefit from the added warmth and reflected light of the waterways.

Most German wine is white. About 88 percent of the German wine cultivation area is devoted to white grape varieties. Of these the Riesling is the undisputed king, producing the country's most sought-after wines. The Müller-Thurgau, a crossing developed in the late nineteenth century, resembles the Riesling in style and taste. Other varieties include: Silvaner, Gewürztraminer, Kerner, Scheurebe, Elbling, Gutedel, and Morio-Muskat.

As soon as the grapes begin to ripen in the fall, the government declares the vineyards "off limits" to everyone, including the owners. This is done to protect the grapes from tampering and from grape thieves.

During the harvest, each vintner must file daily reports to local authorities, recording quality, quantity, origin, and variety of harvested grapes. Inspectors from the Federal Ministry of Food, Agriculture, and Forestry and certain other agencies spot-check the vineyards to verify the accuracy of the daily reports and to ensure that the wine is produced in accordance with the laws of Germany and the EEC. The wine may fall into one of four general classes: *Deutscher Tafelwein, Deutscher Landwein, Qualitätswein bestimmter Anbaugebiete (QbA)* or *Qualitätswein mit Prädikat (QmP)*.

The Wine Label

In Germany any information not expressly allowed by the law is forbidden.

All German wines must indicate Germany as the country of origin and must display the category to which the wine belongs—*Tafelwein*, *Landwein*, QbA or QmP. The bottler or producer will also be identified on the label, as will the bottle capacity.

For German quality wines (QbA and QmP), geographical units as small as individual vineyard sites may also appear if 75

Degrees Öchsle—*Measurement describing how heavy one liter of grape must is in relation to one liter of water. This indicates the grapes' level of natural sugar.*

Edel—*Noble.*

Erzeugerabfüllung, Aus Eigenem Lesegut—*Bottled by the producer.*

Halbtrocken—*Semi-dry.*

Milde (or **Lieblich**)—*Mild or lovely, used to connote sweetness.*

Roseewein—*Rosé.*

Rötling—*Rosé made from a blend of red and white grapes.*

Sekt, Qualitätsschaumwein—*Sparkling wine made using the traditional méthode champenoise.*

Süss—*Sweet.*

Trocken—*Dry.*

Weinkellerei—*Winery.*

Weisswein—*White wine.*

Winzergenossenschaft, Winzerverein—*Winegrowers' cooperative.*

percent of the wine derives from that source. One of the eleven specified wine-growing regions will always be listed. An AP Number will also appear on every quality wine label.

Brand names, alcohol content, an indication of sweetness or dryness (usually with the words *trocken* for dry, *halbtrocken* for semi-dry) and the grape variety are permissible but not mandatory. If a grape variety is listed, 85 percent of the wine is made from that grape. If two varieties are listed, the wine is a blend of both but contains more of the first than the second. No grape variety can be listed if the wine is a blend of three or more types of grapes.

The vintage dates that appear on most German wine labels are not required, but if one is on the label, 85 percent of the wine must have been made in that year.

Deutscher Tafelwein (German Table Wine)

Although very little wine of this category is imported into the United States, in Germany *Tafelwein* is everyday, inexpensive drinking wine, equivalent to the French *vin de table*. The label always indicates one of the four *Tafelwein* regions as the "birthplace" of the wine: Rhein-Mosel, Bayern, Neckar, and Oberrhein. A subregion may also be cited on the label if 75 percent of the wine derives from that smaller geographical unit. Note that if the word *Deutscher* is missing, then it is not a *German* wine, but rather a wine that comes from one or more EEC countries, and that may or may not have been blended with German wine.

Deutscher Landwein (German Regional Wine)

A new category authorized by an amendment to the German wine law in 1982, *Deutscher Landwein* is equivalent to the French *vin de pays*. A step above *Deutscher Tafelwein*, these regional wines tend to be dry and uncomplicated with more body and character than *Tafelwein*. The label will always indicate one of sixteen designated Landwein regions as origin of the wine.

Qualitätswein

Most wine imported into the United States is either QbA or QmP. These are Germany's best wines and must come from one of the eleven designated quality wine regions: Mosel-Saar-Ruwer, Rheingau, Nahe, Ahr, Mittelrhein, Rheinhessen, Rheinpfalz, Baden, Hessische Bergstrasse, Württemberg, and Franken.

These quality wines must undergo rigid controls not only at the time of harvest, but also in the cellar and at time of bottling. After the wine is bottled, each quality wine is chemically analyzed in an approved laboratory and taste-tested by a local board to check color, clarity, aroma, and taste, and to ensure that it is typical of the region in which it was produced. Two sealed bottles of every quality wine produced in Germany are set aside for use as samples should complaints arise. Once it has passed these tests, it is awarded its AP Number (*Amtliche Prüfungsnummer*), its "birth certificate." This is a numerical code that gives information about where and when the wine was tested and bottled. The last number in the code is the year the wine was tested, not the vintage year.

Qualitätswein bestimmter Anbaugebiete (QbA)

The name means "quality wine of a specific region" (French AOC or VDQS) and the label for a QbA wine always indicates a restricted region of origin—one of the eleven designated quality wine regions. In addition, the district (*Bereich*), the community (*Gemeinde*), a collective site (*Grosslage*) or an individual site (*Einzellage*) may be named if 75 percent of the wine derives from that particular unit. The grape variety may also be indicated if 85 percent of the wine is produced from that variety. If a vintage date is noted on the label, 85 percent of the wine is of that vintage.

Qualitätswein mit Prädikat (QmP)

Literally "quality wine with special attributes," these are Germany's best wines, and the labels always tell you not only which of the eleven quality wine regions the wine comes from but also the particular district. If the grapes were gathered from a more restricted area, the label may state the appropriate *Einzellage* or *Grosslage*.

All *Prädikat* wines are made from grapes fully ripened on the vine. They may never be chaptalized—the process of adding sugar to increase alcohol content—although this is allowed for QbA wines, as it is for some of the finest wines from other European countries.

1—The town where the wine was produced. This wine was made in Zeltingen. It is a common German practice to add "er" to the name of a town.
2—Varietal names.
3—Net contents.
4—The importer.
5—The bottler.
6—The shipper.
7—The vintage.
8—The vineyard (*Einzellage*) or commune (*Grosslage*).
9—The wine's grade within the *Prädikat* class.
10—Indicates that this is a QmP wine.
11—The AP number, which provides information about the testing and bottling of the wine.
12—Alcohol content.
13—The specified growing region.
14—Estate-bottled.
15—Location of the bottler.
16—Indicates that the wine bottle is a standard size.

There are six levels of *Prädikat* wines. With the exception of *Eiswein* (described below), each level represents more stringent requirements as regards must weight levels (sugar content of the grape at harvest time) as well as the manner of harvesting.

Kabinett is the entree level of QmP wines, usually light and among the driest of the special distinctions. *Kabinett* wines are made from fully ripened grapes gathered in the normal harvest.

Spätlese (literally "late harvest") is a wine made from grapes that have been left on the vines after the normal harvest and have had extra time to ripen and absorb elements from the soil, adding intensity of flavor.

Auslese is usually a sweeter wine, always made from bunches of late-harvested grapes, specially selected for ripeness and quality.

Beerenauslese is a rare, sweet dessert wine made from overripe grapes often affected with *Botrytis cinerea* (noble mold), a special mold that attacks grapes and causes the water to evaporate, concentrating the natural sugar and flavor. These grapes are individually hand-selected in the late harvest and produce wines with a honey-like delicate aroma and taste—but usually only two to three times each decade.

Trockenbeerenauslese, the noblest of German wines in taste, bouquet, and appearance. Only raisin-like shriveled grapes, affected with *Botrytis cinerea* are hand-selected and pressed to produce these wines. It takes a worker one full day to collect enough grapes to make one bottle of Trockenbeerenauslese. Occurring only once or twice in a decade, these wines are truly rare and consequently among the most expensive wines in the world.

Eiswein is a rarity of a different sort, a wine that occurs only when an early drop in temperature to about 12° F. freezes grapes of the Beerenauslese category still on the vine. The grapes are harvested and pressed while still frozen, and the concentrated juice is made into the rarest of all German wines, Eiswein.

ITALY

Until the late 1950s, Italy's reputation in the wine community had been somewhat suspect as a result of unregulated quality control and labeling practices. All that changed in the early 1960s, when EEC treaties began to open trade barriers and prompted Italy's wine producers to adopt a system of wine-control legislation similar to the system used in France. Italy's *Denominazione di Origine Controllata* (DOC) legislation divided the county's wine into three categories: *Denominazione di Origine Semplice* (DOS), *Denominazione di Origine Controllata* (DOC), and *Denominazione di Origine Controllata e Garantita* (DOCG).

Denominazione di Origine Semplice (DOS)

Vino tipico (typical wine) and *vino da tavola* (table wine) fall into this class, meaning that the wines are "simple" table wines that can claim no special distinction but are often very good. Although some wines are too low in quality to deserve any higher rank, many of the country's best winemakers feel that the DOC laws impose too many restrictions on their craft, and refuse to abide by them. The wines of these artisan producers are banished to the lowest rank and labeled "table wine."

Denominazione di Origine Controllata (DOC)

Many winemakers, particularly those anxious to be part of the export market, aspire to one of the government's higher ratings. *Denominazione di Origine Controllata* wines are those whose origin (although not their quality) is guaranteed by Rome. For a wine to be elevated to DOC status, its producers must petition the National DOC Committee of the Italian Ministry of Agriculture and Forests, and the Ministry of Industry and Commerce. Based on its recommendations, DOC-approved wines are recognized by presidential decree. To date, DOC status has been bestowed on over two hundred wine zones.

It is the wine producers who propose the rules, based on tradition, that they will have to abide by if their petition is approved. The regulations specify areas of land that will be entitled to the DOC-protected name, the grapes that can be used and how they must be cared for, the wine production methods to be used, and the permitted alcohol and acid levels. DOC wines must also pass taste tests. If the proposal is accepted, the words *Denominazione di Origine Controllata* must appear on the label along with the wine's producer, bottler, and location of origin.

Denominazione di Origine Controllata e Garantita (DOCG)

This is the highest of the Italian wine classes. Since the wine's quality as well as its origin is guaranteed by the Italian Government, DOCG wines must meet stricter standards than the DOC wines. So far only four wines—Brunello di Montalcino of Tuscany, Barolo of Piedmont, Barbaresco of Piedmont, and Vino Nobile di Montepulciano of Tuscany—have earned the DOCG rank, but none are on the market yet. All DOCG wines must meet specific aging requirements, and since the first wines have not yet met these standards, they will stay in casks until 1985, when the government has determined that they will be ready.

Their labels will state the grower and bottler, the wine's alcohol content, and the fact that the wine is a DOCG.

Abboccato—*Semi-dry.*

Amabile—*Semi-sweet.*

Amaro—*Tart, bitter, very dry.*

Bianco—*White.*

Classico—*Classic; from the heart of a region, presumably its best area.*

Dolce—*Sweet.*

Fattoria—*Producer.*

Imbottigliato all origine—*Estate-bottled.*

Liquoroso—*Fortified wine.*

Riserva—*Wine that meets longer than usual aging requirements.*

Rosato—*Rosé.*

Rosso—*Red.*

Secco—*Dry.*

Spumante—*Sparkling.*

Superiore—*Wine that meets higher than usual standards of production, aging, and alcohol content.*

Vendemmia—*Vintage.*

Vino Santo, Vino Passito—*Wine made from dried grapes.*

Enforcing the Laws

Enforcement of these laws and control of the quality standards are the responsibility of *consorzi*, teams of government inspectors from the National Institute for the Protection of Denominations of Origin and representatives from local growers' associations.

Before the DOC laws were enacted, *consorzi* were the only controlling bodies in the Italian wine industry. They established minimum standards for each region's growers, although those standards varied considerably from place to place. Those growers who met the requirements were allowed to display the *consorzio*'s logotype on the bottle, a symbol that still appears on bottles of Italian wine. However, since membership in a *consorzio* was voluntary, it had no official disciplinary power. Those who violated the group guidelines could only be threatened with expulsion. Today, those who violate DOC laws face having their wines dropped in rank, fines, and even jail.

Labeling the Wine

A typical Italian wine label will show the wine's rank in the DOC system, the size of the bottle, the alcohol level of the contents, the location where the wine was made, and the name and address of the wine's producer and bottler. Many bottles also carry the seal of the local *consorzi*, and all Italian wine imported to North America will have a small red seal on the neck of the bottle, inscribed with the letters INE. The INE stamp, or National Seal, is a guarantee that the wine has met Italian export standards.

1—Region.
2—Indicates that this is a DOC wine.
3—Guarantees that the wine was bottled where it was made.
4—Net contents.
5—Literally means "Produced and bottled in the region of origin." Alone, it assures only that the wine was packaged somewhere within the same region it was produced, in this case Chianti.
6—The importer, in this case also a brand name.
7—"Classico" means that the wine is from the heart or best part of the region.
8—"Riserva" means that it has been aged for a designated number of years.
9—Alcohol content.
10—Name and location of the producer and bottler.

ARGENTINA

For years the people of Argentina have consumed so much of their locally grown wine that little was left over for export to the rest of the world. Considering that Argentina is the fourth-largest producer of wine in the world, this is not an unimpressive feat.

More than a century ago, Italian immigrants in Argentina began harnessing the melting snow that poured off the Andes and used it to irrigate the plains below. This stable water supply, coupled with the country's constant sunshine, enables Argentina to cultivate in abundance most of the grape varieties found in Europe. Harvests tend to be huge, since there is no legal limit to the amount of grapes that each acre can yield. On half the vine acreage, Argentina produces the same amount of wine as Russia, which vies with Argentina for its place as the world's fourth-largest winemaker.

Enforcing the Laws

Argentine wine laws are enforced by the *Instituto de Vitivinicultura* (INV). All grapes used to make wine must receive the INV's approval. Since it takes several years for vines to mature enough to bear fruit, the INV conducts a census of the nation's grape population every four years to ensure that all of the country's grapes are legal.

Naming the Wine

Except for a few guidelines, Argentine winemakers may call their wines whatever they like. If they wish to name them varietally—after the grape from which they were made—at least 80 percent of the wine in the bottle must have been made from that grape. The INV samples each varietal wine to make certain that it tastes like the grape it has been named for. It also inspects vineyards if there is any doubt that 80 percent of a wine is from one type of vine.

If the vineyard prefers to blend its wine, or is using an unfashionable grape, it may simply make up a name for the wine—*Monte Blanco* (Mountain White) and *Andean* are two common examples.

Labeling the Wine

Labels may carry a vintage date if 95 percent of the wine comes from grapes grown in the vintage year listed on the label.

Certain information is mandatory on all Argentine wine labels. The winery number will tell you where the wine was made and

Wine drinkers in search of quality wines are often surprised to find many of Europe's great grape varieties growing south of the border. The grapes that go into Argentina's finest wines are the same noble grapes that produce the wines of France, Italy, and Germany. The vines grown in Argentina's accommodating soil and climate include:

> *Barbera*
> *Cabernet Franc*
> *Cabernet Sauvignon*
> *Chardonnay*
> *Chenin Blanc*
> *Gamay*
> *Johannisberg*
>   *Riesling*
> *Malbec*
> *Merlot*
> *Nebbiolo*
> *Pedro Ximénez*
> *Petite Sirah*
> *Pinot Blanc*
> *Pinot Noir*
> *Semillon*

bottled. A brand name or description of the grape used is required, as are the wine's alcohol content, the size of the bottle, and the importer's or exporter's name. Any wine that is exported must have INV papers certifying the wine's origin and authenticity.

1—The producer.
2—The varietal name.
3—Alcohol content.
4—Estate-bottled.
5—The importer.
6—Net contents.

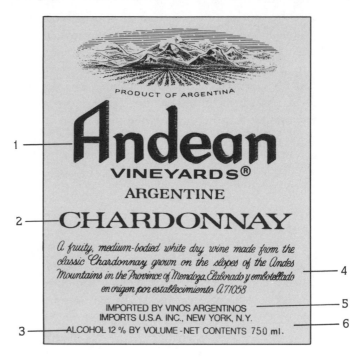

PRODUCT OF ARGENTINA

Andean
VINEYARDS®
ARGENTINE
CHARDONNAY

A fruity, medium-bodied white dry wine made from the classic Chardonnay grown on the slopes of the Andes Mountains in the Province of Mendoza. Elaborado y embotellado en origen por establecimiento a.71058

IMPORTED BY VINOS ARGENTINOS
IMPORTS U.S.A. INC., NEW YORK, N.Y.

ALCOHOL 12 % BY VOLUME - NET CONTENTS 750 ml.

Abocado—*Semi-sweet.*
Aloque—*Wine made from red and white grapes.*
Anejado por . . .
—Aged by . . . (usually the shipper).
Blanco—*White.*
Bodega—*Wine house, château.*
Cava—*Sparkling wine made by the traditional French* méthode cham-penoise; *or the establishment where such wines are made.*

SPAIN

Most of Spain's efforts to regulate the standards of its wines have been directed outside the country's borders, not within them. Its programs have been double-edged. Wine producers from Spain's Rioja region have created new standards to open up new markets for their wines, while Sherry producers attempt to eliminate counterfeit Sherries.

The DOC Laws

Internally, Spain's wine-control laws have barely gotten off the ground. In 1970, as a prelude to gaining membership in the Common Market, Spain borrowed some of the EEC's regulations and set up its "Statute of Vineyards." Although it has many weaknesses, the statute has made the country's wines much more trustworthy.

The 1970 law established the *Instituto Nacional de Denominaciones de Origen Controlado* under the Spanish Ministry of Agriculture. It has classified the nation's finest wine-producing regions as *Denominaciones de Origen Controlado*, or DOC's. With this status, vintners must follow regulations tailored to that region and enforced by local councils called *Consejos Reguladores*. The *consejos* include people from all aspects of the wine trade except shippers. They set standards for sugar content, alcohol level, permissible grape varieties, and additives.

Rioja Laws and Labels

Although all the wine-producing regions in Spain are somewhat similar, many have peculiarities that might drive the average wine lover to drink, particularly while trying to decipher each area's labels.

Thanks to Rioja's aggressive and successful attempt to increase its sales in foreign markets, its labels are among those you are most likely to encounter. Rioja wine labels bear the name of the *bodega* (the wine estate or house) that produced the wine. Below that is usually the name of the town where the winery is located.

The type of wine is also listed on the label—*blanco* for white, *tinto* for red, and *rosado* for rosé. The word *cosecha*, followed by a year, tells when most of the grapes comprising the contents of the bottle were harvested. However, it is a common practice in Rioja to top off barrels of aging wine with wines from different years, so pure vintages are almost never found. Estate-bottled wines carry the designation *embotellado en la bodega*. Some labels also indicate the wine's level of sweetness.

Reservas and *Gran Reservas* are premium Rioja wines. Exceptional wines may earn one of these distinctions in blind taste tests. *Reservas* must have been aged a minimum of four years; *Gran Reservas*, for at least eight years.

Clarete—*Light red. An intermediate shade between red and rosé.*
Cosecha—*Crop or vintage.*
Criado por . . .—*Raised by . . .*
Dulce—*Sweet.*
Embotellado de Origen—*Estate-bottled.*
Embotellado por . . .—*Bottled by . . .*
Espumoso—*Sparkling wine not made by the méthode champenoise.*
Fino—*Very Dry.*
Reserva—*Wine aged longer than usual.*
Rosado—*Rosé.*
Seco—*Dry.*
Tinto—*Red.*
Vendimia—*Vintage.*

1—ALCOHOL 12% BY VOLUME
2—G. C. SUMNER SELECTIONS
3—PRODUCT OF SPAIN
4—NET CONTENTS 730 ML. (24.7 FL. OZS.)
5—RIOJA 1975
6—RED TABLE WINE
OLARRA
Produced and bottled by
Bodegas Olarra
Logroño / Rioja / España
R.E. 5152-LO
7—
8—IMPORTED BY: FOREIGN BRANDS, INC., NEW YORK, N.Y.

1—The alcohol content.
2—The shipper.
3—The bottler and producer's name.
4—The bottle capacity.
5—The region and vintage.
6—The type of wine.
7—The seal of the Rioja region indicating that the wine is a DOC. All wines from this region bear this stamp.
8—The importer.

Storing, Serving, and Tasting

 A first glance through the small shopwindow of Ellis' Son and Vidler in Hastings, England, gives the promise only of a visit to a well-styled, well-stocked retail wine merchant's shop overlooking the English Channel. But to pass into the shop, through a heavy oak door in the rear wall and down a damp passageway, is to enter a time capsule.

Carved first by centuries of high tides and winds, and later by men into the massive, fabled white chalk cliffs of the Channel coast are chalk-walled vaulted spaces—the White Rock Cellars. Although smugglers secreted their booty in the caverns in the sixteenth and seventeenth centuries, the main occupants for the past three hundred years have been countless bottles and casks of wine. Today the bins cut into the cool walls, which are slightly damp to the touch, contain dust-covered turn-of-the-century Ports, fine brandies, and samplings of the great labels and their great—and some good—years. They also hold newly released wines, for in this cellar, and in similar cellaring operations throughout England, the fine wines, wines that demand aging, are purchased and laid down to begin their aging cycles. Much of the current stock is Ellis' Son and Vidler's own, for resale. The remainder, several thousand bottles, is held as reserves for many of England's landed gentry.

For nearly fifty years Michael Card has worked in the White Rock Cellars. During the 1940s he bottled wines that arrived in casks. More recently, his work has been focused on overseeing the storage and shipping of the stocks. "Wine is like a baby," he says. "It starts off young, it grows up, and gets old. And if you try to interfere with it in any way, you're going to have trouble. In these cellars, conditions are ideal. The wine's happy down here—the natural temperature is 54° to 56°F. It's ideal in the summer because it's cool in the day." The White Rock Cellars are unique in the way that all great wine cellars are unique. They have their own history, their legends, stories of individuals and of individual wines, each with its own bottled memories.

Author Ray Bradbury, in *Dandelion Wine*, his bittersweet novel of a late 1920s childhood summer, captured the mystique of the great wine collections and a particular wine cellar. But rather than considering the history and meaning of the '28 Lafites, he made it possible to fully understand a June dandelion, on the last emotional if not official day of the season.

> They went down in the cellar with Grandpa and while he decapitated the flowers they looked at all the summer shelved and glimmering there in the motionless streams, the bottles of dandelion wine. Numbered from one to ninety-odd, there the ketchup bottles, most of them full now, stood burning in the cellar twilight, one for every living summer day.
>
> "Boy," said Tom, "what a swell way to save June, July and August. Real practical."
>
> Grandfather looked up, considered this, and smiled.
>
> "Better than putting things in the attic you never use again. This way, you get to live the summer over for a minute or two here or there along the way through the winter, and when the bottles are empty the summer's gone for good and no regrets and no sentimental trash lying about for you to stumble over forty years from now. Clean, smokeless, efficient, that's dandelion wine."

It would take every day of Michael Card's nearly fifty years of handling and caring for wine, and perhaps the lifetime of the grandfather in Ray Bradbury's story, to understand what—besides fermented juice—a wine bottle contains. Lacking a two-hundred-year-old chalk cellar or a lifetime of handling wine is no reason not to begin to develop a personal store of wine and take advantage of more than just opening, pouring, and swallowing a glassful. It takes only an easy and, for most, a surprisingly interesting effort to become comfortable with storing, serving, and tasting wines.

Wines that heaven knows when,
Had sucked the fire of some forgotten sun,
And kept it through a hundred years of gloom.
—Alfred Lord Tennyson

STORING WINE

To enjoy the advantages of a stock of correctly laid down wines at home, you need to pay some attention to the elements of temperature and humidity, light, and vibrations. In essence, a good wine cellar should be well ventilated and clean, cool, dark, and quiet.

Temperature

Geoffrey Hasler, master sommelier and one of the driving forces within London's Guild of Sommeliers, has followed these guidelines throughout a distinguished career:

With oysters—Champagne, sparkling or still white wines.

With pâtés—Sherry, Marsala, Madeira, full red wines, or Sauternes.

When serving hors d'oeuvres, salads, etc., with dressings that contain vinegar or citrus fruit juice, it is best not to serve wine. Instead, serve a mineral water, as wine and vinegar do not go well together.

With clear soups— Sherry, Marsala, Madeira.

With fish and shellfish —dry Champagne, sparkling or still white wines.

(continued on page 65)

Even though ready for drinking at the time of purchase, most wines will store well for years in an environment that ranges between 55° and 68°F. Steady home temperatures in the low to mid-seventies will be satisfactory for maintaining nearly all drinking wines for several months. Ideally, the temperature should be constant. Realistically, it won't be. But as long as it doesn't vary from hot to cold on a daily basis, wine will hold up. As London wine collector Christopher Selmes points out, one "need not worry, if the house or apartment is air-conditioned and the temperature isn't going up into the nineties. The only real enemies are wild temperature fluctuation and excessive direct light."

One way—albeit costly—to avoid the risk of fluctuation is to install a cooling unit in one's wine cellar or closet. A variety of self-contained air-conditioned wine lockers are available and can be installed in any room, closet, or available space. Their prices range from $1,000 to $5,000.

The drinking wines that most people keep for day-to-day consumption and for entertaining are usually sturdy, and you need not treat the bottles as though they are invalids. Interestingly, the size of the bottle also plays an important part in the longevity of wine. A magnum is the ideal size and half bottles age faster than fifths. However, the ultimate life-span of the occasional rare and fine bottle of wine will probably be somewhat shortened in less than ideal conditions.

If you're planning to hold expensive wines for more than a year or two, they should be professionally stored—held and maintained either within a first-rate wine retailer's cellar or warehouse or in a privately rented wine locker in an air-conditioned commercial warehouse. The more makeshift your wine-storing conditions, the more your wine collection should be made up of wines that need little, if any, aging and are ready or nearly ready for drinking.

Laying Down Wine

All wines, except for fortified wines (Port, Sherry, Madeira, and brandy) and jug wines, should be kept in a horizontal or close to horizontal position. It doesn't matter if the neck is angled slightly up or down. It's important only that the wine in the bottle remain in contact with the base of the cork to guard against air entering and oxidizing the wines. It is, of course, unwise to store a bottle that shows signs of "leaking" due to a faulty or dry cork. Remember that Champagne should never be left in an upright position over an extended period of time or it will turn flat.

There are many excellent, inexpensive, ready-made wine racks on the market; the most useful are those that can hold two or more cases of wine. An alternative to the individual bottle-cradling rack is a simple open-faced bin in which bottles can be stacked on top of one another. Using a bin arrangment, it is possible to store one-third more bottles than with an individual rack that fills the same space.

Vibrations

Regardless of how you store your wine, be certain that the location is reasonably free of vibrations. You can confirm this by placing a full wineglass on the floor of your potential storage area. If wide concentric rings appear on the surface of the liquid, seek another location. If you maintain a small six- to twelve-bottle kitchen wine rack, keep it off the top of the refrigerator and away from the electric dishwasher; even at their smoothest, these appliances can create havoc.

SERVING WINE

Ready for Drinking

Here are a few basic guidelines to keep in mind when determining whether a bottle of wine is ready for drinking. Aromatized wines, fortified wines (with the exception of vintage Port), jug reds and whites, and any wines capped instead of corked are ready to be opened when purchased. Inexpensive red table wines need only a few hours of settling after purchase and delivery to be at their best. The fast-maturing wines, including Beaujolais, most sweet or dry wines, and rosés should rest for a few days after purchase before they are opened. They should never keep their corks for more than three years after their bottling date or the wine will probably begin to break down.

The classic fine red wines, particularly the vintage Burgundies and Bordeaux, the great Italian reds, and the California noble vintage-bottled varietals, require time to reach their fullness. You should discuss with a first-rate wine retailer the time needed for laying down your wines. Even if an expensive fine red wine is sufficiently dated at the time of purchase, you should lay it down for two to three months before serving.

(continued from page 64)

With white fish or salmon with creamy sauce—a dry or medium-sweet white wine, such as a Graves. Some people like a rosé with salmon.

With entrees—clarets, rosé, or light wines such as Rhine wine.

With white roast meat and poultry—clarets, light red wines, Rhine wines.

With red roast meats or game—full, strong, aromatic, top-grade vintage red wines.

With desserts and sweet dishes—dry or sweet Champagne, sparkling wines, Sherry, Port, Madeira.

With fruits and nuts— dry or sweet Champagne or sparkling wines, great sweet wines, cream Sherry, Marsala, Madeira, Port.

With coffee—brandy, liqueurs, Port, Madeira, Marsala.

Opening Wine

One of the relatively few points on which all wine professionals agree is that the most important element of a corkscrew is the screw. It should be a hollow, slightly flattened, worm-edged steel spiral approximately two and a half inches long. Solid, auger-type screws tend to pierce a cork directly down its center and grip poorly when the cork is being removed. A hollow spiral screw takes a firm hold within the corks and will minimize cork breakage. *Sommeliers* most often use a corkscrew-jackknife combination often called "the wine butler's tool" or "the waiter's friend." This multiple-function piece of equipment usually includes a bottle-cap remover, a sharp jackknife blade that can cut bottle neck capsules and their wires, also a lever and a spring-action corkscrew.

A Cork Extractor

A second type of cork remover—actually a tweezer rather than a screw—is an excellent complement to "the waiter's friend." It is an effective tool to use if a cork has broken within the neck of the bottle. If the cork has any firmness, you should be able to remove it in one piece, using the tweezer. The prongs are driven between the inside of the bottle and the outside of the cork. Then, with a slow, upward twisting motion, the cork is carefully drawn.

Removing the Cork

There are four simple steps in removing a wine cork with "the wine butler's tool." First, using the small blade, cut the seal that covers the cork from beneath the mouth of the bottle, and remove the upper part of the capsule. Then clean the cork, the lip of the bottle, the drip ring, and the neck of the bottle with a clean cloth. Line up the screw with the center of the open spiral over the cork's center point. The tip of a spiral screw should touch the cork at a point slightly off true center. (Attempting to pierce the cork in its exact center means only that the actual pressure line will end up at the side.) Then, without any undue pressure, turn the screw into the cork until it is within a quarter inch of the base of the cork (if you *pierce* the cork, the particles will fall into the wine). The lever should then be placed with its inside edge either on the edge of the bottle neck or against the top of the drip ring. Draw the cork by raising the handle against the fulcrum point of the lever. When the cork is nearly out of the bottle, remove the corkscrew and, with your fingers, gently force the cork free from the bottle. Wipe the lip of the bottle thoroughly.

The Wine Butler's Tool

Decanting Wine

The act of decanting—pouring the wine from its original bottle into a decanter—aerates the wine and allows its bouquet and body to begin the process of opening up to its fullest. Decanting a red wine into a clear glass container before serving improves the look of the wine. The colored or toned light-resistant glass in which red wines tend to be bottled camouflages the true color.

The most important reason for decanting, however, is that this process allows you to separate the wine from any sediment, which, if suspended in the wine, can cause a grainy, bitter taste.

Before decanting a bottle of sedimented wine, stand the bottle upright for at least two to three hours or, if convenient, eight to ten hours in the area where you will be opening and decanting the bottle. This assures you that a wine that's been in a bottle for five years or more, and has recently been moved, will have settled.

Decanting should be done with a strong light, or at least a highly reflective white cloth behind the neck of the bottle. Begin decanting as soon as you have uncorked the bottle. A clean glass funnel can be useful if the decanter opening is small, but it should not be necessary if you have a steady hand. To maximize aeration, allow the wine to flow down inside the inside of the neck of the decanter. Watch the neck of the original bottle as you pour the wine; as soon as sediment begins to appear, stop pouring and put the stopper back in the decanter. A small amount of sediment-loaded wine will remain in the bottle, and the wine in the decanter should be clear and attractive. Older, fine red wines should be decanted only a few minutes before serving. Clarets and other big red wines can be decanted one to three hours before serving.

Breathing

Every wine needs some contact with the air to open to its full flavor. White wines, rosés, and low-tannin reds such as Chinon, Arbois, and most light Beaujolais will reach drinking softness within five to fifteen minutes. Red wines, with the exceptions already noted, nearly always require more preparation time than whites. The younger the red, the more breathing time it requires to minimize its acidity and tannin. Sturdy red wines from France, the big reds of the United States, Italian Barolos and Chiantis, Spanish Riojas, and Argentine and Chilean red wines that are less than six years old should be allowed to breathe for an hour or two.

Older and finer reds, however—particularly those that have been laid down for fifteen years or more—may spoil, or at least flatten, if given too much breathing time. You can usually serve and drink them within minutes after opening and decanting. To gauge this, taste them as soon as they are uncorked or, if the wine is already in a stopped decanter, as soon as the stopper is removed a few minutes before you are ready to serve. If the taste is rough (which would be unusual), the wine may require twenty to thirty minutes of breathing. If the taste seems to be at its zenith, get on with the pouring.

Miss Anaïs Nin brought out a bottle of wine, and though there were several other men present she gave it to me to open.

I had worked the screw halfway into the cork when the wooden handle separated. I was given another identical corkscrew. This one broke off in the middle. With an enigmatic smile, Miss Nin produced a third corkscrew of the same type.

I twisted it in very carefully and then pulled slowly and steadily. The corkscrew emerged, straightening out as it appeared, but the cork did not budge. Miss Nin had watched the whole performance closely. Now she took the bottle from my hands. "I can see," she said, "that you are a most interesting young man."

—Anatole Broyard, New York Times

Serving Temperatures

Individual wines should be served at temperatures that maximize their body and flavor. Specific ideal temperatures are nearly impossible to attain, and a few degrees above or below the recommended professional standards will not be noticeable to the palate. Keep in mind that it's best to pour a red wine at slightly lower than its ideal temperature, since within fifteen minutes of being served in a normally heated room a wine will heat 2° to 4°. If a glass of red wine is too cool, warm it by cupping the bowl of glass for a few seconds in your hands.

A rule of thumb that works: the sweeter the wine, the cooler its serving temperature.

At Room Temperature

Keep in mind that the use of the word "room" is more traditional than functional, and the actual ideal temperature range is 60° to 65°F. This is considered the best serving temperature for domestic Burgundy, domestic Zinfandel, Eastern red wines, red Burgundy, red wines of the Rhône, red Bordeaux, red wines of the Loire, Chianti, Barolo, Grignolino, Port, Madeira, Marsala, and Muscatel. Check the bottle with your hand. If it feels slightly cool, not cold, it should be within the correct temperature range. If you think it is too warm, five to ten minutes in the refrigerator and then two to three minutes at room temperature should be enough preparation.

Sweet White Wines: Sauternes and the sweet German wines offer their optimum flavor at 40° to 45°F.

Semi-sweet Wines: The ideal temperature range for serving is 45° to 50°F. The bouquet can reach its potential at this still relatively cool level because of the high sugar content of these wines.

Dry Whites: The delicate, almost brittle taste will lose its edge if the wine is chilled too much. The ideal serving temperature of dry white wine is from 46° to 52°F.

A house with a great wine stored below lives in our imagination as a joyful house, fast and splendidly rooted in the soil.

—George Meredith

Young Red Wines: The light and younger fruity red wines such as Beaujolais, particularly those of most recent vintage, can be served well at 48° to 52°F.

Rosé (Dry): These wines have a body and taste more closely allied to dry white wines than to reds. They can be experienced at their peak at 46° to 52°F.

Rosé (Semi-sweet): As stated, the sweeter the wine, the cooler it can be for serving. Rosé, with its noticeable sugar level, should be served at 45° to 50°F.

Sparkling Wines and Champagnes: The wines of medium and higher levels of sweetness are best chilled between 42° and 45°F. The drier champagnes and sparkling wines should be served slightly warmer, at 40° to 45°F.

Ring Decanter—*Crystal with silver-sheathed neck and faceted stopper. Dutch, late 19th century.*

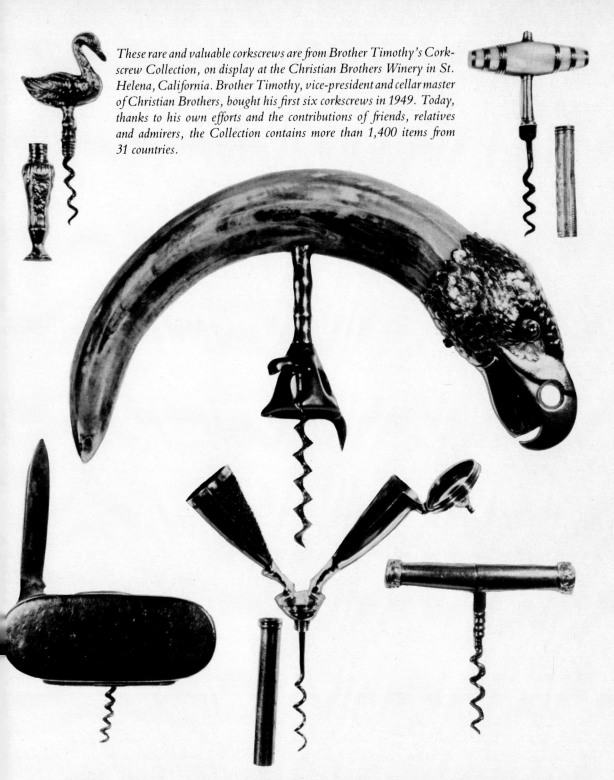

These rare and valuable corkscrews are from Brother Timothy's Cork-screw Collection, on display at the Christian Brothers Winery in St. Helena, California. Brother Timothy, vice-president and cellar master of Christian Brothers, bought his first six corkscrews in 1949. Today, thanks to his own efforts and the contributions of friends, relatives and admirers, the Collection contains more than 1,400 items from 31 countries.

(Top row, left to right) Swan—*The Netherlands, circa 1800. Measures 3.6 x 7.8 x 1.3 cm.* Boar Tusk— *Equipped with a sharp point for breaking wires on Champagne bottles. The United States. Measures 21.1 x 15 x 3.2 cm.* Mother-of-Pearl—*Probably France, circa 1750. Measures 5.1 x 8.5 x 1.5 cm. (Bottom row, left to right)* Snuff Box—*Sweden, circa 1900. Measures 15 x 7 x 2.1 cm.* Nutmeg Grater—*The handle opens to allow access to the nutmeg grater, which was probably used for hot mulled wines or to disguise a poor wine. England, circa 1805. Measures 15.2 x 15 x 4 cm.* Gentlemen's Pocket-Style Cork-screw—*As with all pocket-style corkscrews, the spiral screw can be fully enclosed within the handle. Germany, circa 1897. Measures 8.3 x 7.2 x 1.4 cm.*

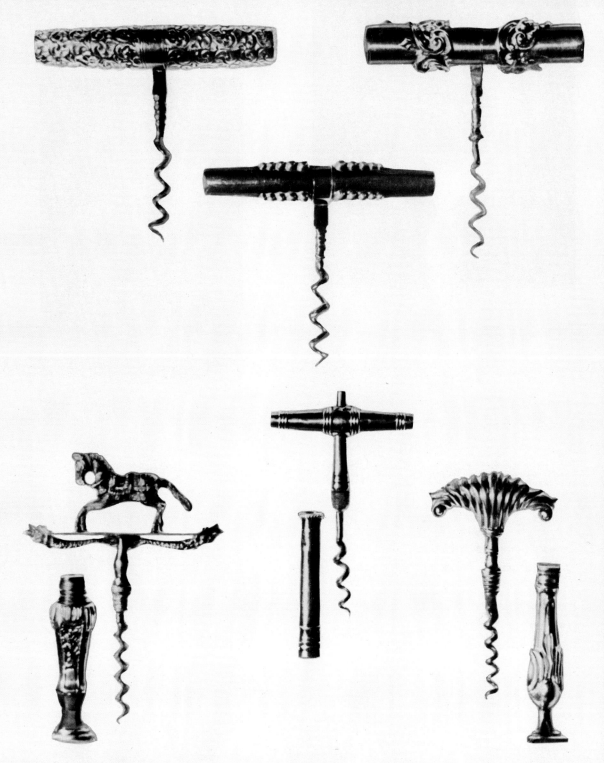

(Top row, left to right) Gentleman's Pocket-Style Corkscrew—*United States, circa 1850. Measures 7.8 x 6.6 x 1.4 cm.* Gentleman's Pocket-Style Corkscrew—*United States, circa 1875. Measures 7.5 x 7.4 x 1.8 cm.* Gentleman's Pocket-Style Corkscrew—*United States, circa 1850. Measures 7.9 x 6.5 x 1.6 cm. (Bottom row, left to right)* Silver Horse—*England, circa 1800. Measures 6.5 x 8.5 x 1.1 cm.* Barrel Handle—*Probably France, circa 1750. Measures 4.7 x 7.3 x 1 cm.* Silver Leaf—*Probably France, circa 1750. Measures 4.5 x 7.5 x 1.3 cm.*

(left, top) **Wineglass**—Flaring bowl with two extended D-shaped wings. Venetian or façon de Venise, early 17th century. *(right)* **Humpen** (Tankard) — Enameled in multi-color with ten figures depicting the "Ten Ages of Man." Bohemian, late 16th or early 17th century. (Bottom, left to right) **Pokal**—Thistle bowl with marine scene. German (Saxony), mid-18th century. **Goblet**—Giant glass with engraved vine motif and legend "The Glorious Immortal Memory of King William III." English or Irish, mid-18th century. **Goblet**—Octagonal in shape, enameled with eight figures. Austrian (Vienna), 1845–50.

Ice Buckets

The quickest and most attractive way to chill a bottle of wine is in an ice bucket. Ten minutes in a correctly prepared (two-thirds ice to one-third cold water) bucket equals an hour in a refrigerator. The bucket, or cooler, should be deep enough so that the bottle can be immersed to its shoulder. Keep a towel or cloth napkin on hand with which to wrap the bottle when serving.

Food and Wine

The harmonizing of food and wine is a matter of personal taste and selection. The goal in this mixing and matching is to put together foods and wines that complement each other, so that neither one dominates the other. This means simply that a delicate food will be most enjoyed if served with a delicate wine. And the converse: a sturdy roast, for example, can be served well with a "sturdy" or big red wine. The final matchings are yours to make.

Pouring

There are a few simple tricks for easy handling of a wine bottle or a decanter. Sommeliers are trained to hold the bottle with the wrist of their serving hand above it, and to spread their thumb and forefinger. They then place the thumb about an inch below the shoulder of the bottle, at a slight angle opposite the second finger, which is pressed against the bottle on the opposite side. The forefinger also presses against the shoulder of the bottle. This gives the server complete control while pouring. A decanter is slightly more awkward to handle and it should be gripped firmly around its neck, just under the lip. When pouring, position the bottle or decanter just above the glass, not in contact with it. Fill each glass no less than one third and no more than half full. If you are serving an older, sedimented red wine directly from the bottle, carry the glasses to the bottle rather than move the bottle around and risk stirring up the tannin-heavy residue.

WINEGLASSES

Your approach to assembling a selection of wineglasses can be as simple or as complex as you wish to make it. You can get along with a few all-purpose wineglasses or a selection of the five basic glasses, or you can attempt to collect the many specific shapes and sizes that hundreds of years of traditional matching of glassware designs to individual grape blends have made traditional. There are four basic elements to keep in mind when stocking your shelves—clarity, shape, size, and breakage.

The All-Purpose Wineglass

The Tulip Glass for Red Wine

The Paris Goblet

Appearance/Clarity: In order to appreciate a wine truly, you must be able to judge its color and clarity. This dictates the use of a clear, simple glass. Regardless of the pleasing aesthetics of ornate, finely cut or etched stemware, or softly tinted glasses, less décor *is* truly more when it comes to wineglasses.

Shape: The top edge of a wineglass should curve slightly inward. This turned-in rim serves to hold and focus the bouquet. The stem of the glass is also important. It should be solid enough that breakage is minimized, but long enough that your hand heat will not negatively affect the temperature and taste of the wine.

Size: Ideally a wineglass should have a capacity, when full to the brim, of seven to nine ounces of liquid. This size glass can comfortably hold a decent portion of wine while no more than half full. With servings of three to four ounces the standard 75mm. bottle of wine yields six to eight glasses. This relationship of wine serving to glass enables you to effortlessly swirl the wine and release the bouquet without risking spills. The giant balloon glasses of twelve to twenty-three ounces frequently seen in restaurants offer a dramatic visual effect, but they add nothing to the experience of tasting and enjoying a wine.

Breakage: Wineglasses break. This is a simple fact and should be kept in mind when buying wineglasses. The nature of the object, its history (a glass dramatically flung into a fireplace is intended to shatter, not bounce), and the nature of commerce (to make and sell more wineglasses next year than last year) dictate a certain temporariness. Breakage can be minimized through proper care in washing, storage, polishing, and serving. When you are stocking wineglasses, it makes sense to always have a few more than you think you will need.

The All-purpose Wineglass

This glass has a long stem, a convex top, and a standard eight- to ten-ounce capacity. A compromise between the traditional tulip glass for red wine, the Burgundy-style goblet, and the classic French white-wine glass, it is accepted as an eye-pleasing addition to any table setting.

The Tulip Glass for Red Wine

Because of its size—eight to ten ounces is now considered standard—this traditional glass is ideal for the strong table reds of France, Italy, Spain, and America. The shape—a masterful blending of art and function—was developed by Venetian glass blowers four hundred years ago, and no one has yet found a way to improve on the original design.

The Paris Goblet

This glass has proved to be ideal for full-bodied reds—the fine wines of Burgundy and Bordeaux, and their equivalents from

California and around the world. A royally decreed adaptation of the tulip shape, the Paris goblet has a capacity of eight to ten and a half ounces, allowing generous portions without spillage. The extreme curve of the inward rim retains and maximizes the bouquet. The rounded bowl allows a reasonable amount of hand warmth to reach the wine and open up the rich flavor. The shape was developed originally in the seventeenth century in answer to an order from Louis XIV. Having declared that the rounded, full-textured Burgundy reds were the "crown gems of France," he directed the winemakers to design a glass matched to his taste. The winemakers did not disappoint him.

The White Wine Glass

The White Wineglass

The French-designed white-wine glass has a definite style and function. Smaller than the standard red wine glass—ideally no more than eight ounces—it is a reminder that white wines, with their acidic levels, are best tasted in smaller quantities. The elongated stem makes it possible to avoid warming the wine with hand heat. The softly curving sides, resulting in a more moderate curve of the inward rim than the classic tulip or more dramatic Paris goblet, make it possible for the bouquet to concentrate effectively. As with all classic designs, the lines are simple and elegant.

The Copita

This glass in its most popular four- to five-ounce size is the standard vessel for Sherry and serves well for Port and Madeira. Developed in Spain and dubbed the "little cup," it has stood the test of time and has highlighted the color, scent, and flavor of wine for over three hundred years.

The Copita

The Champagne

Of the several variations of Champagne glasses available, the elongated tulip shape is the most effective. Its clean and distinct design best allows the wine to effervesce, and its softly curved rim concentrates and maximizes the bouquet. Two other shapes are frequently seen. The *coupe*, with its shallow bowl and broad rim, dissipates the bubbles and the essence of Champagne itself. The *flute*, with its straight and flaring sides, is perhaps better suited for beer.

Washing Wineglasses

The trick in washing wineglasses is in the rinsing. If the glasses aren't thoroughly rinsed, they will dry with a dull luster. Since the rinse cycle on many dishwashers is often less than thorough, it's a good idea to rinse and dry wineglasses by hand. It takes only a few seconds. Pour warm, not hot, water into the glasses, letting it spill over the rim of each glass, or immerse the glasses in water. After rinsing and before drying them, leave a little warm water at the bottom. A warm glass is easier to dry and polish than a cold one.

The Champagne Glass

Drying and Polishing

To dry a wineglass properly, you should polish it. Using a soft, lint-free cloth or dish towel, pick up the freshly rinsed glass and tip the warm water out of the bowl. Push enough of the towel into the bowl to loosely fill it without packing. Rest the bowl in your right hand by inserting your thumb in the bowl, and loosely hold the outside of the cloth-covered bowl with your fingers. Supporting the glass gently with your left hand, wrap the stem and the foot of the glass with the rest of the cloth. Turn the glass clockwise within the towel, rotating it with the fingers of your right hand. Don't grip too tightly with either hand, for if too much pressure is exerted on the top, a sharp triangle of glass may snap off. If too much pressure is exerted on the foot of the glass, the stem may snap. Once the glass is dry, give it three or four more turns with the towel and you will bring up a brilliant shine.

Always polish wineglasses when you take them from a cupboard or glass rack before using. With the rotating towel method, you will keep glasses free of fingermarks and they will look their best.

Storing Wineglasses

It is only logical to store glasses in matched sets—it is easier to keep track of them. Avoid placing them upside down on a shelf, as a glass stored this way may draw up moisture and become cloudy. Also, it will pick up the smell of the shelf—particularly if the shelf is painted or shellacked—and the taste of the wine may be affected. To protect upright glasses from accumulating dust in their bowls, lay a strip of tissue paper across the tops of the glasses. If you use an overhead bar-style hanging glass rack, keep in mind that the inverted bowl will pick up room odors and collect rising smoke and dust. Before using a glass that has been suspended overhead, rinse and polish it.

INSIGHTS FROM A PROFESSIONAL TASTER

Happiness is a wine of the rarest vintage, and seems insipid to a vulgar taste.

—Rudyard Kipling

Draw the cork, pour the wine, and start tasting! Wine is for drinking, and the only way a person can develop a taste is by experiencing the products and the individual blending styles of the world's winemakers. Everything else that is attendant to the world of wine—the books, the lectures, the stylized equipment, the legends—is secondary to the real thing: the wine grapes and the winemaker's skills. The best advice in the midst of all the current enological seriousness is to pull the cork, taste the wine. Think about what you're tasting, how it differs from other wines you've tasted, and how it fits your own palate.

Wine expert Lucio Sorre's job is to taste over four thousand wines each year. As chief wine taster of Villa Banfi, U.S.A., the nation's largest wine importer, he has developed tasting techniques and judging insights that can serve as guidelines, regardless of an individual's degree of wine experience.

Swirling, Sniffing, Sipping

In tasting and giving a personal rating to a wine, it is necessary to consider four general aspects. *Color:* Is it clear, brilliant, limpid? *Bouquet:* Does the wine emit any odor foreign to the grape? Is there any mustiness? Heavy acidity? *Taste:* Do the elements balance? Is there a touch of sweetness mitigated by a touch of astringency? *Memory:* Is the aftertaste a lingering, pleasant sensation?

On Training One's Palate

Many people who are completely comfortable when casually drinking wine feel shy about more formal wine tasting—they feel they have no palate. But if you can distinguish between salt and pepper and other basic tastes in food, you can develop your palate. An exceptional palate is really just an average palate that has been trained by tasting over and over again.

The Wine, Not the Label

When "tasting," pay little attention to what wine professionals say and write about particular wines. Instead, concentrate on and analyze each wine as you would analyze a person you have never met before.

A label is only an indication of what the wine is. You may say to yourself, "This label—this wine—is supposed to be superb," and conclude that there is something wrong with you if you don't like the particular wine. This kind of thinking should be abandoned.

You also must accept this important point: tasting wine can be enjoyed only when you are not distracted by something else. It requires concentration. The focus in tasting several similar wines is not to compare one with another but to notice their differences. It's an important perspective.

A Taster's Sampler

Begin with some very basic red and white wines. Three or four wines of the same type can be sampled comfortably at the same time. And—this is important—make notes. Your notations need not be elaborate. Write down your reactions such as, "It smells of rancid butter" or, "Sour," as a reminder and for later reference.

To try examples of domestic wines, you can begin serious tasting with three white and three red California jug wines—Gallo Chablis and Hearty Burgundy (these best-selling wines are typical of mass-produced wine from California. They are not known for excessive character, but they are pleasant and easy on the palate), Sebastiani Chablis and Burgundy, and Robert Mondavi white and red. As a starting point with imported wines, you could choose Riunite for white and Mateus and Blue Nun for rosé. They do not have complicated characteristics.

If you begin with American jug wines, it is interesting to drink them with meals for a week or two—a different wine each day. Either white or red wine will do, but ideally you would start with Gallo Hearty Burgundy, followed by Sebastiani Burgundy, then the Mondavi. The reason for this particular sequence is that Gallo is an open wine, it is very pleasant, has no sharp edges, and is a broadly appealing wine. Next the Sebastiani, which is recognized as having slightly more complexity and a bit more taste. Then the Mondavi, which has slightly more taste than the other two.

Take a sip of wine without food before a meal. And pay attention to the taste levels as you taste the wine throughout the meal. Record your reactions. Taste a sip again after the meal. Your taste perceptions will diminish and the wine will taste different at each step of the sequence. The characteristics you detected at the beginning will be undetectable at the end.

With imported wines, a logical sequence for tasting would be the Mateus, which is light and has a touch of carbonation; then the Riunite, which has more taste and also a touch of effervescence and sweetness; then the Blue Nun. Although this approach may seem to be running counter to the dogma that one should not drink white wines after reds, it is acceptable because Lambrusco, the grape of both Mateus and Riunite, has a lower alcohol content than Blue Nun.

When you find a type of wine that is pleasing to you, try to find wines of similar consistency but with different tastes. The most important beginning guideline is to taste wines of the same type.

A Taster's Taboos—Odors and Scents

Strong odors interfere with the olfactory tonalities of the wine. Do not smoke before or during a tasting. Men should not wear shaving lotion or cologne while tasting wine, and women should not wear perfume or lipstick. If a woman wearing lipstick tastes a sparkling wine or Champagne, the wine will go flat in the glass.

Glasses: It often happens that a glass will contain a slight soapy residue that, although nearly imperceptible to the eye, is there and can flatten the wine. To guard against this, just pour one third of a glass of wine into the glass. Swirl the wine so that it completely washes the walls of the glass, and then pour the contents into the glass of another wine taster. Repeat the swirling and pouring into the next person's wineglass, and so on. When the last glass is wine-rinsed, throw out the wine. The glasses will be free of residual odor.

Foods: If you drink wine with eggs, the wine will taste of sulfur. Artichokes, fennel, and asparagus destroy the taste of wine—the wine will flatten out and nearly taste like water. You should never drink wine and eat anything containing vinegar if you want to highlight a wine; pickles or peppers or a salad dressing that contain vinegar should be avoided. You can minimize the problem with salad by using lemon juice instead of vinegar, but even so the wine will not taste its best. The taste of white wine is more easily destroyed than that of the sturdier, fuller-bodied reds.

On Smelling Wine

Pour two and a half to three ounces of wine into a stemmed wineglass, then, holding the glass by the foot or stem, swirl it. Swirling the glass so that more of the liquid comes in contact with oxygen releases the alcohol and the elements in the wine that produce the distinctive aroma or bouquet. You can test this yourself. Pour some wine and don't swirl it, then smell it. Pour some of the same wine into another glass, swirl it, and smell it, then smell the still glass again. The swirled glass will tell you much more. You should swirl the wine for five seconds and then sniff it. Far too many people barely let their nose approach the glass, and then they smell the wine shyly. Actually you should put your nose almost inside the glass and take one quick smell.

On Tasting

Take a small sip of the wine into your mouth. Your first sensation will be of the wine's sweetness level, and you'll taste some acidity at the edge of your mouth. Swirl the wine with your tongue, and then breathe air through it. Purse your lips and let some air in so that it will go through the wine to the back of your mouth. Then exhale through your nose, still holding the wine in your mouth. This gives you the full taste of the wine—you don't have to swallow it to taste it.

Inhaling air through the wine should take about three or four seconds. If you are tasting several wines, do not hold the wine in your mouth for too long, since you will eventually dull your taste perception.

If you're tasting white wine, or even if you drink several glasses of the same white wine, the first glass will always taste the best. The second one will not be as definite as the first; the third will be less marked than the second. White wine does not have tannic acid, and without the stimulation caused by the tannin, the mouth becomes tired from glass to glass.

With red wines, the opposite is true: because red wines have tannin, which blends with the mouth, the last glass will always taste the best. The more you sip a red wine, the cleaner your mouth is, and the more you feel the richness of the wine.

Wine Memory
Building a wine memory requires patience. Although a degree of acuity can be gained in two or three months, it takes about a year of daily tasting to have a real sense of the individual values, nuances, and specific tastes of wine.

As mentioned earlier, it is important to limit yourself initially to the wines of a specific region. First gain familiarity with the generic wines of an area, then go into the varietals. If you're going to taste Italian wines, or California wines, limit yourself to the wines of a certain area. Then expand your focus to neighboring areas. It is not a good idea to try to taste a few Italian wines and then jump to California wines, then on to French or German or Spanish wines. It's too confusing.

It is a good idea to attend a basic wine-tasting course, but that can only help to fill in the background. Your own experience and your reaction to wines are what really count.

Annotating A 20-Point Tasting Scorecard

Since 1951, when Dr. Maynard Amerine, former head of the Department of Vinicul-ture and Enology at the University of California at Davis and one of the nation's most important wine professionals, popularized a 20-point system of grading an individual wine, there have been countless variations on his well-founded and well-thought-out theme.

The following sequence of headings and point values is an individual wine-rating system adapted from Dr. Amerine's "scorecard" and used by Rory Roberts, Director of the New York School of Wine, in the tasting courses he conducts throughout New York State and New England.

CLARITY (2 points: cloudy = 0, clear = 1, brilliant = 2): When you look at a wine against a light—never a fluorescent light, but the light of the day, or a candle, or a bulb—the wine should have a luminescence, a shine. The best wines will have a sharpness of color—they will be brilliant, limpid (these are interchangeable terms). The difference between *brilliant* and simply *clear* is similar to the difference between spring water, after the minerals have settled, and tap water. The tap water shows a flatness; its liquid lacks crispness when viewed against a light.

A *cloudy* wine is one in which solid parts suspended in the liquid cut down the limpidity, the brilliance of color. These particles cause a dullness within the liquid. Solid particles natural in the processing of the wine are removed by filtering. A glass of red wine can be cloudy if its bottle has aging sediment and the bottle is shaken before it is poured. Some of the classic French and Italian wines such as Barolo—the very old vintages—will carry sediment, and if the bottle is shaken it will cloud the wine. If you let the glass stand for a while, the sediment should settle. If the cloudiness remains, it can mean that the wine has broken down either because of poor handling and storage or because it has reached the end of its longevity.

COLOR (2 points: distinctly off = 0, slightly = 1, correct = 2): By looking at the color you can surmise the lightness and sweetness of a white wine. The color in a white wine will range from a very pale tone to a honey tone. The dry white wines are at the pale end of the scale, and a rich honey color, with no tinges of brown, is normally an indication of a sweeter white wine.

In a red wine the colors range from brilliant purplish red to a brick color with a tinge of brown. The more purple the wine, the younger it is. A tinge of brown in a red wine is an indication of age. *Distinctly off* means that the wine is past its peak. If a white wine has a brownish tinge, or a red wine has a dullness of color tone, it is *slightly* off.

BOUQUET (4 points: vinous = 1, distinct but not varietal = 2, varietal = 3): The smell, the "nose" of a wine, ranges from a simple aroma—the grapy smell of a young wine—to a full bouquet, which develops as the wine matures in the bottle. The smell is considered *vinous* if, when you sniff, your nose receives a distinct smell of the grape juice instead of a blend of the grape. If you smell a Cabernet Sauvignon and it is pleasant but does not have the pronounced characteristics of a wine made with Cabernet Sauvignon grapes, the wine is considered *distinct but not varietal*.

The smell is considered *varietal* if when you sniff it you can sense the full characteristics of the specific grape and say, "This is definitely Cabernet Sauvignon," or "This is definitely Pinot Noir."

If the wine emits an odor foreign to the grape, such as a slightly cloying smell, that's an indication of dioxidation, the wine's breakdown. If an excessive harsh smell of vinegar is present, the wine is faulty. If too much sulfur is used, it will create a slight burning sensation in the back of the nose which is unpleasant. The presence of sulfur in excessive quantities will also cause the *ring* around the head the next morning. Another off-odor is the baked, burnt smell of oxidized wines. Or there is a skunky or raisiny smell due to the use of overripe grapes. A wine will sometimes smell very musty, which is caused by a diseased cork. If the musty smell doesn't dissipate quickly, that means that the wine hasn't been stored well. If you leave the bottle open for a while or let the glass stand, the odor may diminish but it will not disappear; you can't get rid of it.

As the wine becomes fully aged, the aroma develops its bouquet. It doesn't smell of grape juice anymore; the smell is much more complex. It smells of the full, well-finished wine.

VOLATILE ACIDITY (2 points: obvious off-odors = 0, slight = 1, none = 2): You don't taste the acidity; you discern it with your nose. If you smell the wine and a sharpness shoots through you, you have either a very young wine or a wine that is breaking down. It is a sign of oxidation, the action of oxygen to and within the wine. High oxidation gives a white wine its brownish hue. It also gives off a slightly burned taste. If the oxidation is slight, it is barely noticeable. If the oxidation is very definite, a white wine would be very brown, a red wine would be a dark brick color, and the taste would be musty and heavy.

If there is no off-odor or oxidation, you have a good wine. High levels of volatile acidity are something that winemakers work to avoid. After the grapes are pressed, the juice never receives dosages of oxygen. Oxygen and light are two enemies of wine.

TOTAL ACIDITY (2 points: distinctly high or low = 0, slightly high or low = 1, well-balanced = 2): If the wine has a proper balance of sugar and acidity, your first reaction will be a taste of sweetness, mitigated by an astringency. Your mouth should feel nice and clean. However, if the wine is off-balance and there is more sugar than acidity, it will taste flat. You'll be left with a tired "blah" taste within your mouth. If the acidity overpowers the sugar, the wine will taste sharp and somewhat unpleasant. A white wine with higher acidity is always more enjoyable than one with low acidity. With low acidity the wine won't taste as clean or interesting, and it tires the palate.

SWEETNESS (1 point: too high or low = 0, normal = 1): The quality of sweetness within a wine is always a product of the sugar content and the wine's acidity. A wine should offer a medium, not an excessive, balanced level of sweetness. *Too high* or cloying sweetness results when the wine carries residual sugar, sedimented sugar that has not been effectively fermented or transformed into alcohol. A wine with a great deal of sweetness, such as the Sauternes, *can* be superb *if* it has a lot of acidity. Although Sauternes have high sugar levels, they also have high acidity, which minimizes the sugar.

BODY (1 point: too high or low = 0, normal = 1): Body is the texture you experience, the richness you sense, when you taste the wine. Consider coffee as an example: the difference between an espresso (a wine with full body) and a light American coffee (light body). The taste of a light American coffee will not fill the mouth and is relatively untextured when compared with a cup of espresso. A full-bodied wine will give you fullness of taste—as though you could bite into it.

In some cases a wine may have too high body. This means there is a big "lump" of taste, which, if not mitigated by other factors, is unpleasant. The wine is digestible, but it really doesn't leave a positive taste in the mouth. It's like eating a mealy apple.

Body is, of course, relative to the type of wine. In a light, still wine, *normal* body is considerably lighter than you would expect in a red wine. Within any wine, however, it is a good, pleasant taste.

FLAVOR (2 points: abnormal = 0, slightly off = 1, normal = 2): This is the clean, distinct taste of the wine type, a combination of the wine taste and the grape taste. An *abnormal* flavor is one that has no relationship to what should be expected of a particular wine. If, for example, a wine made from grapes tastes like peach juice, it is distinctly *abnormal*. The flavor is considered *slightly off* if it tastes pleasant but there seems to be something missing. This does not mean that anything is really wrong with the wine, just that the wine is not completely pleasing.

BITTERNESS (1 point: distinctly high = 0, normal = 1): The aftertaste of a wine is *normal* when it is slightly bitter. This touch of bitterness in the aftertaste is inviting and appetizing. At correct levels, it is this quality in the wine that makes you want to drink another glass. Pronounced bitterness will be unpleasant and can indicate that the wine has passed its prime. Distinctly high bitterness is a product of low sugar combined with high acidity.

ASTRINGENCY (1 point: distinctly high = 0, normal = 1): This is the puckering sensation on the upper walls of the mouth which is more noticeable from a red wine than a white. Because tannin lessens as wine ages, young red wines have more pronounced astringency than do older reds. However, if there is too much tannin in a young wine, causing higher than normal astringency, the wine will remain higher than normal in tannin throughout its aging cycle. Astringency is considered *normal*—and ideal—when no element stands out. You would drink the wine and sense the astringency only slightly, if at all. A wine that has *distinctly high* astringency suffers from high acidity and will deliver an unpleasant taste—similar to that of a persimmon that's not perfect.

GENERAL QUALITY (2 points: lacking = 0, average = 1, impressive = 2): A wine is well balanced, of high general quality if, as you taste, your first reaction is a touch of sweetness, mitigated by some astringency and acidity, which leaves a nice clean taste. You have one unit, one whole. If the particular wine fits your palate and stands out in relation to memories of similar wine types and you enjoy it, it should be considered *impressive*. If the wine is not quite what it was meant to be—if it lacks characteristics, color, or bouquet—it should be considered as *lacking*. If the taste experience is pleasant but without any exceptional values, the wine is ranked as *average*.

Adding it up— A wine that, when put to this scoring system, garners 17 to 20 points is outstanding. The point totals for a good commercial wine should range from 13 to 16; 9 to 12 points indicates a defective commercial wine. Anything that tallies 8 points or less should be remembered, only that it won't be repeated.

Wine Auctions

Wine auctions, once an exclusively European institution, are today being held around the world. Thanks to the efforts of Heublein, Christie's, Sotheby's, and other leaders in the wine auction field, Americans now have the opportunity to do what overseas wine lovers have been doing for centuries—use wine auctions to round out or thin their collections, mingle with those in the wine trades, sample fine bottles, and, most important, buy fine wines at a fair price.

Wine auctions began receiving wide American attention in 1970, when New York City wine merchant Peter Morrell purchased a double magnum of 1865 Château Lafite from Christie's, the London-based auction house. The $480 Morrell paid for the wine seems modest by today's standards (an 1865 Lafite sold for $10,000 at Heublein's 1982 auction), but at the time it shocked the American wine community and drew national attention to both Morrell and the wine auction industry. That same year, Sotheby's established a wine department in London. In the United States, Heublein had held its first wine sale in 1969. The wine auction was coming of age.

Despite resistance from some retail merchants and legal restrictions dating back to Prohibition, wine auctions are on the increase. Heublein's first sale sold $55,000 worth of wine. Today, a Heublein sale may gross ten times that amount. Christie's and Sotheby's, two English auction giants, have recently gotten their U.S. wine sales off the ground. And a wide range of non-profit organizations now use wine auctions as fund raisers.

You need not be a major charity, wine grower or wine merchant to profit from selling wines at auction. For an estate left with an extensive wine cellar, for the wine collector who wants to winnow down his stock, or for those whose collections are now so valuable that they feel they can't afford to drink them, wine auctions are one of the few legal ways to sell wine without a liquor license.

But it is the wine drinker who can benefit most from the wine auction. Few retailers can offer the assortment of vintages and vineyards that the regular auction-goer will find available to him. And the alert buyer can still find something rarer than any wine in today's market: the bargain. Those willing to do some homework and bid carefully can often purchase fine wines at a fraction of their worth.

Wine auctions, large and small, are cropping up everywhere in affiliation with an array of sponsors and organizers. It is likely that as the U.S. acquires a taste for such sales, the industry, still in its infancy, will expand at an explosive rate. What follows is a cross section of those wine auctions that have a head start.

Heublein's Alexander C. McNally pours Bouchard Pere & Fils Beaune Burgundy 1865 at an auction preview tasting.

HEUBLEIN, INC.

Memphis restaurateur and wine merchant John Grisanti holds a jeroboam of 1864 Château Lafite, purchased at Heublein's 1978 sale for a then record price of $18,000.

Heublein, the international food and beverage company, is responsible for one of the finest wine auctions in the country. Each year, following months of preparation and weeks of preview tastings, Heublein moves into a major American city and, like a posh mobile gourmet shop, puts on the block some of the most sought-after wines in the world.

Although Heublein—a major wine importer and distributor, and the second-largest wine producer in the U.S.—originally organized the auction as a not-for-profit promotional venture to showcase its wares, in recent years the sales have been the scene of some record-setting purchases. Businessmen who benefit from the publicity they receive when they make record bids use the Heublein sale as an opportunity to draw attention to themselves. In fact, when John Grisanti, a Memphis restaurant owner and wine merchant, bought the most expensive bottle of wine ever—a $31,000 bottle of 1822 Château Lafite in 1980—he was competing against a Washington retailer who also wanted to set a record.

Grisanti's previous record purchase, $18,000 for a jeroboam of 1864 Château Lafite, stood for only a year. It was toppled at Heublein's 1979 sale by Syracuse wine merchant Charles Mara, who paid $28,000 for a bottle of 1806 Château Lafite.

Grisanti and nine others paid $3,100 each for a share of that record bottle, which was opened at a gala charity wine tasting in Memphis in 1981. There, 250 people paid $200 each to sample rare wines donated by local families, and to watch 20 people (five of the original investors who showed up, and 15 people selected by lot) sip the most expensive wine in the world. The event raised $70,000 for St. Jude's Children's Research Hospital, and those who donated wines were able to deduct the cost from their taxes.

Alexander C. McNally, Heublein's International Wine Director, prides himself on his ability to include exotic wines in Heublein's sales. Two years ago, he sold several bottles of Port, Bordeaux, and Madeira that divers had retrieved from a sunken ship off the coast of Georgia. The wines had been submerged for 140 years. Last year he sold the contents of a lost French cellar, forgotten 150 years ago when its original owners died. In 1977, McNally removed the most important cache of wines ever discovered in America from the Ten Broeck Mansion in Albany, New York. The cellar, the legacy of two nineteenth-century businessmen and wine connoisseurs, Dudley and John Josiah Olcott, had been untouched for almost three quarters of a century. In all, McNally has assembled nearly $5 million worth of rare wines in the sale's 15-year history.

Heublein has also offered some bargains along with the exotic wines. While a handful of record setters have been paying thousands of dollars for single bottles, the merchants, restaurateurs, wholesalers, and connoisseurs who typically attend have bought cases for as little as two dollars a bottle. The 1982 Boston auction is one of the best examples. At that sale, a bottle of 1865 La Romanée from the cellars of Bouchard Père et Fils sold for $1,700. Numerous cases of Portuguese Perquita 1970 were purchased for just $40 per case, or $3.33 a bottle. Although a large number of private collectors attended and bought many individual lots, trade buyers were the biggest spenders. They broke no records, but prices were generally high. The highest single bottle buys were $13,000 for a jeroboam of 1929 Château Mouton-Rothschild and $10,000 for a double magnum of 1865 Château Lafite—a bottle from the same producer and vintage that cost Peter Morrell a record-breaking $480 back in 1970.

You needn't attend a Heublein auction to place a bid. Bids can be commissioned. "We have a form in our catalogue on which you put down the highest price that you would be willing to pay for a wine, say one hundred dollars for lot number twenty-eight," McNally explained. "The auction commissioner puts it in his book, and will bid on your behalf. For example, say the bidding in the room goes as high as fifty dollars. It is knocked down to you at the next highest step, which is fifty-five dollars. So that means you are not necessarily going to pay the full hundred dollars that you commissioned. You pay just fifty-five dollars in this case, or as

Newspapers publish the sales that make the headlines, and people think that's all that you can get here. The good news of the auction is that it provides some unsung values. You can buy for thousands, but you can also buy for just a few dollars.
—Alexander McNally, International Wine Director of Heublein.

Auctioneer Reeder Butterfield at the '82 Heublein sale is aided by major domo Hendrik Groot.

You start with the level of fill. Ullage—the space between the cork and the top of the liquid—gives some idea as to the chance of air getting into the wine. The capsule and cork should be intact, and the color of the liquid through the neck of the bottle should conform to the wine's appellation and vintage. In the case of red wine, you should get a red hue. If the wine has spoiled or oxidized, it will have lost its color and become a yellow, watery shade. In the case of white wine, the depth of the golden or white color is an indication. If a white wine has oxidized, it will be amber, brown or sometimes black.

—Alexander C. McNally

much as is necessary to surpass the highest bid from the floor. Now if the bidding in the room had gone up over one hundred dollars, then you would be dropped out. It would get sold to someone else at one hundred and five dollars or higher. Usually about one third of the sales will go to commissions, and two thirds to the floor."

If you wish to bid in person, you register when you arrive and receive a bidder number card. Each time you want to place a bid, you raise the card toward the auctioneer, who acknowledges it by pointing to you. If yours is the last number in the air when all the others have dropped out, the auctioneer will close the bidding with a rap of the gavel, and sell you the wine.

About ten days after the sale, successful bidders receive an invoice, which should be returned with payment and instructions for delivery. All sales are FOB Hartford, Connecticut, where the warehouse is located, and all taxes, local charges, and markups, where applicable, are up to you. Heublein makes certain that everything conforms to the regulations, and prepares the wine for shipping. It may take up to two months for you to get your wine.

Heublein receives a 25 percent commission from the seller— in addition to a great deal of well-earned publicity. If you would like to sell wine through the Heublein auction, send an inventory of your collection to Heublein, attention Alexander C. McNally, Farmington, CT 06032. Include a description of the wine (its name, appellation, vintage, etc.) and a description of the cork, label, capsule (the seal over the cork), and bottle. Of particular importance is an honest description of the conditions under which the wine has been stored. "When I appraise wine I try to go to the cellar where the wine has been and still is stored," McNally said.

Carl Mayhue of Florida (card number 177) purchased a record $83,495 in rare wines at Heublein's 1982 auction.

After evaluating the wine's storage conditions, McNally examines the bottles themselves.

If there is a sufficient quantity of wine, it is sampled. "What we do in a sampling," McNally said, "is to open deeply ullaged bottles that are probably not salable and taste them. If they are good, you get an idea of the style of the wine. When you open a full bottle, it will probably be even better."

The public is invited to attend pre-auction tastings held around the country and abroad. Extreme rarities are not tasted, but one or two bottle from large lots will be sampled. At the average tasting 150 wines may be sampled.

The auction catalogue serves as an admission ticket to the tastings. Catalogues cost $30 each, $35 at the door (these prices may increase slightly at upcoming auctions; check with Heublein, Inc., Box 505, Farmington, CT 06032. Heublein's next sale is scheduled for May 26, 1983, in Los Angeles.

CHRISTIE'S

Christie's has been selling wine at auction since 1766, and European wine lovers have long relied upon Christie's frequent sales as a steady source of reasonably priced wines. Although now in the process of establishing a regular auction schedule in the United States, Christie's initial attempt to hold a sale in New York City in 1980 was blocked by the legal action of three local retailers. The merchants feared that the auctions, not subject to the high operating expenses of conventional wine outlets, would provide consumers with an inexpensive alternative to their own retail stores.

Renowned auctioneer Michael Broadbent directs bidding at a Christie's auction.

After the setback in New York, Christie's held its first wine auction in Chicago on April 25, 1981. There, prices ranged from $120 for a dozen bottles of Château Fombrauge 1962 to a staggering $13,000 for a jeroboam of 1961 Château Petrus.

Christie's held its second sale in October 1981 in Washington, DC. Among the offerings was a rare bottle of 1806 Château Lafite, which brought $9,800. Two years earlier, an 1806 Château Lafite sold for $28,000 at a Heublein sale.

The third sale, in April 1982, featured an acknowledged "star" —one bottle of 1945 Romanée-Conti. "That was right after the war," Christie's Jacqueline Quillen explained. "Very little was made." The bottle sold for $1,980.

To sell your wine collection through Christie's, send a description of the wines to Jacqueline Quillen, Christie's Wine Department, 219 East 67th Street, New York, NY 10021. Wines accepted for sale will be moved to the temperature-controlled cellars of the Morgan Manhattan Warehouse in Montclair, New Jersey. After the sale, it is the buyer's responsibility to have them picked up or

This bottle of Sherry, once owned by one of Napoleon's marshals, was purchased by Manuel Domecq-Zurita at a Christie's sale held to commemorate the 250th anniversaries of the founding of both the House of Domecq and Christie's. The bottle is now in the Domecq Museum in Jerez.

Sotheby's auctioneer and wine expert, Patrick Grubb.

arrange to have them remain stored in the warehouse at a nominal charge. If you want to ship your wines home, Quillen warns that "there are some very confusing laws about moving wines from one state to another." Although many of these laws are holdovers from Prohibition, Christie's recommends that you check with your local liquor authority before transporting wines.

Christie's plans to hold four wine auctions a year, in various cities. For catalogues and information about upcoming sales, you can write to Christie's Wine Department at the above address. If you'd like to purchase any of the wines offered, bids may be phoned or written in. If you prefer to attend, a catalogue serves as your admission ticket. Christie's collects a commission of 10 percent of the hammer price from both buyers and sellers.

SOTHEBY'S

International wine lovers have been attending Sotheby's regular worldwide wine sales since 1970. Their more than twenty sales each year span several continents, from North America to Africa. The offered wines range from "finest and rarest" to "fine and inexpensive" selections, with occasional sales devoted to Burgundy, Port, Maderia, cognac, and other spirits. Sotheby's also runs fund-raising sales for some charitable organizations.

Sotheby's first American wine auction was about what might be expected from one of the world's leading auction houses. The sale, held November 17, 1981, in Chicago, featured over 6,000 bottles of wine from a vast assortment of vineyards and vintages. Among the selections were wines from leading French vineyards, including Château d'Yquem, the Domaine de la Romaneé-Conti, and some notable Italian, German, and California wines.

Although there was no tasting held prior to the Chicago sale, some of the bidders were invited to a reception the day before the auction to hear Master of Wine Patrick Grubb, director of Sotheby's Wine Department, conduct a seminar concerning the wines to be offered.

Buyers pay no commission. Individuals selling wine through Sotheby's must pay 15 percent of the sale price as a commission. Members of the trade pay a 12.5 percent commission.

If you would like to sell wine through Sotheby's, send a list of your collection to Patrick Grubb at Sotheby's Wine Department, 34-35 Bond Street, London, WIA 2AA, England. He will send you more information.

A catalogue is required for admission to a Sotheby's wine sale. To date, there is no schedule for auctions to be held in the

United States, but any information that is available can be obtained by writing Sotheby's Subscription Department, 980 Madison Avenue, New York, NY 10021.

NAPA VALLEY

The hot afternoon sun that has been responsible for many great vintages of Napa Valley wine hung over the Meadowood Country Club in St. Helena, California. It beat down on the white tent that had been set up near the eighteenth fairway to shade the nearly 500 buyers, workers, reporters, and spectators who had assembled on June 21, 1981, for the First Napa Valley Wine Auction. By the time the sun had set, 600 lots of wine, either donated or consigned to the event by local wineries, had been sold for a total of over $324,000.

Each of the 260 bidders paid $100 for a bidding paddle; for many, as bids rocketed to record levels, the admission price turned out to be the cheapest purchase of the day. The most noteworthy wine offered was bought by Syracuse, New York, wine merchant Charles Mara, who paid $24,000 for a case of wine he had never tasted, smelled, or even seen.

That case will be the first ever bottled of a wine made jointly by noted California vintner Robert Mondavi and Baron Philippe de Rothschild, proprietor of Château Mouton-Rothschild. The Baron and Mondavi agree that no one, not even its purchaser, will taste the wine until it has finished aging, probably in late 1983 or 1984.

The Second Napa Valley Wine Auction, held June 20, 1982, at the same location, boasted nothing quite so spectacular, but it did offer some excellent buys and raised over $240,000 from 250 registered bidders.

The record purchase of the day was $5,400 for a case of 1978 Diamond Creek Cabernet Sauvignon. A 1970 Cabernet Sauvignon from Chappellet Vineyards brought the highest price for a single bottle—$3,300 for a jeroboam.

The "big spender" of the '82 auction was Fred Halimeh of Atlanta, who bid on behalf of a restaurant called Midnight Sun. His purchases, including the $5,400 case of Cabernet Sauvignon, totaled nearly $35,000.

Thanks to its two years of success, the Napa Valley auction is on its way to becoming an annual summer event at the Meadowood Country Club, with Christie's renowned auctioneer, Michael Broadbent, donating his services. The 1983 auction is already set

Californians or Texans will have a couple of fine cars and a fine wine cellar, but New Yorkers will use a taxi or hire a limo and complain that a ten-dollar bottle of wine is too expensive.
—Christopher Selmes

for June 19 and 20 (the actual auction is always preceded by a day of tastings). Proceeds from the sale, after expenses, benefit two local hospitals. For information or a catalogue, write Napa Valley Wine Auction, 1118 Pine Street, St. Helena, CA 94574.

SONOMA COUNTY

The first Sonoma County Wine Auction, held August 9, 1981, was notable not for record-breaking prices or especially rare wines. It was notable, however, for the labels affixed to a case of Kenwood Vineyards 1975 Cabernet Sauvignon—labels that were later banned by the Bureau of Alcohol, Tobacco and Firearms as "obscene and indecent." The labels, showing a line drawing of a nude woman reclining on a hillside, were the work of California artist David Goines, and had been commissioned as part of Kenwood Vineyards' Artist Series. A case of the wine with the controversial labels sold for $480, the highest price of the day.

At that first auction, the most expensive single bottle of wine, a 1976 Chateau St. Jean Johannisberg Riesling, went for $110. At the second auction, held August 8, 1982, the most expensive offering brought considerably more—$4,750. A San Francisco restaurateur paid that amount for a future bottling of one case of Piper-Sonoma Tete de Cuvee Champagne, product of a collaboration between California's Sonoma Vineyard and France's Piper-Heidsieck Champagne Cellars. When the wine, which has never been tasted, is released to the purchaser, its label will be signed by both the French and American winemakers and the label's designer. Since the wine is not yet ready to be released, a label artist has not yet been commissioned.

The Sonoma County Wine Auctions are organized by a local Kiwanis Club and the Sonoma County Wine Library, and are deliberately low-keyed. A local winemaker is selected to serve as auctioneer, and mail bids are not accepted. A barbecue lunch is included in the reasonable admission fee. After the sale, buyers simply pick up their purchases and leave. No shipping arrangements, no commissions, no insurance—just a chance to taste and purchase Sonoma Valley wines. The auction is an annual summer event, and information and catalogues are available by writing to Sonoma County Wine Auction, P. O. Box 434, Healdsburg, CA 95448.

Art panel from the Kenwood label banned by the Bureau of `Alcohol, Tobacco and Firearms as "obscene and indecent."

KQED

Public Broadcasting Systems are noted for creative fund-raising campaigns, and San Francisco's PBS station, KQED, boasts one of the most innovative—the San Francisco International Wine Auction.

Since 1979, KQED has held wine auctions that benefit both the station and the individuals who donate wines to the sale. "The donors don't receive any money from the sale of the wines," explained KQED's auction director John Loder, "but their donations are tax deductible."

Loder is especially proud of a unique feature of the KQED sales. "We now handle wine artifacts," he explained. "Most wine auctions don't." At the April 3, 1982, sale held in the KQED television studios, several wine-related treasures were offered to bidders. Among them were a signed, original Ansel Adams photograph of the vaulted barrel aging room of the Paul Masson wine cellars, donated by the Masson winery; two nineteenth-century corkscrews donated by Brother Timothy, owner of one of the finest corkscrew collections in the world (see page 00); and an offer by famed Napa Valley artist Sebastian Titus to design an exclusive wine label for the private cellar of the highest bidder.

A selection of wines offered at KQED's fund-raising wine auction.

In addition to the artifacts, there was, of course, wine. "There was a tremendous response to the California wines, especially the ones from the '60s and early '70s," Loder noted. For example, three bottles of 1972 Stony Hill Chardonnay valued at $90–100, sold for $225. The most expensive offerings at the sale were two magnums of 1870 Château Lafite, one of which sold for $4,000, the other for $4,500.

In the past, KQED auctions had been noted for low bidding and a preponderance of retailers purchasing wines cheaply for markup on their shelves, but at the April '82 auction that seemed to be changing. "We're still young," Loder said, "and there wasn't any really high-powered bidding, but there was a large number of write-in bids from Canada, England, and the East Coast. Our prices are probably still the most reasonable of any major auction in the country, but we're getting up into fair market value now."

The auction is run by Sotheby's Wine Department, and follows its standard auction procedures. Purchases are paid for on the day of the sale, and should be picked up within four or five days thereafter. The buyer is responsible for taxes, shipping charges, and any other expenses.

Catalogue information and a schedule of events can be obtained by writing KQED Auction, 500 Eighth Street, San Francisco, CA 94103.

Port and Sherry

The names of these remarkable wines are synonymous with their sources—Port from Portugal and Sherry from Spain. And despite attempts at duplication by winemakers throughout the world, the true wines have been impossible to match. They are unique, and they set the standards.

Each is the product of skilled winemakers who, although they use modern machinery and technology, produce wines according to methods and directed by standards that have existed for hundreds of years. The character of the wines are the result of growing conditions that exist solely at their sources—the Douro River for Port and Jerez de la Frontera for Sherry. The international markets for these wines were originally developed by English wine shippers and traders. And the traditions which over the years have become vested with the grapes mirror the wines' origins and history.

There are excellent port-type and sherry-style wines produced throughout the winemaking world, but to taste and appraise them properly requires experience with, and an understanding of, the originals.

PORT WINE

Once tasted and savored, a fine Port wine becomes a fixed element of virtually everyone's wine memory. Known as the Englishman's drink, Port, a red or white fortified blended wine made from grapes grown in a strictly defined part of northern Portugal's Upper Douro River Valley, has been a part of worldwide wine language and lore since the early seventeenth century. Perhaps no wine offers more history and more consistency of style and taste than does a true Port wine *(Porto)*.

Although France has been, since the mid-1970s, the largest importer of Port wine (throughout France it is considered an apéritif), British firms have been dominant factors in its production and distribution since the Methuen Treaty was signed in 1703. It was this English-Portuguese trade agreement that led to the development of international trade in Port wine. British names are still dominant in the Port wine lexicon and in many major Port operations in Portugal; in many cases the companies are still overseen from London or Bristol. Called "shippers," the organizations might be better termed the Port maker/sellers. They buy the grapes from the wine farmers of the Upper Douro Valley; many shippers also grow and harvest some of their own wine grapes. They process the wines, age them, and blend them. They are also the bottlers, the exporters, and the marketers of this remarkable wine. There is no Port establishment—Portuguese or British-Portuguese—that does not continue to feel the steadying influence of the wine's English connection. Some of the leading shippers are Cockburn (owned by John Harvey and Sons), Croft, Sandeman, Graham, Warre, Martinez, Calem, and Mackenzie.

The small grape-growing area known as the Upper Douro is the only part of the world that can produce wine carrying the name Port or Porto without any qualification. The region through which the Douro River flows is a wild, rocky area varying between 20 and 40 miles wide (from north to south) and 60 miles long. The river flows west, entering Portugal from Spain, twisting its way through a harsh, rugged valley whose steep hillsides are terraced by small vineyards, and reaches the Atlantic Ocean a mile beyond the city of Oporto (Portuguese for "the port"). Until the early 1960s the river was the primary lifeline and thoroughfare of the wine farmers. *Barcos rabelos*, single-sail flat-hulled boats, moved up and down the river carrying the casks of new wines to the warehouses and blending facilities at Vila Nova de Gaia, the port town that faces Oporto on the south shore of the Douro River.

The vineyards of the Upper Douro district are considered generally the most difficult and expensive to cultivate in the

If worldwide Port sales increased by more than twenty-five percent, there wouldn't be enough Port to go around.

—Tim Sandeman
—HOUSE OF SANDEMAN

The River Douro at Ferradosa. Tiny terraced Port vineyards, carved into the rock of the hillside, are visible in the background.

wine-producing world. They are planted on terraces carved out of the steep canyon walls to withstand the heavy seasonal rains.

Perhaps the most outstanding impression of a first-time visitor to the Upper Douro district is that there appears to be no soil, only stones. The surface, actually composed of schist (a crystalline rock whose component minerals are arranged in more or less parallel layers), is in effect broken pieces of extremely hard rock varying in size from small boulders to chunks the size of a fist. No spade can turn this surface so that a vine can be set in it. Today bulldozers churn the terrain prior to the systematic planting of new vines, but 20 years ago the schist was either dynamited or broken with sledgehammers. The Port grapevine thrives in this. The taproot of a mature vine descends for at least 12 feet, penetrating through broken rock to fight for water throughout its life in this inhospitable area.

The climate of the Upper Douro region ranges from scorching heat in summer to below freezing in winter. The growing of grapes is indeed a struggle against the soil and the elements, but it is these difficult, arduous conditions that are responsible for the full, mellow flavor uniquely associated with Port.

GOVERNMENT REGULATION

Since 1933 the Portuguese Government has maintained and administered a system of control, regulation, and certification to assure the authenticity and quality of Port from the wine to the glass. The *Instituto do Vinho do Porto* (the Port Wine Institute) is the official government body that oversees and coordinates the activity of the *Casa do Douro* (the Farmers' and Winegrowers' Association) and the *Grêmio dos Exportadores de Vinho do Porto* (the Port Wine Shippers' Association).

The *Instituto* directs and controls Port production and trade, monitors the storage and movement of all wines, conducts laboratory and tasting analyses of Port quality, and is responsible for the issuing of the Certificate of Origin and the seals of guarantee that are printed on the neck label attached to each bottle before shipping. Working with the *Casa do Douro*, the institute establishes minimum and maximum grape yields and prices and additive brandy price levels at the beginning of each wine-growing cycle. The *Grêmio* reports to the Port Wine Institute concerning all activity in Vila Nova de Gaia—that is, storage, blending, and shipping. The effect of these controls is the assurance that Port is a genuine product of the Douro region and has been produced as a true Port wine.

FROM GRAPE TO PORT

There are 28 red and 19 white grape varieties grown in the Douro region's wine farms *(quintas)* for blending into Port wine. Malvasia Paeta, Mourisco, Tinta Sousao, Tinto Avarsla, Tinto Carvalha, Tuite Francisca, Tinta Cão, Tina Roriz, and Gouveia are grapes used to blend red wine; and Malvasia Fino, Malvasia Rei, Moscatel Taxa and Rubigato are the distince blending grapes of white Port.

A *quinta* in the Douro Valley can be a magnificent well-groomed estate producing the finest wine grapes, or it can be (as is most often the case) a humble building adjacent to a small patch of land supporting a few lines of grapevines. The word simply means "property." Some of the larger and finer *quintas* in the Douro Valley are owned by the leading Port shippers.

The harvest takes place toward the end of September. The grapes are brought in from the vineyards to the shippers' own Douro region lodge facilities where the grapes are crushed. It is usual for the shipper to purchase his grapes from the same vineyards year after year in order to maintain continuity and house style.

Until recent years the grapes were trodden during the evening of the day on which they were picked. Now, less romantically but

Claret is for boys,
Port is for men.
—Dr. Samuel Johnson

more efficiently, modern mechanical methods are employed. Usually the stems are removed and the grapes are lightly crushed to release their juice. The resulting pulp is transferred to large vats, where fermentation begins.

Sugar is soon converted into alcohol and color is extracted from the skins. When the shipper decides that enough color has been acquired and the sugar content is at the desired level, the half-fermented wine is drawn off and mixed with a predetermined quantity of grape brandy. This stops the fermentation, leaving the wine at the desired level of sweetness. The new wines are stored in pipes (large oak casks with a capacity of 116 gallons) in the Upper Douro lodges until the following spring. Then they are transported by road or rail in large oak casks from the storage lodges and processing facilities in the mouth of the Douro River. Although deriving its name from Oporto, Port by law must be stored and processed in Vila Nova de Gaia and be shipped to the outside world over the bar of the Douro.

Blending and Maturing in "Gaia"
Each shipper's facility or lodge complex in Vila Nova de Gaia contains several maturing storage areas, laboratories, a tasting room, and a bottling hall. The tasting room and the laboratories are the hub of the business. It is here that the individual Port wine blends are determined and the blending is achieved.

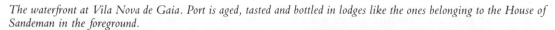

The waterfront at Vila Nova de Gaia. Port is aged, tasted and bottled in lodges like the ones belonging to the House of Sandeman in the foreground.

A blender examines a glass of Port in the tasting room of a Sandeman's lodge. Experienced tasters check the Port at every stage of its development during the aging process.

The actual blending is the most important step in the creation of the final wine. A continuity of style is critical to the individual shipper; the character of the blending, differences are overridden or balanced by adding controlled quantities of sweeter or drier, or lighter or heavier wines of various harvests to the shipping lot—the wine that will ultimately be bottled and sent out to the markets. (A point to remember! When the age rather than the vintage date is mentioned on the label, it refers to the average age of the various wines that make up the final blend, not the year when the grapes were harvested.)

TYPES OF PORT

Port can be divided into two major categories: wood Ports (Ruby, Tawny and White), which is matured in oak casks and is ready to drink when bottled and shipped; and vintage (and vintage-style) Port, which after a few years in casks continues to mature in the bottle.

Ruby Port

This is considered a young Port, aged in the cask for an average of three to eight years. When it is bottled, it is ready to drink. It is full-bodied, comparatively sweet, and has a rich ruby color—hence the name. In effect, it is the excellent *vin ordinaire* of the Port family. It is also the least expensive.

Tawny Port
Older than ruby Port, the wines are aged in wood for ten years. During the aging process, Port loses body, gains softness, becomes increasingly pale in color and slightly drier. These well-balanced, mature blends are ready for drinking when bottled.

White Port
This wine is made in a similar manner to ruby Port, but from white grapes. It is popular as a chilled dry or medium-dry apéritif in France, throughout Scandinavia, and Portugal.

Vintage Port
This is the wine of an outstanding year. The shippers deem a particular harvest to be worthy of vintage appellation 18 months after the harvest, when the wines have already been in casks and questions concerning superiority have been answered. This occurs on an average of three times in each decade.

Only a small portion of the finest early wines of designated vintage harvest actually are handled as vintage Port. The best wines of the harvest are matured for two to three years in wood casks, blended only with Port wines of the same vintage, and then bottled. The wine is not ready for drinking, however, until at least eight to ten more years have passed. Even at this age, the wine may offer a certain roughness. Fifteen to twenty years is considered the time needed for the wine to reach its full character and maturity. A fine Port will maintain its peak in bottle for 30 to 55 years. While in bottle, vintage Ports produce a sediment. Because of this they must be carefully decanted before serving.

A fully aged vintage Port is a wine of great character, bouquet and balance. The vintage Port market traditionally has been dominated by Cockburn, Croft, Sandeman, Delaforce, Fonseca, Dow, Taylor, Martinez Gassiot, Warre, Ferreira, and Noval.

"Wood" Ports aging in oak casks in a lodge in Vila Nova de Gaia.

Crusted Port
Although rarely the wine of a single year, this style of Port—always of high quality—is a blend of wines from different harvests, matured in wood for from two to four years. After the blending it is laid down in bottles for four to five years, when it becomes sedimented. Crusted Port offers a deep, full red color similar but not quite equal to that of vintage Port, combined with a firm, fruity taste. Crusted Port must be decanted. It is usually ready for drinking by the time it is shipped.

Late-bottled Vintage
Also known as "Port of the vintage," this is not a vintage Port. Where a true vintage Port is aged in wood for two to three years before being bottled, a wine marked "of the vintage" or "late-bottled" may rest in wood for ten years or more. The lengthy time in wood creates a soft, well-rounded wine, but it lacks the full body and richness of true vintage Port. Although it creates a deposit in the cask, this is left behind when the wine is blended and bottled. Late-bottled vintage Port is perfectly clear in the bottle and can be served without decanting.

Vintage-character Port
Wines carrying this designation, although blended from the grapes of several harvest years, are similar in taste to the late-bottled vintage Ports. They are matured in wood longer than traditional ruby Ports but for a shorter length ot time than a Port of the vintage. Although ready for drinking when bottled, these dark and fruity wines can be laid down and will continue to mature in the bottle.

PORT-STYLE WINE

Port wine (without a capital P) is also produced and consumed in volume in other wine-growing areas of the world, particularly the United States. Of course, it is not the proper Port made in the Douro Valley, but Americans, Australians, and South Africans buy their native red dessert wines and enjoy their "ports."

The main differences between "domestic port," such as California port, and Port *(Porto)* are the grape varieties used, the sun and rain ratios, the soil, and the fermentation processes. California port has traditionally been made with the heavy, sweet Tinta Madera grape variety grown in the severe heat of the San Joaquin Valley. Newcomers to the California port-producing scene are now using table wine grape varietals, with some varietals reaching 15 to 18 percent alcohol naturally, without fortification.

Approximately half of the wineries in the United States producing port are in California, as well as almost all of the largest producers in the United States: E. & J. Gallo, Paul Masson, Christian Brothers, and United Vintners (Taylor is in New York).

The firm of E. & J. Gallo is the largest port producer in the country, although Christian Brothers produces the largest volume of premium port. Gallo uses Carignane, the indigenous Zinfandel, the Tinta Madera, and some Grenache grapes. They have also developed two vinifera hybrids, Rubired and Royalty, at the University of California at Davis, specifically for port production. During any given year, Gallo produces probably as much port in Modesto, California, as is shipped from Portugal to world markets.

The Gallo operation is immense. They transport the freshly picked grapes in 20-ton gondola tank trucks. The grapes are then crushed and centrifugally pumped into 100,000-gallon fermentation tanks where frequent pumping is carried out to extract the proper amount of color from the skins, Neutral grape spirit is added at the desired critical time to arrest fermentation, and the resultant wine is 18 to 19 percent alcohol by volume.

Most California port is produced from grapes grown inland to the east of San Francisco, where the sun is torrid and constant. Because the soil is fertile and the land is flat, the grapevines have an easy life, not struggling for survival as in the case of the Upper Douro Valley. The result is that the ports produced in California traditionally have a rather cooked "nose," or smell, and a grapy taste.

Although the mass producers of port cater to broad general tastes, there are several smaller companies in the United States that produce vintage ports. Companies such as Beringer Vineyards, Ficklin Vineyards, J. W. Morris Port Works, Quady Vineyards, and Woodbury Winery are representative of the trend in California port. As yet they do not export their ports outside the United States.

Beringer produces port that combines richness with the definite varietal fragrance of the Cabernet Sauvignon. Their decision to use Cabernet Sauvignon grapes reflects the desire to experiment and improve on existing varietals. Ficklin is recognized throughout the world as producing the California port most closely styled to Portuguese Port, achieved in part by using certain Portuguese grape varietals. The style is always steady and the result is a well-balanced, generous dessert wine. J. W. Morris Port Works produces vintage and late-bottled vintage ports. Its first port, called Founders Port, which was produced in 1974, is quite different from mass-produced California blends; the wines are fruity and young, sensual and fragrant, and do not have the "grapy raisin" hallmark of early mass-produced California ports. Andrew Quady selected Amador County for his vineyards, as he believes that Amador Zinfandels have the necessary grip and spice needed for port. He produced his first vintage port in 1975 when he made 1,600 cases; he has since doubled his production. The Woodbury Winery, a family winery located in Marin County, produces full and robust wines known to have a definite port grip and a keen stalkiness that gives the wine a backbone seldom achieved in California.

STORING AND SERVING

There is no need to age ruby or tawny Port. It is, however, critical to the development of vintage Ports to allow them to age; ask your wine merchant how much time is necesssary and when your vintage port will be ready for drinking.

All vintage Ports should be laid down so that the cork is kept moist through contact with the wine. It is a good idea to lay down all bottles so that the label is facing upward for easy identification. To avoid disturbing the sediment, the angle should remain the same until the bottle is ready for drinking.

Port looks its finest in a decanter. However, there is no need to decant the wine unless it is a vintage or vintage-style crusted port. Before decanting vintage Port, carefully take the bottle from your wine rack and allow it to stand upright for 24 hours. This gives the sediment time to settle.

An old-fashioned method of opening vintage Port is to snap the neck off the bottle. The neck of the bottle is firmly gripped for half a minute or so with specially made red-hot tongs. The tongs are removed; then a wet rag is applied to the neck. With a sharp twist, the neck will break off cleanly and easily. Removing the cork in the usual, slightly less dramatic way requires a corkscrew— ideally an especially long screw, because a vintage Port cork is longer than most.

The well-known adage of Port decanting is: "The older the wine, the nearer the meal." Old Ports, 50- or 60-year-old vintage Ports, will lose their bouquet very quickly after being exposed to air. Old Port should never be left to breathe. A younger vintage, 10 to 15 years old, may need three or even five hours to breathe. There is no hard-and-fast rule; the best way to judge is by tasting the wine at intervals. For the wine to breathe, the decanter should be left unstoppered in a clean atmoshpere. Never let it breathe in a room where people are smoking or it will absorb the cigarette smoke and lose its lush bouquet.

There are many traditions attached to drinking this venerable wine. Among the best-known is the British custom of passing the decanter clockwise around the table. Even if someone refuses Port and then changes his mind, the decanter must complete the circuit around the table before returning to the empty glass.

I drink it
as the Fates ordain it,
Come, fill it,
and have done with
*   rhymes;*
Fill up the lonely glass,
and drain it
In memory of dear old
*   times.*
—William Makepeace
*   Thackeray*

SHERRY

Sherry is regarded as a drink you can offer any-body without offending them.

—David Pallengat,
LUIS GORDON
(DOMECQ)

Customs change slowly in all of southern Spain, but in Jerez de la Frontera they change slowest of all. For years the frontier *(la frontera)* was here, when the North African Moors resisted the Christian advance for control of all Spain. Now, in a way, Jerez is on a different border: one with time. The town's pace resembles that of the infinitely patient aging process in the soleras, where *all* the world's Sherry is slowly coming to term. They boast of men here, of bullfighters and bulls. They point to the exquisite grace of their young women—often an enticing mixture of Moorish, Spanish, and Gypsy blood. They are proud of their racing grey-hounds, among the finest in Spain, and of their finely bred horses, exported all over the world as show, riding, and carriage horses. There is even a *Feria del Caballo,* an entire fair showcasing the hand-some and arrogant horseflesh of the region.

But all that is nothing compared to the wine, because the wine is everywhere. The dusty golden grapes brush the land with color everywhere you look. The wine is steeped in the wood-rich smell of the cafés where asking for a *vino* will only get you Sherry. It has made dynasties. Oddly, virtually none of these dynastic families were originally Spanish. The Browns, Sandemans, Williamsons, Terrys, and Harveys established themselves in Jerez in the eighteenth century, coming from England in order to export the local wine back home. The Domecqs, the most fabled of all the Sherry families, came from Béarn in the French Pyrenees.

Even today, in this land where time moves slowly, many still refer to these "Sherry-rich" families as *los extranjeros*—the foreigners —although they have been established in Jerez for centuries. It is no wonder. Although proud to be Spanish and often active in Spanish politics, the Sherry families have made every effort to set themselves apart, to retain their foreign heritage. The children are tutored in English from birth, often knowing it better than their native tongue until later in life.

Don José Ignacio Domecq, patriarch of the Domecq Sherry dynasty, experiments with wines in a laboratory adjacent to his office.

A Sherry vineyard in Jerez during the harvest. In the foreground, harvested Pedro Ximénez (PX) grapes are spread on espartos *(grass mats) to dry in the sun. In two to three weeks, when the grapes have turned to raisins, they are pressed and their juice used as a sweetening agent in Sherry.*

The wine is everywhere—life itself—in the Marco de Jerez, where the only true Sherry in the world has been made for hundreds of years. Prior to the eighteenth century the Sherry trade was conducted by small individual merchants and independent growers, but in the early 1700s large aboveground structures called *bodegas* were erected in and around Jerez, and the *solera* system of aging the wine began to come into general use.

Today's Sherry is a unique wine that owes its inherent qualities to several factors: geography, climate, grape species, soil, vineyard procedures, method of vinification in the bodegas, aging by solera, and the art of blending. True Sherry cannot be duplicated. No wine region outside of Jerez has the same growing conditions or employs the same techniques for making authentic Sherry.

Geography

All of the Sherry vineyards are situated in a limited, triangular growing area of 50,000 acres bounded by three historic towns: Jerez de la Frontera, Puerto de Santa María, and Sanlúcar de Barrameda. Since 1933, the territory that may be cultivated has been precisely defined by the Sherry Control Board *(Consejo Regulador de la Denominación de Origen Jerez-Xérès-Sherry),* which also regulates all other aspects of Sherry production and trading.

Climate

The region averages 295 days of sun and 70 days of rain annually. About 40 percent of the rain falls in October, November, and December; the remaining 60 percent falls between February and mid-May, providing moisture for the vines when they need it. Rain seldom falls when the grapes are pollinating and ripening.

Grapes

The most important grape grown in the region is the Palomino, which accounts for 90 percent of the planted vineyards. Second is the Pedro Ximénez, or P.X., which yields a sweet wine used in

During the harvest in September, workers load the grapes into baskets made of olive shoots and carry them to the press houses.

blending. These species, together with some Moscatel (which yields a dark wine used for coloring), are the only varieties that may be planted in the delimited zone.

Soil

The three soils of the area are now graded according to their relative chalk content. *Albariza* is the best soil for Palomino grapes and averages about 40 percent chalk. Although difficult to cultivate and low in yield, it produces grapes of the highest quality because it retains moisture. *Barro* contains a lower proportion of chalk, and consists mainly of clay. It is higher in yield, but its wine is of less quality. *Arena,* a sandy soil with a chalk content of 10 percent, is the poorest and is good for sweet wines only.

The Vines

A Sherry vine is productive for only about 25 to 30 years. With luck it will yield an adequate vintage in the fourth year after it was planted, but it will have to be dug up some 25 years later when its yield becomes small. After the old vines are pulled out, the vineyard is rested for five years.

Harvesting

The harvest usually begins during the first week of September and lasts about a month, as each vine must be picked several times before it is stripped of fully ripened grapes. Depending on the weather in the district and the type of wine desired, the harvested grapes are left in the sun for several hours.

Processing

The traditional method of treading the grapes by foot has virtually disappeared, although it is still performed ceremonially every year for the *Fiesta de la Vendimia,* the week-long vintage festival in Jerez. Today mechanical presses designed to leave the pips and stalks intact are used to extract the juice from the grapes.

The fresh grape juice is then immediately taken to the nearby bodegas where it is put into new oak barrels to begin fermentation. From its initial fermentation, through its maturity, fractional blending and final bottling seven to eight years later, Sherry remains in wooden casks, or butts.

The bodegas were designed and constructed especially for the making of Sherry. High, vaulted ceilings and windowed walls encourage the circulation of air, and the dirt floors are sprinkled regularly to maintain proper humidity. Ideally, the temperature throughout the structure should remain constant and the air moist.

(left) The process of preparing the vineyard to receive new vines, known as the agostado, begins in July or August when weeds are pulled and the soil is broken mechanically. The broken ground is soaked by winter rains, and this moisture will be trapped beneath the soil's hard-baked surface in the spring to nourish the Sherry vines. (below) Since the sun reduces grapes' moisture content and increases their level of sugar, many vineyards use protective awnings to shield the grapes. The awnings also protect the fruit from the evening dew.

The harvest takes place in September when the grapes are ripe. Once the grapes are removed from the vines by workers using knives (above), the larger stalks are removed and the spoiled fruit is discarded. The grapes are then placed in boxes (right) that hold about 30 pounds of fruit. They will be carried to the press houses to be dried in the sun.

(above, left) A Sherry press removes the stalks from the grapes, then presses the fruit. After pressing, the grape must is transferred to butts for fermentation. Before the Sherry is transferred, these oak casks are "fired" to make them flexible and destroy bacteria. (above, right) A cooper douses the flame with water from a bull's horn. (below, left) A stack of casks bearing the names of notables, including Spanish royalty, who have visited this bodega.

(right) Flor *developing on the surface of a new Sherry. Since this* yeast *is a living growth, it will continue to develop, thickening in the spring and fall and thinning out in the summer and winter. The* flor, *which imparts distinctive characteristics to Fino and Amontillado Sherry, occurs naturally and cannot be induced. (below) Within the bodega, Sherry develops and matures in butts stacked on top of one another in tiers three or four levels high. Over the years the Sherry ages and is fractionally blended to achieve a wine of uniform and consistent quality.*

Even the location of casks within the bodega is important; if one butt is exposed to a continuous draft while another is sheltered in a corner, the wines within them will be appreciably different.

For a week or so after the September crushing, the freshly pressed wine ferments rapidly as the grapes' sugar is converted into alcohol. The fermentation then slows for two to three months until the new wine, in loosely stoppered casks, is absolutely dry— retaining no residual sugar. It is, however, not yet Sherry.

By December or January the wine "falls bright." Suspended impurities have descended to the bottom of the cask, leaving the wine clarified. The wine is then tentatively classified.

The bodega foreman draws samples from the butts which are judged by sight and smell and are put through laboratory tests for alcoholic strength, acidity, and other natural components. Categorized as potentially Fino or Oloroso, or undetermined, according to what seems to be its natural inclination, the wine is transferred from its casks to vats and lightly fortified. The blend is then returned to the casks and grape brandy is added, bringing the alcoholic strength to 15½ percent. The wine is now said to be *sobretabla* (fortified on top of wood) and ready for the next stage, the *añada*.

The word *añada* derives from *año*, the Spanish word for "year." It is the name given to a harvest's wines during their initial stage, when they have not yet revealed their characteristics. One of Sherry's profound mysteries is the way a particular new wine decides for itself whether it will become Fino or Oloroso. No one can influence this basic decision, and no one understands why casks containing wine pressed at the same time, from the same grapes, grown in the same vineyard, develop differently.

Within 18 to 24 months, a wine destined to be Fino develops a thick coating of yeast cells on its surface called *flor* (Spanish for "flower"). Flor is encouraged to form when the undisturbed surface of the wine is exposed to air, the temperature is 60° to 70° F., and alcoholic strength is 15 to 16 percent. Given these conditions, flor will thicken in the solera each year during the spring and fall, and float on the Fino Sherry indefinitely.

A wine that will become an Amontillado Sherry also forms flor, but it is thinner than that of the Fino. Its flor will live for perhaps two or three years, and then die and fall to the bottom of the cask. A Fino could become an Amontillado if it were allowed to age in a solera without being refreshed with new Finos; hence, the description of Amontillado as an aged Fino.

Sherry destined to become an Oloroso develops no natural flor and is immediately fortified to 18 percent alcohol.

A good sherris-sack hath a two-fold operation in it. It ascends me into the brain; dries me there all the foolish and dull and crudy vapours which environ it; makes it apprehensive, quick, forgetive, full of nimble fiery, and delectable shapes; which deliver'd o'er to the voice, the tongue, which is the birth, becomes excellent wit. The second property of your excellent sherris is, the warming of the blood; which, before cold and settled, left the liver white and pale, which is the badge of pusillanimity and cowardice; but the sherris warms it and makes it course from the inwards to the parts extreme.

—Shakespeare's Sir John Falstaff

A worker uses a jarra *(jug) to pour Sherry drawn from a solera in a Sandeman lodge for testing.*

The Solera System

At the end of the *añada* stage the new Sherries are ready to be introduced into their respective soleras. This is the system by which fine old Sherries are joined to the new wine to produce a wine of consistently high quality year after year.

Stated simply, a solera system consists of row after row of identical butts, each holding 130 gallons. Each row is known as a "scale." The number of scales is not fixed; it is common for a solera to have 10, 12, or even more. Wine for shipment is always drawn from the oldest (the lowest) row of the solera. This is replenished from wine drawn equally from casks of the first *criadera* (the second scale); the second *criadera* (the third scale) in turn is topped with wine drawn from the third *criadera* (the fourth scale), and so on, until all the casks in the system make their contribution.

This complex and costly method, known as "running the scales," eliminates any marked differences from year to year. By continuous fractional blending, the great Sherry establishments create and style the same type of Sherry year in and year out. To maintain quality levels, not more than one third of the solera scale may be drawn off in any one year. As a result, by the time the small quantity of new wine introduced to the system each year has reached the final solera scale, it has taken on all the noble characteristics of the older wines in the system.

Wines drawn from a solera for shipment are not yet completely finished Sherries. They may be too dry, too pale, too cloudy, and have not been fortified to shipping strength.

Egg whites are beaten into a gallon of wine, which is then added to a cask. After allowing time for the egg to coagulate and settle to the bottom, taking the impurities along with it, the wine is racked off. Alcohol content is adjusted by adding neutral grape brandy. The finished Sherry wine is somewhere between 16 percent and 20 percent alcohol (32 to 40 U.S. proof) for shipment overseas.

Dryness and paleness are corrected by the blending in of a sweet P.X. wine (which has also passed through a solera system), and of the deep amber-colored Spanish Moscatel. Since most Sherries are sold under a brand name, it is essential that there be no variation in style from year to year. The final blending may therefore involve mixing the wines of several soleras to ensure uniformity before shipment from Jerez.

TYPES OF SHERRY

All Sherries are permutations and combinations of five basic styles.

Fino

Pale and straw-colored, light and very dry, Fino Sherry is crisp, delicate, and slightly pungent. Its distinctive aroma, reminiscent of almonds, comes from the flor yeast that grows on the surface of the wine during development in the solera. Served chilled, Fino is often used as an apéritif wine.

Manzanilla

This is the palest, driest, and lightest-bodied of all Sherries. It is produced in only one place within the Sherry zone, the town of Sanlúcar de Barrameda on the Atlantic coast. It is said that if a Manzanilla is taken to Jerez and aged there, it will acquire the characteristics of a normal Fino. And conversely, if a Jerez Fino is taken to a bodega in Sanlúcar, it will tend toward Manzanilla.

Like the Jerez Fino, Manzanilla is chilled before serving. It is favored as an apéritif wine. Production is limited, and this type of Sherry is not always available in the United States.

Amontillado

This amber-colored medium-dry Sherry has a light, pungent aroma and a nutty taste. Shipped at somewhat higher alcoholic strength than Aroma Fino, it is sometimes blended with Fino for the American market. It is correct to pour Amontillado at room temperature, chilled, or on the rocks, depending on the taste preference of the user.

Oloroso

In Spanish, *Oloroso* means "fragrant," and this Sherry typically has a strong bouquet. The wine may be dark gold or amber in color, and is softer and mellower, with more body than the Amontillados. Oloroso can be served either at room temperature or over ice.

Cream

A full, smooth, rather sweetish wine, cream Sherry results when Oloroso is blended with a sweetening wine such as Pedro Ximénez or Moscatel. Cream Sherry, the most widely consumed of all Sherries, is accepted as being suitable at virtually any time of day.

Storage

All Sherries are fully aged and ready for drinking when they are shipped. They need not be laid down for additional aging in the bottle. Except for the Fino, exposure to air will not affect Sherry. It has a long life, and may therefore be kept in a decanter. (Finos should be chilled before being served, and the bottles refrigerated after being opened.)

Because World War II meant a virtual cessation of shipments, some marvelous old stocks of Sherry and Port date from that time, and these form the heart of our soleras in Spain and our lots in Portugal today.
—Michael Hobbs,
—HARVEY'S

Visiting the Vineyards

America has been known for its vines since A.D. 1000 when it was described as one vast land of vines by Norse explorer Leif Ericsson. Today the United States is second to no country in viticulture and enological research, and is the producer of some of the best quality wines and *vin ordinaire* in the world. The nation's scientific approach to winemaking dates from 1933, when the wine industry was forced to start afresh after the repeal of Prohibition, which lasted thirteen years. Instead of continuing traditional European methods, American winemakers adopted and developed modern techniques that elevated wine production to even greater heights.

There are roughly three categories of winegrowers throughout the United States. Some wineries are owned by large conglomerates such as Heublein, Coca-Cola. There are family operations that date back over 100 years. And there are many winemaking entrepreneurs who have recently set up business on their own or in partnership, or who have started a family company. Many of these people have restored and put back into use pre-Prohibition wineries that had fallen into disuse. Most wineries offer guided tours, although smaller operations may prefer visitors to make an appointment in advance.

California is the most internationally famous and the largest wine-producing state, boasting some of the world's best table wines, high quality jug wines, first-rate sparkling wine (California champagne), and fortified wines. The majority of vineyards are within a day's journey of San Francisco. The earliest wineries were located near Sonoma and the Napa Valley to the north. Until the 1960s these were considered California's most important wine regions, but the need for expansion has led to the development of new areas which today produce splendid wines.

Washington and Oregon share similar growing conditions with California. Washington is the third largest wine-producing state. New York, which produces a considerable volume of sparkling wines as well as fortified wines and table wines, ranks second in wine production. The fundamental difference between wine production in the Eastern states and on the West Coast lies in the vines. The native American vine, *Vitis labrusca*, is at the heart of wine made in the East, whereas the European grape stock, *Vitis vinifera*, is important for wine made on the West Coast.

Visiting a winery is perhaps the most enjoyable way to learn how wine is made. Throughout the wine-producing nations of the world, wine estates are open to the public. The properties range from small historic vineyards to large modern complexes. Each one offers its own fascinating insight into how wine is produced.

The following pages contain a representative list of the many wineries that can be visited. Also included is a small selection of wine museums that offer the visitor a unique glimpse into the winemaker's craft.

**THE WINE MUSEUM
OF SAN FRANCISCO**
633 Beach Street,
San Francisco, CA 94109
(415) 673-6990

LOCATION: America's most famous wine museum is located on Beach Street near Fisherman's Wharf in San Francisco. *HOURS:* Tuesday to Saturday, 11 A.M. to 5 P.M.; Sunday, 12 noon to 5 P.M. Guided tours every afternoon, 2 P.M. to 4 P.M. Closed Monday and major holidays. *POINTS OF INTEREST:* This magnificent collection toured the country until the museum was established in 1974. The permanent exhibits were built up over a 30- to 40-year period under the aegis of Alfred Fromm, chairman of the board of Fromm and Sichel, Inc. The company is the sole distributor of Christian Brothers wines and brandies.

Guests will enjoy seeing 500 years of wine portrayed in graphic and decorative art, works by Picasso, Chagall, Kokoschka, and others. There is also the wonderful Franz W. Sichel Glass Collection, which spans nearly 2,000 years, from Roman times to the present.

Alabama

PERDIDO VINEYARDS
Rt. 1, Box 20-A
Perdido, AL 36562
(205) 937-WINE

THE WINERY: Perdido Vineyards, Alabama's first farm winery, was established by Jim and Marianne Eddins "to preserve the uniqueness of Southern wine growing." Acreage was purchased in 1972; the first crush was in 1979. The acres of vineyard which surround the simple Spanish-style winery are capable of producing 50,000 gallons of top-quality wine annually. The winery is located one hour away from Mobile at the I65 Rabun-Perdido exit.
THE WINES: Magnolia, White Muscadine, Sweet Muscadine, Noble, Rosé, Cou Rouge, Red Muscadine.
THE TOUR: Perdido's winery is open Monday through Saturday, 10 A.M. to 5 P.M., and is closed on Sunday. The vineyard is open year-round, allowing guests to observe wintertime pruning and the spring and summer growth of the vines. In addition, visitors are free to pick their own grapes off the vines daily, including Sundays, from August 15 until the end of September. A guided tour of the facility features a slide presentation on winemaking. The tour ends in the tasting room, where guests have a chance to sample and discuss the wines, which they may purchase.

Arkansas

THE WINERY: The Swiss chalet-style wine cellar is set in the mountains off Champagne Drive, near the outskirts of Altus, in the Ozark Mountain region of Arkansas. Wiederkehr is the largest winery in the state, with about 575 acres of land planted to vines. The firm, founded in 1880 by Johann Andreas Wiederkehr, remains family-owned.
THE WINES: Table wines are bottled under the Wiederkehr label. Sparkling wines are marketed under Hanns Wiederkehr and Château du Monte labels. Dessert wines are also produced. *THE TOUR:* Open Monday through Saturday from 9 A.M. to 4:30 P.M. The winery's 30-minute guided tour is followed by a tasting. Wine and wine-related items are available at the retail store. There is also a Weinkeller restaurant. Festivals are held during October.

WIEDERKEHR WINE CELLARS, INC.
Wiederkehr Village
RR 1, Box 14
Altus, AR 72821
(501) 468-2611

California/Alameda County

WENTE BROTHERS
5565 Tesla Road
Livermore, CA 94550
(415) 447-3603

THE WINERY: Wente Brothers has remained a family operation since the nineteenth century. The company was founded in 1883 by Carl H. Wente, who bought 50 acres in the Livermore Valley. His sons, Herman and Ernest, continued the family business. Ernest's son, Karl Wente, expanded the winery and vineyards, and today there are 1,450 acres under vine. Since Karl's death in 1977, his children, Eric, Philip and Carolyn, have managed the winery and vineyards. *THE WINES:* Wente Brothers produces 14 different table wines. Traditionally known for white wines, particularly Chardonnay and Sauvignon Blanc. Recommended: Chardonnay, Grey Riesling, Blanc de Blancs. *THE TOUR:* The winery is open Monday through Saturday from 9 A.M. to 5 P.M., Sunday from 11 A.M. to 5 P.M. Guided tours Monday through Friday. Last tour, 3 P.M. Closed New Year's Day, Easter, Thanksgiving, and Christmas. An appointment is necessary for group tours. The tour of facilities lasts 30 to 45 minutes and is followed by a tasting. Guests can buy wine-related items from a small gift counter. Limited picnic facilities are available.

California/Madera County

THE WINERY: This small winery, 20 miles north of Fresno in the heart of the San Joaquin Valley, produces some of the finest port-type wines in the country. Walter C. Ficklin came to Fresno as a grape grower in 1911. As an experiment, his son Walter, Jr., began planting port wine grapes among the table grapes in 1945. Another son, David, studied enology at UC-Davis and began making wine in 1948. Over several years a large inventory of aging wine was built up, and from these lots the port wine was blended. The first Ficklin Tinta Port was released in 1952. Ficklin Vineyards remains a family winery. David continues to run the winery with his son Peter. Walter Jr., has retired and his son Steven is vineyardist. *THE WINES:* Ficklin port wine is made from four varieties of premium Portuguese grapes: Tinta Cao, Tinta Madeira, Souzao, and Touriga.
THE TOUR: As this is not a large winery, there are no general tours. However, tours can be arranged by appointment.

FICKLIN VINEYARDS
30246 Avenue 7½
Madera, CA 93637
(209) 674-4598

California/Monterey County

THE MONTEREY VINEYARD
800 South Alta Street
Gonzales, **CA 93926**
(408) 675-2481

THE WINERY: This modern winery was built in time to harvest the 1974 vintage. It was purchased in 1977 by the Coca-Cola Company. Dr. Richard Peterson, the winemaster and president of The Monterey Vineyard, directs the production of excellent white varietal wines and red wines for The Monterey Vineyard label. *THE WINES:* Fine vintage varietal wines, primarily of Monterey County appellation. The company also produces three varietal blend Classic California wines and Signature Selection wines of outstanding quality, notably Thanksgiving Harvest Johannisberg Riesling. *THE TOUR:* Tours are conducted daily from 11 A.M. to 4 P.M. They include the crushing area, centrifuges, and stainless-steel temperature-controlled fermenters. The upper-level aging cellars are full of redwood casks and thousands of small oak barrels where all red wines and a few selected whites are aged. The tour ends in the tasting room, where wines can be sampled. The tasting room is open from 10 A.M. to 5 P.M. Advance notice is requested for groups of 20 or more. Guests can purchase The Monterey Vineyard wines at the winery.

California/Napa County

THE WINERY: The vineyard and estate are in Rutherford, a small town 15 miles north of Napa. Beaulieu was founded in 1900 by Georges de Latour, who imported from his native France the cuttings that ultimately led to the production of Beaulieu Vineyard Cabernet Sauvignon and other varietal and generic wines. All of BV's wines come from approximately 15,000 acres of Napa Valley premium vineyards. A part of Heublein since 1969, BV has always been proud of the distinct character of its wines, which are among the finest produced in the United States.
THE WINES: The principal varietal wines include Dry Sauvignon Blanc, Cabernet Sauvignon, Pinot Noir, Pinot Chardonnay, Johannisberg Riesling, and Muscat de Frontignan, a rare dessert wine. Generic wines are Burgundy and Chablis. Sparkling wines include Brut Champagne and Champagne de Chardonnay. In addition, BV bottles limited selections known as Georges de Latour Founder's wines. These are 100 percent varietal wines and include the outstanding Private Reserve Cabernet Sauvignon. BV also bottles special lots of vintage wine of individual grape varieties from particular locations or unusual vintages. An excellent example of these wines is Carneros Pinot Noir.
THE TOUR: The winery is open daily for tastings and tours from 10 A.M. to 4 P.M. (the last tour begins at 3 P.M.). Visitors are greeted with a glass of wine at the Visitors' Center before a tour, which lasts 30 to 45 minutes and is followed by a 15-minute film on the winery and the art of winemaking. Special tours are possible if requests are made in advance. The winery is closed on Good Friday, Easter, Thanksgiving, Christmas, and New Year's Day. Most Beaulieu Vineyard wines can be purchased at the winery.

BEAULIEU VINEYARD
1960 St. Helena Highway
Rutherford, CA 94573
(707) 963-2411

THE CHRISTIAN BROTHERS
Mont LaSalle
Napa, CA 94558
(707) 963-2719

THE WINERY: Mont LaSalle Monastery and Novitiate are in the foothills of the Mayacamas Mountains, eight miles northwest of the town of Napa. The Mont LaSalle winery is on the grounds, surrounded by its own vineyards.

The Christian Brothers, members of the Brothers of the Christian Schools, is the largest church-owned wine-making organization in the world. In California it is one of the leading winemakers, producing approximately four million cases per year. Properties include six wineries, 1,500 acres of vineyard land in the Napa Valley, and over 1,000 acres in Fresno County and the San Joaquin Valley. *THE WINES:* The winery, traditionally known for producing nonvintage wine, distributed its first vintage-dated varieties in 1979. A full line of apéritif and dessert wines is produced, as well as champagne and brandy.

THE TOUR: The winery is open daily from 10:30 A.M. to 4 P.M. The tasting room is open until 5 P.M. but is closed New Year's Day, Good Friday, Easter, Thanksgiving, and Christmas. Guided tours last approximately 30 minutes. Each stage of winemaking is shown and detailed as visitors are taken through the winery. The tour ends with a tasting.

THE WINERY: Freemark Abbey is a small, highly respected winery four miles north of St. Helena in Napa Valley. A late-nineteenth-century stone building houses modern winemaking facilities. Also in the building are a candle shop, a gift and gourmet shop, and a restaurant called The Abbey. In 1970, three years after a partnership of seven men took over and revitalized the winery, new wines were released on the market and enjoyed enormous success. Today, 25,000 cases are produced annually. *THE WINES:* Freemark Abbey is famous for its excellent varietal wines. Of note: Chardonnay 1980; Cabernet Bosché 1979; Edelwein 1978. *THE TOUR:* The winery is open every day from 10 A.M. to 4:30 P.M., and closed on Easter, Thanksgiving, and Christmas. A 45-minute guided tour is given at 2 P.M. and ends with a tasting.

FREEMARK ABBEY
3022 St. Helena Highway North
St. Helena, CA 94574
(707) 963-9694

HANNS KORNELL
CHAMPAGNE CELLARS
P. O. Box 249
St. Helena, CA 94574
(707) 963-9333

THE WINERY: The gray stone winery houses three million bottles of California champagne made by the traditional French *méthode champenoise.* Hanns Kornell's distinctive champagne is made up of still wines produced from carefully selected Johannisberg Riesling, Chardonnay, Pinot Blanc, and Semillon grapes. *THE WINES:* Only champagne is produced here. *THE TOUR:* The cellars are located on Larkmead Lane, five miles north of St. Helena. They are open seven days a week from 10 A.M. to 4 P.M. Guests are given an informal guided tour of the cellar. The tour lasts 15 to 20 minutes and ends in the tasting room, where visitors are given a free sample of the superb Hanns Kornell champagne. Champagne can be purchased.

INGLENOOK VINEYARDS
Highway 29
Rutherford, CA 94573
(707) 263-2616

THE WINERY: The winery and vineyards were founded in 1879 by Gustave Ferdinand Niebaum, a wealthy sea captain. After his death in 1908 the family estate passed to his nephew, John Daniel, Jr. In 1964 the winery and vineyards were sold by the Daniel family to United Vintners, a large cooperative group of grape growers. United Vintners came under the ownership of Heublein in 1969. The Inglenook facilities have expanded since then, and additional plantings have been carried out to provide more top-quality varietal grapes. **THE WINES:** The top of the Inglenook line is composed of premium varietal, vintage-dated and estate-bottled. Superior wines produced from Napa Nalley vineyards are available as cask selections. Inglenook's most prestigious wine is the Cask Cabernet Sauvignon.

THE TOUR: Public tours are conducted daily from 10 A.M. to 4 P.M. Although the actual wine production, which is carried out in Oakville, is not open to the public, you do see the largest wine-aging building in the Napa Valley (13,000 barrels of wine). The guided tour of the winery lasts 30 minutes and is followed by a tasting. An eight-minute film on the history of Inglenook and the art of winemaking is also shown. Special tours are possible, and catering arrangements can be made in advance. The winery is open seven days a week. It is closed Thanksgiving, Christmas, and New Year's Day.

THE WINERY: The winery was established in 1861 by Charles Krug, one of the most prominent names in California wine history.

In 1943, Cesare Mondavi, founder of C. Mondavi and Sons, purchased the company and restored and expanded the winery. Today, 1,200 acres of vineyards throughout the valley are under the ownership or control of Charles Krug Winery. Cesare Mondavi's son Peter is the president. **THE WINES:** Charles Krug is distinguished for varietal wines, although generics are also produced. Among the best known are Chenin Blanc, developed by the Mondavis in the 1950s. Good jug wines are also available under the C. K. Mondavi label. These should not be confused with the wines of Robert Mondavi. **THE TOUR:** The winery is open daily from 10 A.M. to 4 P.M. and closed on major holidays. An appointment is necessary for large groups. Wine tastings are held.

CHARLES KRUG WINERY
2800 Main Street
St. Helena, CA 94574
(707) 963-2761

ESTABLISHED 1861

ROBERT MONDAVI WINERY
Highway 29
Oakville, CA 94562
(707) 963-9611

THE WINERY: The Robert Mondavi Winery in Oakville is 12 miles north of the town of Napa, a short distance from Charles Krug Winery (the original Mondavi family winery where Robert Mondavi was a partner for many years). In 1966 he left Krug to pioneer his own winemaking methods in association with his eldest son Michael. Since then, his wines and ingenuity have had an exciting and significant impact on the premium wine market.
THE WINES: Fumé Blanc, Chenin Blanc, Johannisberg Riesling, Moscato d'Oro, Cabernet Sauvignon, Napa Gamay, Gamay Rosé, Pinot Noir. A limited quantity of the first Mondavi-Rothschild wine is to be released in 1983 or early 1984. *THE TOUR:* Open daily May through October, 9 A.M. to 5 P.M; November through April, 10 A.M. to 4:30 P.M. Closed New Year's Day, Good Friday, Easter, Thanksgiving, and Christmas. The 45-minute guided tour of the facilities covers all aspects of winemaking. Afterward, selected wines are sampled and discussed in the tasting room. Robert Mondavi also sponsors special programs at the winery. These range from tastings and dinners to cooking classes, art exhibits, jazz concerts, and a seven-day touring and tasting program.

THE WINERY: Visitors take an aerial tramway ride to reach the winery, which boasts a spectacular view 500 feet above the Napa Valley floor. The first vineyards were planted in 1964 and the winery was completed in 1973. In 1977 it was sold to the Coca-Cola Company by founders Michael Stone and Peter Newton. *THE WINES:* Cabernet Sauvignon (Vintage and Reserve), Chardonnay, Merlot, and Sauvignon Blanc. These are vintage-dated, estate-bottled, 100 percent Napa Valley wines.
THE TOUR: Open daily, April through October, 10:30 A.M. to 4:30 P.M. Open Wednesday through Sunday, November through March. Closed New Year's Day, Easter, Thanksgiving, and Christmas. There is a nominal tramway fee for visitors aged 16 and over. Public viewing galleries are located throughout the cellar area, and information is displayed to assist the self-guided tour. Of interest is the first U.S. *chai* (a two-story cellar), where Sterling Vineyards Reserve wines are aged. The ceramic art, stained-glass windows, sculptures, and Moorish fountains within the winery complex, as well as the magnificent view, make this a memorable place to visit. Wines can be purchased. Sterling also hosts group tours, special tastings, lunches and dinners by advance arrangement.

STERLING VINEYARDS
111 Dunaweal Lane
Calistoga, CA 94515
(707) 942-5151

TREFETHEN VINEYARDS
1160 Oak Knoll Avenue
Napa, CA 94558
(707) 235-7700

THE WINERY: In 1968 the Trefethen family acquired a nineteenth-century winery and renamed it Trefethen Vineyards. The winery has since become one of the most respected operations in California. The vineyard has been expanded to encompass 600 acres, and their cellar has been modernized and enlarged to hold 150,000 gallons of wine. The winery is just off Highway 29, three miles north of Napa. *THE WINES:* Chardonnay, White Riesling, Cabernet Sauvignon, and Pinot Noir. Proprietary wines: Eshcol red wine, Eshcol white wine. *THE TOUR:* By appointment only. Winery hours: 9 A.M. to 5 P.M. Closed Sundays.

California/Riverside County

THE WINERY: Callaway Vineyard and Winery was the first to produce premium varietals in Southern California, where the climate had previously been considered too hot to produce top-quality wine. Callaway purchased land 23 miles inland from the Pacific Ocean, in the foothills of Mount Palomar, northeast of San Diego.

The first wines, released in 1975, met high praise. Since then, Callaway has increased production and currently sells 85,000 cases per year. All grapes come from their own or adjacent vineyards. The company has recently been taken over by Hiram Walker & Sons.
THE WINES: Fumé Blanc, Chardonnay, Chenin Blanc, Sauvignon Blanc, White Riesling, Cabernet Sauvignon, Zinfandel, Petite Sirah. A specialty is Sweet Nancy, named for founder Ely Callaway's wife. It is a botrytised Chenin Blanc. Nonvintage port is also produced.
THE TOUR: Tours leave on the hour seven days a week. The Visitors' Center is open from 11 A.M. to 5 P.M. The winery is closed Thanksgiving, Christmas, and New Year's Day.

Visitors see the vineyards and are given an instructional tour of the winery. During the week guests can watch wine production in progress. The tour ends in the tasting room, where the wines are discussed in an informal lecture. The tour is free, but there is a small charge for tasting. Wines can be purchased.

A picnic area is on the grounds, and barbecue lunches are hosted by the winery.

**CALLAWAY VINEYARD
AND WINERY**
32720 Rancho California Road
Temecula, CA 92390
(704) 676-4001

California/Santa Barbara

FIRESTONE VINEYARD
Zaca Station Road
Los Olivos, CA 93441
(805) 688-3940

THE WINERY: The first crush from the 300-acre vineyards was 1975. The most important winery in the Santa Ynez Valley, Firestone Vineyard is owned jointly by the family of Leonard Firestone and the Japanese distillers of Suntory. From the beginning they have had the guidance of André Tchelistcheff, internationally renowned for his integral role in establishing the California wine industry of today. Ambassador Firestone's son, Brooks, is managing partner of the Firestone Vineyard. **THE WINES:** Firestone produces premium varietal table wines. It is distinguished for Johannisberg Riesling, Gewürztraminer, Chardonnay, Cabernet Sauvignon, Merlot, Pinot Noir, and Sauvignon Blanc. **THE TOUR:** The winery is open Monday to Saturday from 10 A.M. to 4 P.M. It is closed on major holidays. An appointment is necessary for groups of ten or more. Wine tastings are held and wines may be purchased.

California/Santa Clara County

THE WINERY: Almadén was founded in 1852 by Etienne Thee and Charles Lefranc, on land now known as Almadén's home winery in San Jose. According to eminent California wine historian Charles Sullivan, Almadén Vineyards is California's oldest producing winery. The present empire of several wineries and several thousand acres is due in large part to Louis Benoist, a San Francisco businessman who purchased the winery in 1941. In 1967 Almadén was acquired by National Distillers, and it has continued to be one of California's fastest-growing wineries.
THE WINES: Most of Almadén's wines are varietal, bearing the grape name on the label. It is perhaps best known for Mountain Red and Mountain White jug wines and for Almadén Grenache Rosé. In 1978 Almadén presented a new super-premium line, Charles Lefranc Founder's Wines. These are select lots of the best vintages and are produced in limited editions. Almadén also markets dessert wines, California champagne and sparkling wines, California port, California sherry and brandy.
THE TOUR: Guided tours begin at 10 A.M., 11 A.M., and 2 P.M. on weekdays and last 40 to 45 minutes. Visitors see the original wine cellar, which is still in use, as well as the bottling house, one of the most modern facilities in the world.

ALMADÉN VINEYARDS
1530 Blossom Hill Road
San Jose, CA 95118
(408) 269-1312

**PAUL MASSON CHAMPAGNE
AND WINE CELLARS**
13150 Saratoga Avenue
Saratoga, CA 95070
(408) 257-7800

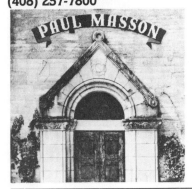

THE WINERY: The winery to which Paul Masson gave his name was founded in 1852 and is the oldest continuous wine producer in California. Masson's nearly 4,500 acres of vineyards are principally in Monterey County, close to its winery in Soledad. A second winery is located in Madera County, and the Paul Masson Champagne and Wine Cellars are in Saratoga, three miles south of Highway 280.
THE WINES: The wide variety of Paul Masson wines includes the Pinnacles Selection Estate wines, several classic varietal wines, Emerald Dry and Masson Light Chablis, Rosé, and Rhine, Sparkling wines and dessert wines are also produced. *THE TOUR:* The Champagne and Wine Cellars are open daily from 10 A.M. to 4 P.M. and are closed on New Year's Day, Easter, Thanksgiving, and Christmas. A self-guided audio tour includes a 12-minute slide presentation. During the tour visitors see modern winemaking facilities and aging cellars. Tastings are offered. Wine and wine-related items are available at the retail store.

California/San Joaquin County

THE WINERY: Established in 1906 in California's fertile North San Joaquin Valley, Franzia Winery has grown to become one of the leading winemakers in the country. It is privately owned and situated on the original 80 acres upon which it was founded. *THE WINES:* Franzia produces varietal table wines, premium champagne, and vermouth. *THE TOUR:* Open daily from 10 A.M. to 7 P.M. Closed New Year's Day, Easter, Thanksgiving, and Christmas. Wine tasting only. Wines, cheeses, bread, and deli items are available. A tree-shaded picnic area is adjacent to the tasting room.

FRANZIA BROTHERS
17000 East Highway 120
Ripon, CA 95366
(209) 599-4111

California/Sonoma County

CHATEAU ST. JEAN
8555 Sonoma Highway
Kenwood, CA 95452
(707) 833-4134

THE WINERY: The Mediterranean-style villa is situated just below Sugarloaf Ridge in the hillside benchlands of Kenwood in Sonoma County. Brothers Robert and Edward Merzoian and brother-in-law Ken Sheffield are the owners of this impressive winery, whose first vintage was in 1974. *THE WINES:* Winemaster Richard Arrowood makes several vineyard-designated bottlings of the distinctive Chateau St. Jean Chardonnays, as well as late harvest Johannisberg Rieslings each year. He also produces several vineyard-designated Fumé Blancs and Gewürztraminers. At its separate facility in Graton, Chateau St. Jean produces vintage sparkling wine made in the traditional *méthode champenoise*. The first bottles are scheduled for release in late 1983 or early 1984. *THE TOUR:* The chateau is open from 10 A.M. to 4:30 P.M. Guests can see the chateau and sample the wine before strolling in the garden, where picnicking is encouraged. Wines can be purchased.

F. KORBEL & BROTHERS
13250 River Road
Guerneville, CA 95446
(707) 887-2294

THE WINERY: Internationally famous, Korbel is America's largest producer of premium sparkling wines. The estate is situated along the Russian River at Guerneville, 17 miles northwest of Santa Rosa on River Road. During the 1880s the three Korbel brothers began producing a sparkling wine using the traditional French *méthode champenoise*. In 1954, the Heck family purchased Korbel, and since that time Adolf Heck has been president **THE WINES:** Champagnes include Korbel Natural Brut, Extra Dry, Rosé, and Rouge. Also Blanc de Noirs, Blanc de Blancs, champagne, and a small amount of estate-bottled table wines. The winery also produces brandy. **THE TOUR:** Guided tours and tastings are held every day from 10 A.M. to 3 P.M. at no charge. The winery is closed New Year's Day, Easter, and Christmas. The 45-minute tour focuses on the history of the winery and includes a step-by-step explanation of the *méthode champenoise*.

THE WINERY: Established by Samuele Sebastiani in 1904, Sebastiani Vineyards, still family-owned and operated, is the largest winery in Sonoma Valley, with a storage capacity of six million gallons. **THE WINES:** Vintage premium varietals, Proprietor's Reserve wines, champagne (*méthode champenoise*), and sherry bottled under the Sebastiani Vineyards label; red and white country varietals, mountain wines, and champagne (bulk process) under the August Sebastiani Country label. **THE TOUR:** Informative tour mingles winery history with facts about winemaking. Visitors are shown enormous redwood aging vats (several with a 59,000-gallon capacity), early-twentieth-century equipment brought around Cape Horn, and the California wine country's largest collection of carved wine barrels depicting scenes of early California Franciscan Fathers making wine at Sonoma Mission, created by renowned woodcarver Earle Brown. During harvest (September and October) visitors are shown grapes being put through the crushers. Tour culminates in a tasting, during which guests may sample up to five wines of their choice from an extensive wine list. The winery is open daily.

SEBASTIANI VINEYARDS
P.O Box AA
389 Fourth Street East
Sonoma, CA 95476
(707) 938-5532

California/Stanislaus County

GALLO VINEYARDS
P.O. Box 1130
Modesto, CA 95353
(209) 521-3111

THE WINERY: Gallo, the world's leading winery, is headquartered in Modesto. Other Gallo wineries are located in Livingston, Fresno, and Healdsburg. Gallo's total storage capacity is 250 million gallons. Most grapes come from growers in Napa, Sonoma, and Monterey Counties. Although they are now in their seventies, brothers Ernest and Julio Gallo still run the company. Since it was founded in 1933, Gallo has played a major role in familiarizing Americans with wine. **THE WINES:** The wine cellars of Ernest and Julio Gallo produce the leading varietal wines at retail. Chardonnay and Sauvignon Blanc are among this group. Chablis Blanc, Hearty Burgundy, and Livingston Cellars Cream Sherry are perhaps the best known Gallo generic wines. **THE TOUR:** The wineries are not open to the general public.

Indiana

BANHOLZER WINE CELLARS, LTD.
5627 East County
Route 1000 North
La Porte, IN 46350
(219) 778-2448

THE WINERY: Located 60 miles east of Chicago, near the village of Hesston in La Porte County, this wine cellar is the largest in Indiana. It was established by owners Carl and Janet Banholzer in 1971. *THE WINES:* Sparkling wine and table wines include: Pinot Chardonnay, Carbernet Sauvignon, La Fleur, Kaisertahl, Madame La Femme, Picnic Rosé, and Vidalesque. Banholzer has its own wine society. *THE TOUR:* The winery is open during the year Friday through Sunday, 11 A.M. to 5 P.M., except on Christmas and New Year's Day. The full guided tour, which includes a 30- to 45-minute sight and sound show, lasts two hours. The shows start at noon, 2 P.M. and 4 P.M. For a small fee, guests can purchase a food- and wine-tasting package, including cheese and homemade fresh bread. Snacks are available for picnics. Wines can be purchased. Special events are held four times a year at the winery.

Maryland

THE WINERY: Author, editor, and winemaster Philip Wagner, who planted the first French hybrid grapes in this country in 1940, founded Boordy vineyards with his wife Jocelyn near Baltimore in 1942. Today, in its new location in Hydes, the winery is managed by the Deford family under the direction of winemaker Robert Deford, with Philip Wagner as consultant. *THE WINES:* French-American hybrids. These include Maryland Red, Maryland White, Maryland Rosé and, Maryland Vin Gris; vintage-dated red wines and varietal white wines.
THE TOUR: Winery tours are available by appointment. Informal guided tours last from 1 to 2½ hours and are followed by a tasting. Wines can be purchased.

BOORDY VINEYARD
Hydes
Long Green Pike
MD 21082
(301) 592-5015

Michigan

BRONTE WINERY AND VINEYARDS
Keeler, MI 49057
(616) 621-3419

THE WINERY: President Robert Wozniak's father, Dr. T. Wozniak, founded Bronte with a group of investors in 1933. The company expanded in 1943, moving to the present location at Keeler in Van Buren County.
THE WINES: Table wines, sparkling wines, sherry and port. Bronte is best known for being the first winery to bottle Cold Duck, a mixture of red and white sparkling wines. Best-sellers include Rheinhaus, Pink Delaware, Hartford Cream Sherry. Award-winning wines include Bronte Baco Noir and Bronte Champagne. *THE TOUR:* The winery is open daily except New Year's Day, Easter, Thanksgiving, and Christmas. Tours begin hourly from 10 A.M. to 4 P.M., Monday through Saturday, and from noon to 4 P.M. on Sunday. The tour includes a visit to the champagne and sherry rooms and to the main cellar, where there are vast wooden storage tanks, several of which were used in Al Capone's breweries. The tour is followed by a tasting. Wine can be purchased.

Missouri

STONE HILL WINE COMPANY
Rt. 1, Box 26
Hermann, MI 65041
(314) 486-2221

THE WINERY: The turreted Stone Hill winery is on a hilltop at the southern edge of the town of Hermann. Built in 1847, it was once America's largest winery, but at the start of Prohibition it closed and the vineyards fell to ruin. In 1965 James Held and his family restored the winery and slowly replanted the vineyards, which now total 60 acres. *THE WINES:* Table wine, sparkling wine. Notable selections are Missouri Riesling and Norton. Golden Rhine is an excellent seller. *THE TOUR:* The winery is open Monday through Saturday, 8:30 A.M. to 5:30 P.M., and Sunday, noon to 6 P.M. The one-hour guided tour through the facilities includes a look at vaulted cellars over 100 years old. The tour ends with a wine tasting. There is a shop where wine and wine-related gifts are available, a restaurant, and a wine museum.

New Hampshire

THE WINERY: John and Lucille Canepa, the first people to establish a winery in New Hampshire, were so successful with their first wines in 1964 that five years later they bought a 150-acre farm and built and equipped an ultra-modern winery. Since then, White Mountain Vineyards has been enlarged to a 100,000-gallon capacity. Approximately 15,000 cases are marketed annually. The White Mountain winery is situated seven miles from Laconia on Durrell Mountain Road, just off Route 107. *THE WINES:* They include Aurora, Seyval Blanc, Rayon D'Or, Chancellor, Chelois, Maréchal Foch, Landot, Rosés, and fortified wines. *THE TOUR:* The winery is open June through August, Monday through Friday, 9 A.M until noon and 1 P.M. until 4:30 P.M. On Saturday it is open only by appointment. The winery is closed on Sundays and during harvest, September 1 through October 15. There is a guided tour through the winery, followed by a tasting of New Hampshire wines. After the tour, visitors are allowed to walk through the vineyards. Wines can be purchased.

WHITE MOUNTAIN VINEYARDS
R.F.D. 6, Box 218
Laconia, NH 03246
(603) 524-0174

New Jersey

RENAULT WINERY
R.D. 3, Box 21B Bremen Avenue
Egg Harbor City, NJ 08215
(609) 965-2111

THE WINERY: Renault Winery, founded by Louis Nicholas Renault over 100 years ago, was acquired in 1919 by the D'Agostino family. Maris D'Agostino transformed the old winery into a showplace and in 1966 established a museum that houses an outstanding collection of wineglasses dating back to the thirteenth century. Since 1977 the winery has been owned and run by Joseph Milza.
THE WINES: Sparkling wines, table wines, and dessert wines. Specialty wines include Noah, Blueberry Champagne, Blueberry Duck, and Pink Lady. *THE TOUR:* The winery is open Monday through Saturday, 10 A.M. to 5 P.M., Sundays, noon to 5 P.M. Closed on New Year's Day, Easter, Thanksgiving, and Christmas. The 45-minute guided tour includes the Champagne Room with equipment dating back 100 years, and the glass collection. The tour ends with a tasting. A candlelight buffet is hosted on Saturday evenings, by reservation, all year round.

New York/Finger Lakes District

BULLY HILL VINEYARDS
Greyton H. Taylor Memorial Drive
Hammondsport, NY 14840
(607) 868-3610 or
(800) 252-5408
(for New York State residents)

THE WINERY: The Bully Hill Wine Company was established in 1970 by Greyton H. Taylor and his son Walter S. Taylor. At his father's death, Walter Taylor became sole owner. He is the direct descendant of the founder of the nearby Taylor Wine Company. *THE WINES:* Chiefly "French-born" grapes. All Bully Hill wines are vintage-dated and either estate-bottled or produced strictly within New York State. The latter appear under the Special Reserve label. All wines are bottled in 750 ml. bottles. Bully Hill wines include Seyval Blanc, Vidal Blanc, Aurora Blanc, Chancellor Noir, Maréchal Foch, Baco Noir, and Founder's Red. *THE TOUR:* The winery is open April through November, Monday through Saturday, holidays included. Advance reservations are necessary for groups of more than 10 people. Tours start at 10 A.M. The last tour is held at 3:30 P.M. On Sundays they start on the hour, 1 P.M. to 3 P.M. The 45-minute guided tour includes the vineyards, winery, and tasting. Wines are sold at the retail shop. Picnicking facilities are available or you can visit the Champagne Country Café. Visitors should also see the Greyton H. Taylor Wine Museum in the original nineteenth-century winery.

THE WINERY: Walter Taylor, a cooper, started the Taylor Wine Company in 1880 with a seven-acre plot of land overlooking Keuka Lake in the Finger Lakes region of New York State. Taylor has grown and flourished ever since. In 1962 the company went public, and in 1977 it merged with the Coca-Cola Company. It is now the largest producer of premium sparkling and dessert wines in the United States. *THE WINES:* Most famous for Taylor sparking wines, of which the best known is Taylor New York State Brut Champagne. Notable table wines are Lake Country Red, White, and Pink. Taylor has recently introduced Lake Country Soft Red, White, and Pink, a line of low-alcohol, lightly carbonated Lambrusco-style wine. *THE TOUR:* The winery is located off Route 54, 1½ miles from the village of Hammondsport, New York. Free guided tours are held July through October, Monday through Friday, 10 A.M. to 4 P.M. From November through June tours are held from 11 A.M. to 3 P.M. Reservations are necessary for group tours. The tour includes a visit to the traditional aging and storage cellars and ultramodern bottling and packaging facilities. It ends with a tasting of Taylor wines and champagnes in the hospitality room. Guests can picnic on the grounds. Wines can be purchased at the gift shop, which also sells wine-related items.

TAYLOR WINE COMPANY
Old Bath Road
Hammondsport, NY 14840
(606) 569-2111

New York/Hudson Valley

BENMARL WINE COMPANY, LTD.
Marlboro, NY 12542
(914) 236-7271

THE WINERY: This unique, family-owned winery is only an hour away from New York City. The 72-acre vineyard is one of the finest in the Hudson Valley, and potentially among the most important in America. It was founded in 1956 by Mark Miller, who replanted a century-old vineyard. He also developed a cooperative called the Société des Vignerons, which entitles members to wine from each vintage in exchange for financial support in growing the vines. At the start, all of his wine went to the Société members, but after two years he was producing enough to make Benmarl wines available in restaurants and retail stores.
THE WINES: Benmarl Vineyard and Cuvée du Vigneron table wines. These include: Seyval Blanc, Baco Noir, Chardonnay, and Marlboro Village white and red wines. Sparkling wines are produced under Cuvée du Vigneron label.
THE TOUR: Tours of the winery are for persons considering Société membership, by appointment only.

THE WINERY: The Hudson Valley Wine Company is only an hour away from New York City on the New York State Thruway, off Route 9W South. Founded at the turn of the century, it is now owned and run by Herbert Feinberg. *THE WINES:* French hybrids. Chelois. Premium regional wines; Pink Catawba, Chablis, Haute Sauterne, Burgundy, and Blanc de Blanc champagne. *THE TOUR:* Open year-round Monday through Friday 11 A.M. to 4 P.M. There is a modest admission charge. Advance reservations are necessary for groups of 15 or more. Guided tours and tastings are accompanied by bread, fruit, and cheese. For groups of 30 people, a country buffet is served in the wood-paneled dining room by appointment. Special events are sponsored by the winery during the year.

HUDSON VALLEY WINE COMPANY
Blue Point Road
Highland, New York 12528
(914) 691-7296 or
(212) 594-5394

Oregon

AMITY VINEYARDS
Route 1, Box 3488
Amity, OR 97101
(503) 835-2362

THE WINERY: Amity Vineyards is about 45 miles southwest of Portland, Oregon. It was established by Ione Redford, her son Myron, and Janis Checchia in 1976. For the past six years the company has introduced their wines at two annual festivals planned around the solstice in June and December. *THE WINES:* Amity's reputation was built on its Nouveau and Dry Rieslings. It is also notable for Pinot Noir, made both in the Nouveau and conventional barrel-aged styles, and for Gerwürztraminer made in the dry Alsatian style. Merlot and Cabernet Sauvignon are produced under the Redford Cellars label.
THE TOUR: The winery and vineyards are open every day, June through September, from noon until 5 P.M. From October through May, they are open Saturday and Sunday from noon until 5 P.M. Amity is closed from December 24 through January 30. Advance notice is required at other times. There is a modest charge per person for groups over 20 or for those wishing to take the Grand Tour, a personalized guided tour of the vineyards and winery, followed by a tasting. Wine can be purchased. Picnic facilities are available.

Rhode Island

SAKONNET VINEYARDS
West Main Road
Little Compton, RI 02837
(401) 635-4356

THE WINERY: The Mitchell family more than doubled their production from 9,000 gallons in 1976 to 20,000 gallons in 1981. The 40-acre vineyard is the largest winery in New England and produced Rhode Island's first home-grown wines. **THE WINES:** Rhode Island Red and America's Cup White, and more recently Compass Rosé, Light House Red, and Spinnaker White. Varietals include Vidal, Riesling, Chardonnay, and Pinot Noir.
THE TOUR: Sakonnet Vineyards is open to the public from May 30 through October, Wednesdays and Saturdays only, 10 A.M. to 4 P.M., otherwise by appointment. Wines can be purchased Monday through Saturday. Visitors may walk through the vineyards (where over 200 flowering plants are in bloom in July and August) before joining a guided tour through the winery. This is followed by a tasting. Picnicking is permitted.

Washington

THE WINERY: Chateau Ste. Michelle is Washington State's foremost winery with holdings of over 2,000 acres of premium vineyards. The winery itself is in the style of a classic Bordeaux château, standing amid 85 arboretum-like acres in Woodinville, 25 minutes northeast of Seattle. All of the grapes are grown in Washington's dry eastern half, in the Columbia Valley, where soil, climate and latitudinal position combine to create an ideal growing region for classic grape types. **THE WINES:** Premium varietal table and sparkling wines. Notable are the Johannisberg Riesling, Grenache Rosé, Chardonnay, Cabernet Sauvignon, and Blanc de Noir Sparkling Wine. **THE TOUR:** The winery is open every day from 10 A.M. to 4:30 P.M., closed on New Year's Day, Thanksgiving, and Christmas. A 20-minute guided tour of the wine cellar is followed by a 15-minute tasting of the wines. Picnic items as well as wines may be purchased; visitors are welcome to picnic.

CHATEAU STE. MICHELLE
P. O. Box 1976
14111 NE 135th Street
Woodinville, WA 98072
(206) 488-1133

Wisconsin

WOLLERSHEIM
Highway 188
Prairie du Sac, WI 53578
(608) 643-6515

THE WINERY: Before traveling west to California, the celebrated Count Haraszthy planted vines near Prairie du Sac. The winery and family house were built in 1858 by Peter Kaehl of Germany. Closed in 1889, the winery was reopened by the Wollersheim family in 1972.
THE WINES: French hybrids and Riesling grapes bottled as varietals and proprietary wines. Award winners include Foch, Estate Red, Baco Noir. **THE TOUR:** Wollersheim is open daily from 10 A.M. to 5 P.M. It is closed on New Year's Day, Easter, Thanksgiving, and Christmas. Advance notice is requested for groups of ten or more. Highlights of the guided tour include a slide show and a visit to the original limestone aging cellar carved into a hillside, where wooden casks date back to the Civil War. A tasting session follows the tour. Wines and wine-related items are available at the gift shop.

France

Most wine lovers agree that of all the world's wine-producing countries France reigns supreme. For although France does not produce the most wine, it does produce the greatest number of highly respected wine types. Bordeaux is the chief wine region. It boasts the peninsula of Médoc, where some of the greatest red wines are made, and the famous white wine districts of Graves and Sauternes. A smaller quantity of equally fine wine is produced in Burgundy, which stretches from the commune of Chablis in the north through the Côte d'Or to the Beaujolais region in the south.

The Champagne vineyards fall into four large districts in the environs of the famous Champagne towns of Reims and Épernay. Millions of bottles lie in the natural chalk cellars beneath these towns, where the traditional champagne-making process, known as *méthode champenoise*, is carried out.

Visitors touring the legendary wine districts of France can taste and purchase local wines at roadside wine bars called *caves touristiques* and *salles de dégustation*. Those run by the local wine cooperative are especially recommended. When visiting châteaux, advance notice is usually required. It is also a good idea to confirm times of opening. Contact the U.S. importer whose name is on the wine label, write to the château, or within France telephone direct. For further information, contact the French Government Tourist Office, 610 Fifth Avenue, New York, NY 10020.

France/Bordeaux

CHÂTEAU HAUT-BRION
Domaine Clarence Dillon S.A.
33600 Pessac Graves
(56) 48.73.24

THE WINERY: Haut-Brion produces the only wine in France to be classified as a *Premier Cru* of both the Médoc and the Graves regions. In the nineteenth century its reds were considered so magnificent that they ranked as *Premier Cru* in the Médoc classification of 1855, even though Haut-Brion is not in the Médoc region, but in the area called Graves, which wasn't classified until the 1950s. The estate lies in Pessac, a suburb west of Bordeaux, barely 15 minutes away from the city center. Château Haut-Brion is one of the few venerable French properties that is foreign-owned. Since 1935 the proprietors have been the heirs of the late American financier Clarence Dillon. **THE WINES:** Fine Bordeaux red and white wines. Château Haut-Brion Blanc is one of the best dry white wines of Bordeaux. **THE TOUR:** By appointment only. Monday to Friday, 9 A.M. to 11 A.M., and 2 P.M. to 5 P.M. English-language guided tours of the winery last 1 to 1½ hours. Over the last two decades the château has been redecorated and restored, and in 1973 a magnificent underground cellar was built which is open to visitors. Tastings are limited to members of the wine trade, and bottles cannot be purchased.

CHÂTEAU LAFITE-ROTHSCHILD
33250 Pauillac
(56) 59.01.004

THE WINERY: Described as the ultimate connoisseur's wine, Lafite was already famous in the Middle Ages. In the eighteenth century it was the favorite wine of Louis XV, and a century later it was designated *Premier Cru* in the Bordeaux classification of 1855. In 1858 the Rothschild family bought the estate at auction, for a little more than $3,000,000. Château Lafite has remained in the Rothschild family ever since. The vineyards border those of Mouton, the great wine estate which is owned by another branch of the family. Château Lafite lies in the hills of the Pauillac commune. **THE WINES:** Only the highest-quality wine is designated Château Lafite. **THE TOUR:** By appointment only. Monday to Friday, 8:30 A.M. to 11:30 A.M. and 2 P.M. to 5:30 P.M. English-language guided tours last 30 minutes to an hour. Of exceptional interest are the magnificent vaulted cellars. The wine library that contains bottles dating back to 1797 may also be included in the tour. Tastings are held only for people in the wine trade. Wine is not for sale.

THE WINERY: One of the four Bordeaux châteaux classified as *Premier Cru* in 1855, Latour is famous throughout the world for its outstanding ability to maintain a high standard in adverse years that affect the excellence of other *Premier Cru* wines. From the end of the seventeenth century until 1963, the château belonged to members of the Ségur family. Then, in 1963, descendants of the family sold three quarters of their holdings to Lazard Brothers, a British company. Another British firm, Harvey's of Bristol, bought one fifth of the Lazard interest. Since then Lazard has carried out a modernization and restoration program, which has included the repair of the tower that is depicted on the label. **THE WINES:** Fine red Bordeaux. Also, Les Forts de Latour, a secondary wine of this great château. **THE TOUR:** As this is a small organization, it is open by appointment only, Monday to Friday, 9:30 A.M. until noon and 2 P.M. to 4:30 P.M. Tours of the cellars and modern operational facilities last 30 minutes to an hour. No tastings are held except for members of the wine trade, and wine cannot be purchased.

CHÂTEAU LATOUR
33250 Pauillac
(56) 59.00.51

CHÂTEAU
LA MISSION-HAUT-BRION
67 Rue Peybouquey
33400 Talence
(56) 48.76.54

THE WINERY: The vineyard dates from the seventeenth century, when it was established by the Mission of St. Vincent de Paul. The property is now owned by the Société Civile des Domaines Woltner. The Woltner family acquired the property in 1919, and achieved the high standard of excellence for which the château is renowned. In the Graves classification of 1953 and 1959 the red wine was accorded *Premier Cru* status, and it rivals the celebrated red wines from the neighboring vineyard Château Haut-Brion. La Mission-Haut-Brion is in Talence, a suburb less than a mile away from Bordeaux, off the N650 road leading to Arachon. *THE WINES:* Fine Bordeaux red wines. A second vineyard, Laville-Haut-Brion, produces a fine dry white Graves. A third vineyard, La Tour-Haut-Brion, makes an excellent red Graves. *THE TOUR:* By appointment only. Monday to Friday, 9 A.M. 11 A.M., 2 P.M. to 5 P.M. Closed July 14 to October 20. The French- or English-language guided tour of the winery takes from 30 minutes to an hour. Visitors see the cellars where wines spend two or three years maturing in casks before being bottled at other cellars in Bordeaux. The tour includes a visit to the Lazarite Mission Chapel, where a collection of Holy Water stoups and antique Delft dishes is on exhibit. Visitors also see the remarkably beautiful château where tastings are held.

THE WINERY: This venerable estate is only 15 miles from Bordeaux, near the village of Cantenac in the Médoc district. It has had many proprietors, among them King Edward III of England, who is said to have owned the vineyard in the fourteenth century. The château, however, was built in the early nineteenth century, and it sits in grand style surrounded by parkland. For many years it belonged to M. Pierre Ginestet, but in the late 1970s the property was sold to M. Mentzelopoulos, owner of the Potin Supermarket chain. The château has remained in this family, although M. Mentzelopoulos died in 1981.
THE WINES: Bordeaux red classified as a *Premier Cru* at the Paris Exposition in 1855. Some dry white Bordeaux is sold as Pavillon Blanc du Château Margaux. (It is the only *Premier Cru* estate in the Médoc district to make white wine.) *THE TOUR:* By appointment only. Monday to Friday, 9.30 A.M. until noon, and 3 P.M. to 5 P.M. English-language tours of the winery last 30 minutes to an hour. The wine is made in "sheds" termed *chais* where visitors can see the presses, the huge fermenting vats, and oak casks. The château is open to the public. It was superbly redecorated by M. Mentzelopoulos, and is well worth seeing. Tastings are held for members of the wine trade only, and bottles of wine cannot be purchased.

CHÂTEAU MARGAUX
33460 Margaux
(56) 58.40.28

CHÂTEAU MOUTON-ROTHSCHILD
B.P. 32, 33250 Pauillac
(56) 59.01.15

THE WINERY: This great château has been in the Rothschild family since 1853. During the past sixty years Baron Philippe de Rothschild has presided over the estate. In 1973 Château Mouton-Rothschild was raised from *Deuxième Cru* to *Premier Cru* in the only revision ever made in the 1855 classification by the French Ministry of Agriculture. Some of Baron Philippe's spectacular innovations have been to commission the original illustration of the bottle labels by a different artist each year and to establish a magnificent wine museum. The château, surrounded by its own acres of vines, is in the village of Mouton, two kilometers north of the village of Pauillac. **THE WINES:** Fine red Bordeaux. Secondary wines are best-selling Mouton-Cadet red and white wines from a selection of Bordeaux vineyards, Château Mouton-Baron-Philippe, and Château Clerc-Milon, which were classified as *Cinquième Cru* in 1855. These are produced and marketed by La Bergerie. **THE TOUR:** By appointment only. Open weekdays, 9:30 A.M. to 12:30 P.M. and 2 P.M. to 5:30 P.M. Closed during the month of August. There is a museum charge of five francs. The hour-long guided tour includes the cellars and the production facilities at the château, as well as the museum. Particularly impressive is the great *chai* which houses the casks, and the cellars and tunnels at a lower level which store 200,000 to 300,000 bottles of Mouton at a constant temperature of 52°F. The museum contains a superb collection of wine artifacts. Tastings are available on request, but wines cannot be purchased at the château.

THE WINERY: Forty percent of this château's great Sauternes—indisputably the best dessert wine in the world—is sold in the United States. It has been famous for hundreds of years. Thomas Jefferson called it the greatest white wine of France. In 1855 it was the only wine to be awarded a *Premier Grand Cru* at the Paris Exposition. The Lur-Saluces family have owned Château d'Yquem since 1786 and Count Alexandre Lur-Saluces now runs the estate. The turreted château and its 250 acres of surrounding vineyards lie on and around a hill overlooking the Garonne River, south of Bordeaux. **THE WINES:** Bordeaux white wine: Château d'Yquem, of which 1921 is considered the greatest vintage. Only the highest-quality wine from the best harvest is sold as Yquem; the rest is bottled as regional Sauternes. The château also produces a dry white wine called Château Y *(i grec)*. **THE TOUR:** By appointment only. Monday to Friday, 9 A.M. to noon and 2 P.M. to 5 P.M. Saturday, 10 A.M. until noon. English-language guided tours last 30 minutes to an hour. Tours of the cellars are usually restricted to members of the wine trade. Bottles are not for purchase. During the Bordeaux festival in May, concerts of chamber music are held on the ·grounds of the château.

CHÂTEAU D'YQUEM
33210 Langon
(56) 62.61.05

France/Burgundy

BOUCHARD PÈRE ET FILS
Au Château
Beaune 21201 Beaune
Côte d'Or
(80) 22.14.41

THE WINERY: Bouchard Père et Fils, one of the most admired shippers or *négociants* in Burgundy, is also one of the few producers to own over 200 acres of premium Côte de Beaune vineyards. The firm, founded by Michel Bouchard in 1731, is today the leading company in the Côte de Beaune. The cellars are located on the eastern side of the town of Beaune along Avenue du 8 Septembre.
THE WINES: Fine red and white Burgundies.
THE TOUR: Open by appointment, Monday to Friday, 9 A.M. to 11:30 A.M., 2 P.M. to 5:30 P.M. Closed during August. French, German, or English guided tours of the old cellars last from 30 minutes to an hour. The tour is followed by a comparative tasting of wines of the current and preceding years. Bottles of wine can be purchased.

THE WINERY: The 125 acres of the Clos rank as one of the largest vineyards in Burgundy. It has upheld this distinction since the twelfth century, when the vineyard was first planted by monks on the slopes above their monastery in the village of Vougeot. Today the vineyard is shared among a number of owners in a syndicate. Depending on the skill of the winemaker and the acreage he owns, the quality of wine varies from the great Burgundy for which Clos de Vougeot was granted the designation *Grand Cru*, to wine of lesser quality. After completing the monastery and planting the Clos, the monks built a 10-foot-high wall around their property and added a magnificent stone château and press house to the enclosed area. Since 1944 the château has been owned by the members of the International Wine Brotherhood known as the *Chevaliers du Tastevin*. The order celebrates its love of good Burgundy by serving Clos-Vougeot at grand banquets and at pageants held in the great halls of the château. *THE WINES:* Clos de Vougeot is fine red Burgundy. A small proportion of white Burgundy called Clos Blanc de Vougeot or Vignes Blanches de Vougeot is also produced. *THE TOUR:* Open daily, 9 A.M. to 11:30 A.M. and 2 P.M. to 5 P.M. The entrance fee is six francs. Group tours, four francs. English-language guided tours leave every 30 minutes and include the sixteenth-century courtyard, the vast cellars where banquets are held, and the original oak winepresses.

CHÂTEAU DU CLOS DE VOUGEOT
21640 Vougeot, Côte d'Or
(80) 06.86.09

France / Champagne

CHAMPAGNE J. BOLLINGER S.A.
16, Rue Jules-Lobet
51160, Ay, Marne
(26) 50.12.34

THE WINERY: This distinguished Champagne house was established in 1829 by M. Jacques Bollinger, whose father-in-law owned vineyards in Ay. Christian Bizot, president of the company, is a direct descendant. The firm has remained small, producing only 100,000 cases a year. Bollinger uses 75 percent of its own grapes. These are grown on 300 acres of vineyards lying in the Côtes des Noirs and on the outskirts of Epernay, in the Champagne region of France. *THE CHAMPAGNES:* Bollinger Special Cuvée (nonvintage), Bollinger Vintage, Bollinger Tradition RD, Bollinger Vielles Vignes Françaises. The last-matured is sold at a high price and in small quantities. *THE TOUR:* As this is a small operation, an appointment is necessary. Open Monday to Friday. Closed public holidays and the month of August. French- and English-language guided tours of the vineyards and cellars, which hold some 600,000 bottles, last about an hour. Visitors see traditional Champagne-making processes, including the riddling (*remuage*) and disgorging (*dégorgement*) of the Champagne bottles, which are carried out by hand. Tastings are included by request. Bottles cannot be purchased.

THE WINERY: Moët et Chandon is the largest producer of Champagne in the world. The firm was established in 1743 by Claude Moët. His grandson, Jean-Remy Moët, expanded the company and purchased the vineyards and monastery buildings of Hautvillers, where 100 years earlier the Benedictine monk Dom Pérignon had perfected the method by which Champagne is made. Jean-Remy was succeded by his son Victor and son-in-law Pierre Gabriel Chandon in 1832. From that date on, the firm has been known as Moët et Chandon. *THE CHAMPAGNES:* Dom Pérignon Vintage; Brut Impérial Vintage and Non-vintage; White Star Extra Dry Non-vintage; White Star Demi-sec Non-vintage; Brut Impérial Rosé Vintage. *THE TOUR:* No appointment necessary. Open all year, except national holidays. Tours leave on the hour, from 10 A.M. to 12:30 P.M. and 2 P.M. to 5:30 P.M. From March 30 to October 31 the cellars are open Saturday, 9:30 A.M. until noon and 2 P.M. to 8 P.M., and Sunday, 9:30 A.M. until noon and 2 P.M. to 4 P.M. The Maison Moët et Chandon is located 100 meters east of the Place de la République, Épernay's main square. The English-language guided tours take visitors through the Moët et Chandon Museum where Champagne-making equipment is on display. Then you can visit the magnificent cellars, which stretch for 18 miles beneath the city of Épernay and hold approximately 40 million bottles. All tours (which last approximately an hour) are followed by a tasting. Guests can purchase bottles in gift packs. Visitors can make a separate trip to Hautvillers to see the vineyards and visit the abbey where Dom Pérignon is buried.

CHAMPAGNE MOËT
ET CHANDON
18 Avenue de Champagne
51200 Épernay, Marne
(26) 51.71.11

Germany

Germany, the northernmost wine-producing nation in the world, is also one of the smallest in terms of the amount produced. The country is renowned for its superb white wines. The premier grape is Riesling. Germany makes very little red wine, and virtually none is exported.

There are many beautiful and historic wine estates throughout the nation's eleven wine regions, as well as a number of modern cooperative wineries. These are staffed full-time by experts who buy grapes from a membership of growers. The wine, which ranges from the most ordinary to the very best, is then marketed as Cooperative German wine.

Most wineries offer tours but require advance notice. This can be arranged by writing directly to the winery or telephoning from within the country. Otherwise, in the United States you might contact the importer whose name is on the bottle label. For further information, contact the German Wine Information Bureau, 99 Park Avenue, New York, NY 10016. For travel information, contact the German National Tourist Office, 630 Fifth Avenue, New York, NY 10020.

Germany/Franconia (Franken)

JULIUSSPITAL WEINGUT
8700 Würzburg
Juliuspromenade 19
Franken, West Germany
(0931) 51610 or
(0931) 50067

THE WINERY: Juliusspital wine estate is one of the largest and best known in Germany. The winery is situated in the center of the city of Würzburg in Juliusspital Park. The vineyards are in various villages in lower Franconia. The estate belongs to the Juliusspital Charitable Foundation, established in 1576 to maintain a hospital and home for the aged. *THE WINES:* Franconian varieties. *THE TOUR:* Open Monday through Friday, 8 A.M. to 3 P.M., and occasionally evenings. Tours are available for groups of 20 to 50 people. Four weeks' advance notice is required. The 45-minute guided tour is conducted in German. The fine carvings and rows of barrels in the old cellar are well worth seeing. There is a range of nine different wines at the wine tasting, at a cost of 20 DM. Wines can be purchased. A superb restaurant is in the east wing of the Juliusspital. This is closed on Wednesday and during the month of February.

Germany/Mosel-Saar-Ruwer

THE WINERY: The most famous vineyard of the Saar is two kilometers east of Wiltingen toward Oberemmel. It was monastery-owned from 1030 until 1796, when it was secularized by Napoleon during the French Revolution. The following year the vineyard was purchased at auction by Jacques Koch. Egon Müller, the present owner, is a direct descendant of Koch. *THE WINES:* Riesling.
THE TOUR: Tours are conducted Monday through Friday, 8 A.M. to 6 P.M. For groups of up to 50 people, four weeks' advance notice is required. Only German- or French-language guided tours are available. Tastings are offered free but no wines are available for purchase.

WEINGUT EGON MÜllER
511 Scharzhof bei Wiltingen
Saar, West Germany
(06501) 2432

Germany / Rheingau

KLOSTER EBERBACH
Administered from Verwaltung der
Staatsweingüter in Rheingau
Schwalbacherstrasse 56-62
6228 Eltville-am-Rhein
West Germany
(06123) 4155-6

THE WINERY: This magnificent former Cistercian monastery was founded in 1135, and the majority of its vineyards date from that period. The monastery and winery were secularized during the French Revolution. Kloster Eberbach is now a state-owned winery. To reach it from Wiesbaden, turn right at Eltville and approach from the village of Kiedrich. *THE WINES:* Riesling. *THE TOUR:* Open Monday through Friday, 9 A.M. to 5 P.M. Four weeks' advance notice is required for tours. The winery is open for tours and tastings to groups of ten or more people. There is a minimum 4 DM charge which includes tasting three wines. A five-wine tasting costs 9 DM; a ten-wine tasting costs 20 DM; and a twelve-wine tasting costs 25 DM; tastings and sensory evaluations are held after 6 P.M. Only the German language is spoken throughout the hour-long tour and at the tasting. Of note at the monastery is a collection of ancient winepresses in what was once the lay brothers' refectory. Wines can be purchased and there are two restaurants, closed Monday and Tuesday respectively. Kloster Eberbach is famous for its festivals: wine fairs, wine auctions, and the harvest thanksgiving of the Rheingau Vintners Association. During the summer months classical music concerts are given. The German Wine Academy holds English-language wine seminars for foreign students at the abbey.

THE WINERY: For over 1100 years, some of Germany's finest wine has been produced at Schloss Johannisberg, situated on a hill north of Winkel and Geisenheim in the middle of the Rheingau. From the twelfth century to the start of the nineteenth century, the vineyards were part of the Benedictine monastery. When the monasteries were secularized during the French Revolution, the property passed through the hands of Prince William of Orange, Emperor Napoleon, and Marshal Kellermann, to Emperor Francis I of Austria. In 1816 he presented it to Prince Metternich, provided that Metternich would give the Austrian Crown a tenth of his annual yield. This tithing is still honored today by the proprietor of Schloss Johannisberg, Fürst von Metternich. *THE WINES:* Riesling.
THE TOUR: Open Monday through Thursday, 8 A.M. to 4 P.M.; Friday, 8 A.M. until noon. Four weeks' advance notice is required for tours. Visitors see the church, terrace, vineyards, and cellar on German-language guided tours, which last half an hour without a tasting, or slightly over an hour with a tasting. Tastings are charged according to the type of wine that is sampled. Wine can be purchased. A restaurant on the estate is open to the public every day except Tuesday, from mid–April through October.

SCHLOSS JOHANNISBERG
6225 Johannisberg
Rheingau
West Germany
(06722) 8027

SCHLOSS VOLLRADS
6227 Winkel
Rheingau, West Germany
(06723) 3314

THE WINERY: Situated near the village of Winkel, Schloss Vollrads has been the property of the Matuschka-Greiffenclau family since the fourteenth century. Internationally famous for its fine wines, it is one of the largest and most venerable wine estates in private hands. *THE WINES:* Riesling. *THE TOUR:* Open Monday through Friday, 8 A.M. until noon, 1 P.M. until 5 P.M. Four weeks' advance notice for tours is required. There is no fee for tours without wine tasting; tours and tasting cost 30 DM. The 45-minute German- and English-language guided tours include the courtyard of the estate and parts of the garden and vineyards. Also of note is the small wine museum where single bottles of old vintages are preserved. The tour is followed by a six-wine tasting. Wine can be purchased. A restaurant on the estate is closed on Monday.

Germany/Rheinpfalz

THE WINERY: This is perhaps the greatest wine estate in the region, producing Rheinpfalz Riesling at its very best. Since 1816 it has been in the hands of the Jordan family, who have owned vineyards in the Rheinpfalz since 1718. The estate is close to the village of Deidesheim, on Route B-271. The Kirhgasse goes directly from the marketplace at Deidesheim to the entrance of the winery. *THE WINES:* Predominantly Riesling. *THE TOUR:* Open Monday through Friday, 8 A.M. until noon, 2 P.M. to 6 P.M. Two weeks' advance notice is required for tours. The one-hour German and English tours include a fascinating visit to the extensive medieval cellar. The estate also has a remarkable wine museum that should not be missed. Tastings are tailored to suit each group. Cost depends on the range of wines sampled. Wine can be purchased.

DR. VON BASSERMAN-
JORDAN'SCHES WEINGUT
6705 Deidesheim
Postfach 20
West Germany
(03626) 206

Italy

Italy, the largest exporter of wine to the United States, produces the greatest volume and widest range of wines in the world.

Asti Spumante, Italy's famous sparkling wine, as well as fine red wines such as Barolo and Barberesco from the hearty Nebbiolo grapes, are produced in the Piedmont region. Barbera is the most widely drunk Piedmontese wine, and the Barbera grape is grown in abundance north and south of Asti.

Tuscany is the home of Brunello di Montalcino, an outstanding red wine made in the environs of Siena. It is also the home of Chianti and Chianti Classico. The wine zone stretches from Florence to Siena, and Chianti Classico comes from the heart of this area.

The hinterland of Venice and Verona produces twice the amount of wine made in Tuscany. The best wines are Bardolino, Valpolicella, and Soave. These are made in the districts that bear their names and lie north of Verona. Soave Classico, Italy's premier white wine, comes from the Classico area in the Soave district.

Most wine estates are family-owned and family-run. They offer informal, fascinating insights into winemaking, but few estates host regular guided tours—those that do may alter their hours of opening. Because of this it is advisable to tell the winery well in advance of your visit. This may be arranged by contacting the U.S. importer whose name is on the bottle label. Otherwise you can write or, within Italy, telephone direct to the winery. For further information, contact the Italian Wine Center, 499 Park Avenue, New York, NY 10020.

Italy/Lazio

VINI DI FONTANA
CANDIDA S.p.A
Casella Postale 52
00044 Frascati (Roma)
(06) 944131

THE WINERY: Fontana Candida is only 24 miles from Rome, set in a horseshoe of volcanic hills overlooking the city, in the heart of the Castelli Romani district. The company is respected throughout Italy and the United States for specializing in superior quality Frascatis, the premier Castelli wine. Currently a member of the Winefood group of companies, the 31-year-old firm recently enlarged its production capacity to five million liters. **THE WINES:** Frascati, Frascati Superiore. **THE TOUR:** Appointment necessary. The winery is open only to members of the wine trade.

Italy/Lombardy

THE WINERY: Nino Negri is the leading firm of the Valtellina district, about 90 miles from Milan. The firm, located near the town of Sondrio, was founded in 1897 by Signor Nino Negri. It is under the aegis of the Winefood group of companies. **THE WINES:** Sassella, Inferno, Grumello, Fracia (Valgella). All four are defined as Valtellina Superiore. **THE TOUR:** By appointment. Monday to Friday, 9:30 A.M. to 11:30 A.M. and 2:30 P.M. to 4:30 P.M. Guided tours include the old cellars and modern operational facilities at the winery. Tours are followed by a tasting, and bottles of wine can be purchased.

CASA VINICOLA
NINO NEGRI S.p.A
23030 Chiuro (Sondrio)
(0342) 54207

Italy/Piedmont

FONTANAFREDDA
Tenimenti di Barolo e di
Fontanafredda
12051 Alba (Cuneo)
(0173) 53.161 or
(0173) 53.162

THE WINERY: Visitors will enjoy touring Fontanafredda, which is housed in the Royal Hunting Lodge that once belonged to King Victor Emmanuel II. It is set amid its own vineyards, nine kilometers southwest of Alba. The firm belongs to the Monte dei Paschi di Siena bank, and is considered one of the most progressive and highly regarded companies in Piedmont, the hilly region in northwestern Italy where Piedmontese wines are grown. *THE WINES:* Asti Spumante, Barolo, Barbaresco, Barbera, Pinot Bianco, Grignolino. *THE TOUR:* By appointment. Monday to Friday, 9:30 A.M. to 11:30 A.M. and 3 P.M. to 5:30 P.M. Closed the first three weeks of August. Before the tour starts, visitors can see the splendid royal apartments. A guided tour of the stone cellars is followed by a tasting.

Italy/Tuscany

THE WINERY: Biondi-Santi is famed for its super-expensive red wine Brunello di Montalcino, known to outlast some of the longest-lived Bordeaux and considered by some to be Italy's most prestigious wine. In 1865 Clemente Santi won a citation to use the name, but his son Ferrucio Biondi-Santi is generally considered the founder of Brunello. Biondi-Santi remains a family-owned firm. Dr. Franco Biondi-Santi, Ferrucio's grandson, runs the family estate at Il Greppo, 20 miles south of Siena. He is assisted by his son Jacopo in personally overseeing 45 acres of vineyards. Only vines over 10 years old are used to make Brunello, and only the best grapes are used for making the highest quality, worthy of the designation of Riserva, in fine years. *THE WINES:* Brunello Riserva, Brunello, Brunello Annata, Greppo. In poor growing years, Biondi-Santi sells his wines in bulk rather than produce Brunello. *THE TOUR:* By appointment. Monday to Friday, 9 A.M. until noon and 3 P.M. to 5 P.M. Visitors are shown the cellars where this fine wine is aged· After the tour there is a tasting. Bottles cannot be purchased.

BIONDI-SANTI
Cantina del Greppo
53024 Montalcino (Siena)

CASA VINICOLA
BARONE RICASOLI S.p.A.
Castello di Brolio
Brolio-in-Chianti
Siena

THE WINERY: The name Ricasoli has been synonymous with Chianti since the time of Bettino Ricasoli, who became prime minister of Italy in 1861. At his castle in Brolio, 15 kilometers from Siena, he devised a method of making Chianti that is still in use today. In the mid-1970s the company left the consortium and the family sold their controlling interest in the firm to Joseph E. Seagram and Sons, Inc. *THE WINE:* Chianti Classico, Chianti Classico Riserva, Torricella, Ricasoli Vin Santo. *THE TOUR:* By appointment only. Monday to Friday, 9 A.M. until noon and 2 P.M. to 5 P.M. Closed during the month of August. Visitors can combine an English-language guided tour of the winery with a visit to the historic castle. The winery is at the foot of the hill leading to the castle 1,600 feet up. The climb is well worth it, as there is a magnificent view of the towers of Siena from the grounds and the public can visit the castle, which is a national monument.

CHIANTI RUFFINO S.p.A.
50065 Pontassieve
Firenze
(055) 83.023.07

THE WINERY: The firm was established in 1877 by two cousins, Ilario and Leopoldo Ruffino. Today it is owned by the Folonari family and continues to be best known throughout the world for its Chianti and Chianti Classico made from its own vineyards in Tuscany. Ruffino also makes a range of wines from vineyards in other regions, but the headquarters are at Pontassieve outside Florence. **THE WINES:** Chianti Ruffino, Chianti Classico Ruffino, Riserva Ducale, Gold Label, Orvieto, Galestro. The last-mentioned wine was introduced in mid-1980. **THE TOUR:** Open Monday to Friday, 9:30 A.M. to 1:30 P.M. and 2:30 P.M. to 5 P.M. Closed mid-August to mid-September. There are guided tours of the aging cellars and the winery's operational facilities. Visitors can see the vineyards by prior arrangement. The English-language guided tour lasts 45 minutes and is followed by a tasting. Bottles can be purchased.

THE WINERY: Lamberti, one of the leading wineries in Verona, is known throughout the United States for its competitively priced fine wines. Although a member of the Winefood group of companies, Lamberti takes its name from a noble tenth-century family of Verona, where their tower, the Torre dei Lamberti, still stands. The cellars at Lazise are on the southeast shore of Lake Garda, 23 kilometers from Verona. The company also has a bottling plant at nearby Pastrengo. Both are in the Bardolino Classico district where the company owns 247 acres of vineyards. Lamberti has other wineries producing Soave and Valpolicella wines. The grapes come from their own vineyards as well as from individual growers within these wine regions. **THE WINES:** Bardolino, Soave, Valpolicella, Recioto della Valpolicella Amarone. **THE TOUR:** By appointment. Open Monday to Friday, 10 A.M. until noon and 3 P.M. to 5 P.M. English-language guided tours of these large cellars show visitors how wine is fermented and aged.

LAMBERTI, S.p.A.
34017 Lazise
Verona
(045) 71.70.043

S.V.I.P. S.p.A.
Vicola Ghiai 7
37100 Verona
(045) 59.4055

THE WINERY: These shippers are the sole distributors of Bolla wines, which are well known throughout the United States for being good-quality wines sold at competitive prices. Although more than half of Bolla's production is exported to this country (totaling some ten million bottles), the firm is perhaps best known for its Soave Bolla. Bolla has remained a family firm, founded in 1883 by Alberto and Luigi Albano Bolla, and is currently headed by Bruno Bolla. **THE WINES:** Soave, Valpolicella, Bardolino, Recioto Amarone, Rosé, Trebbiano. **THE TOUR:** By appointment. Monday to Friday, 9:30 A.M. to 11:30 A.M. and 2:30 P.M. to 4:30 P.M. Closed August. There are English-language guided tours of the cellar and the bottling plant where the bottle is corked, sealed, and labeled by sophisticated machinery. The tour is followed by a tasting.

BENMARL

The Société des Vignerons, a cooperative association of more than 1,500 wine lovers, was created by Mark Miller of Benmarl Vineyard in Marlborough, New York, in 1971. The cost of membership in the Société is $575 for the first year (with one vineright) and $75 dues and sponsorship fees each year thereafter. Additional vinerights (two vines) are $40 each. In exchange for this investment, each Société member is guaranteed one case of wine produced by the vineyard, bottled under his own signature or estate label. Members may also purchase other Benmarl wines at reduced prices.

These "vicarious vignerons" receive more from membership in the Société than simply fine wines. Members are encouraged to visit the vineyards. They are invited to observe the grapes' progress, taste the wines, and become involved in Benmarl's plans for the future.

Their investment enables Benmarl to continue experimenting with grape varieties and producing consistently superior wines that win high praise from wine experts. A New York Times wine columnist summed them up as "remarkable examples of what dedication can produce." The Millers and the Société continue in their determination to improve the art of winemaking in the United States. As a Miller family friend observed, Benmarl is "more of a crusade than a business."

Wines for Tasting

The best place to experience wine is in your own home, with wine you've bought yourself and can enjoy with wine-minded friends. And your most valuable ally in selecting and tasting specific wines is a good wine merchant —one who knows as well as sells wines and, more important, who will take pleasure in helping you set up and maintain your own wine stock.

Finding such a merchant may not be easy, but any effort put into the search is, in the long run, more than worth it. You can start by asking wine-drinking friends where they buy their wines, and who in their wine store has been particularly helpful. If this approach fails, make your own inspection tour of wineshops in your neighborhood or city. See whether, without being too obvious, you can sniff out how much the merchant knows about wine and how comfortable you're going to be placing your business in his shop.

The store itself should give you a good indication. First see how much wine the store sells. Take a look at how it's displayed: all bunched and mixed together (if so, go somewhere else), or laid out systematically with bottles stored on their sides and displayed in various categories. Variety is important. A first-rate wineshop should offer not just a single brand of varietal grape, but a selection of wines from a number of regions and countries.

Make sure none of the wine is exposed to direct sunlight, and take note of the temperature. Careful wine merchants in warm and hot seasons will keep their air conditioners running throughout the night—you can tell if the air conditioner has been running by visiting the shop in the morning and feeling the bottles to see if they're cool. During winter months it is important that the shop have an air circulator and maintain temperatures in the mid-60's to low 70's.

Next, talk to the merchant (or manager or salespeople). If the person simply hands you a bottle and says, "You'll like this," look elsewhere for a mentor. On the other hand, if the merchant begins to answer your question with questions of his own—How many people? What are you serving? What style of wine do you like? —you're probably in good hands.

Once you find a wine merchant in whom you have confidence, pay attention to his suggestions but make sure that you are also involved in the decision process. The number and variety of the wines you buy depend, of course, on how much money you want to spend, but also on why you want the wines: to enjoy those you already know, or to acquire knowledge of and a taste for new wines. Most knowledgeable wine merchants stress variety in any basic collection.

From 40 to 50 percent of your opening stock will probably consist of wines capable of being "laid down" (that is, kept for up to a year or two or more, until their peak) and 50 to 60 percent of wines ready for drinking on the spur of the moment. Most likely, too, there will be far more reds than whites in your first cellar. Balance is crucial. You want not only wines that you already enjoy, but wines for which you can acquire a taste.

Don't be in a hurry. Some wine merchants, in fact, won't set up a wine cellar for you until you've sampled a dozen or so different wines and have reported back your responses. And once you've assembled a basic wine cellar, don't get lazy. Continue to restock, keeping your cellar at a comfortable level, and establish some sort of system for keeping track of each bottle of wine you drink and how you responded to it.

Recommendations from the Pros

No one is better qualified to set up a collection of wines for home consumption than a wine merchant who knows the business and understands and cares about the wines he or she sells. What follows are recommendations, based upon current stock and pricing, from 32 leading wine merchants throughout the United States. In each instance the retailer has compiled a "recommended" list for either a $250 or $600 purchase, or both, as basic or beginning cellaring suggestions, along with a few words of advice. Individual wine prices are indicated within dollar categories (see below), since the actual prices for specific wines will shift both up and down from time to time.

Price Key	C = $6—$10
A = $4 and under	D = $10—$15
B = $4—$6	E = Over $15

California

HI-TIME GOURMET FOODS AND SPIRITS   Costa Mesa, California

"I like to see a truly international flavor in a beginning wine list, with a nice balance between California wines and European. Beginners should usually start out with sweeter wines like Rieslings and Chenin Blancs and then graduate to Chardonnay and Bordeaux and like wines."

—Charles Hanson, Wine Buyer

$250 Wine List

Qty.	REDS	Cost
	California	
1	Cabernet Sauvignon, Bel Arbres 1979	B
1	Cabernet Sauvignon, Fetzer, Lake County, 1979	B
1	Cabernet Sauvignon, Fieldstone 1978	C
1	Gamay, J. Lohr 1981	B
1	Merlot, Rutherford Hill 1979	C
1	Petite Sirah, Wente Brothers 1979	B
1	Pinot Noir, J. Pedroncelli 1979	B
1	Zinfandel, Ahern 1980	B
	France	
1	Beaujolais, Jadot 1981	B
1	Bordeaux, Château Clerc-Milon 1976	D
1	Bordeaux, Château Gloria 1978	D
1	Burgundy, Côtes de Nuits-Villages, Lupé-Cholet 1978	D
1	Côtes-du-Rhône, E. Guigal 1978	B
	Italy	
1	Chianti Classico, Catignano 1979	A
1	Torgiano, Rubesco Lungarotti 1975	C

Qty.	WHITES	Cost
	California	
1	Chardonnay, Conn Creek, Château Maja 1980	B
1	Chardonnay, Château St. Jean, 1980	C
1	Chardonnay, Alexander Valley Vineyards 1980	C
1	Chenin Blanc, Parducci 1981	B
1	Gewürztraminer, Navarro 1981	C
1	Johannisberg Riesling, Obester 1981	C
1	Sauvignon or Fumé Blanc, Dry Creek 1981	C

Qty.	WHITES	Cost
	France	
1	Alsace, Gewürztraminer, Klug 1979	C
1	Bordeaux Blanc, Barrière Frères 1980	A
1	Burgundy, Mâcon-Vire, A. Bonhomme 1979	B
1	Burgundy, Pouilly-Fuissé, J. Jacoby 1980	D
1	Vouvray, Château Montcontour 1980	C
	Germany	
1	Mosel-Saar-Ruwer, Ockfener Bockstein Fischer, Spätlese 1979	C
1	Mosel-Saar-Ruwer, Piesporter Goldtröpfchen, QbA., Barrington 1980	B
	Italy	
1	Valdadige, Pinot Grigio, Bollini 1981	B
1	Orvieto, Decugnano dei Barbi 1980	C

Qty.	ROSÉ	Cost
1	Gamay, Robert Mondavi 1981	B
1	Travel, Château d'Aqueria 1980	B

Qty.	APÉRITIF/DESSERT WINE	Cost
1	Panache, Domaine Chandon	B
1	Port, Graham's Royal Consort	C
1	Sherry, Gonzales & Byass Cream	C

Qty.	CHAMPAGNE/SPARKLING WINE	Cost
1	Chandon Brut	D
1	Stanford Governor's Cuvée	A
1	Veuve Clicquot Brut	E

THE WINE HOUSE   Los Angeles, CA

"Anyone can buy wine with a famous label—the trick is to buy good wine intelligently. One of the best ways of doing this is to store wines that come of age at different times. It is a European practice to lay down wine. This practice is becoming more prevalent in the United States as California wineries release their wines earlier."

—Greg Gillooly, Retailer

$250 Wine List

Qty.		Cost	Qty.		Cost
	REDS			**REDS** (continued)	
	California			France	
1	Cabernet Sauvignon, Heitz Cellars 1978	D	1	Burgundy, Mâcon-Lugny Louis Latour 1979	B
1	Gamay Beaujolais, Charles Shaw 1981	B	1	Graves, Château La Gravières 1979	C
1	Petite Sirah, Stag's Leap Winery 1978	C	1	Vouvray, Château Montcontour 1980	B
1	Zinfandel, Fetzer 1978	B		Germany	
	France		1	Mosel-Saar-Ruwer, Deinhard Green Label 1979	B
1	Bordeaux, Château Gloria	D		Italy	
1	Bordeaux, Château Greysac 1978	C	1	Pinot Grigio, Brigl 1980	C
1	Bordeaux, Château Larose-Trintaudon 1978	C	1	Torre de Gano, Lungarotti	B
1	Côtes-du-Rhône, E. Guigal 1979	B		**ROSÉS**	
	Italy		1	Gamay Rosé, Robert Mondavi 1981	B
1	Chianti Classico, Monte Vertine 1978	B	1	Grenache Rosé, McDowell Valley 1981	B
1	Dolcetto, L. Einaudi 1979	B		**APÉRITIF/DESSERT WINE**	
	Spain		1	Boardroom Port, Dow	C
1	Gran Coronas Riserva, Torres 1977	C	1	Panache, Domaine Chandon	B
	WHITES			**CHAMPAGNE/SPARKLING WINE**	
	California		1	Langlois, Château Samur	B
1	Chardonnay, Clos du Bois 1980	C	1	Blanc de Blanc, Domaine Chandon	D
1	Chenin Blanc, Stag's Leap Winery 1981	C			
1	Johannisberg Riesling, Grgich Hills 1981	C			
1	Sauvignon Blanc, St. Clement 1981	C			

WINE COUNTRY   Newport Beach, CA

"Get into the habit of taking notes anytime you drink a wine you really like! Jot down how it looked, the color, the smell—that sort of thing. Keep it brief—three or four lines—and keep a file so that you'll have a feeling for when you want to open other bottles of the same wine."

—Linden Knighten, Retailer

$250 Wine List

Qty.		Cost
	REDS	
	California	
3	Cabernet Sauvignon, Durney 1979	D
2	Cabernet Sauvignon, Kenwood, Jack London Vineyard 1979	D
2	Zinfandel, Sycamore Creek	C
	France	
2	Bordeaux, Château Cos D'Estournel 1979	E
2	Bordeaux, Château Pichon-Lalande 1979	E
	WHITES	
	California	
2	Chardonnay, Beringer Private Reserve 1980	E
2	Chardonnay, Jekel 1980	C
2	Sauvignon (Fumé) Blanc, Napa Cellars 1981	C
	France	
2	Burgundy, Meursault 1979, François Jobard	D
	APÉRITIF/DESSERT WINE	
2	Port, Dow 1977 (375 ml.)	D

$600 Wine List

Qty.		Cost
	REDS	
	California	
3	Cabernet Sauvignon, Beaulieu Vineyards, Private Reserve 1978	E
3	Cabernet Sauvignon, Durney 1979	D
2	Petite Sirah, McDowell Valley 1979	C
2	Zinfandel, Sycamore Creek 1980	C
	France	
2	Bordeaux, Château Margaux 1979	E
2	Bordeaux, Château Palmer 1979	E
2	Burgundy, Bonnes Mares 1978, Robert Groffier	E
	WHITES	
	California	
2	Chardonnay, Beringer, Private Reserve 1980	E
2	Chardonnay, Château Montelena 1979, Napa Valley	E
2	Chardonnay, Château St. Jean, Robert Young Vineyard 1980	E
2	Sauvignon (Fumé) Blanc, Château St. Jean, Murphy 1980	C
	France	
2	Burgundy, Meursault-Genevrières, Michelot-Garnier 1978	E
	APÉRITIF/DESSERT WINE	
2	Port, Dow 1977 (375 ml.)	D
2	Port, Taylor-Fladgate 1977 (375 ml.)	D

THE VINEYARD San Diego, CA

"The best way to learn about wines is to go to as many wine tastings as possible. We hold a tasting at our store every week. We try to offer as many different styles of wine as possible, so that people can decide what they like and tune into what their palate prefers."

—Ted Tiege, Retailer

$250 Wine List

$600 Wine List. These wines should be added to the $250 list.

Qty.	REDS	Cost	Qty.	REDS	Cost
	California			France	
1	Merlot, Stag's Leap Winery 1979	D	2	Bordeaux, Château Léoville-las-Cases 1978	E
3	Red Table Wine, Raymond 1979	A	2	Bordeaux, Château Pichon-Lalande 1979	E
1	Zinfandel, Raymond 1979	C	1	Burgundy, Côte Rôtie, Jaboulet 1979	E
	France		2	Burgundy, Volnay, La Bousse d'Or 1979	E
2	Bordeaux, Château Latour 1979	C	1	Rhône, Hermitage, Jaboulet 1979	E
1	Bordeaux, Château Prieuré-Lichine 1979	D		Italy	
1	Burgundy, Santenay, B. Bachelet 1979	E	1	Barbaresco, Gaja 1978	E
2	Côtes-du-Rhône, Guigal 1979	B	1	Barolo, Scanavino 1971	D
	Italy				
3	Chianti Classico, Catignano 1979	A		**WHITES**	
1	Chianti Classico Riserva, Badia a Coltibuono 1975	C		California	
1	Gattinara Riserva, Dessilani 1974	D	1	Chardonnay, Château Montelena 1979	E
				France	
	WHITES		2	Chablis "Mountmain," Domain de la Tour Vaubourg 1980	C
	California				
2	Chardonnay, Lefcourt Cellars 1981	C	2	Burgundy, Puligny-Montrachet "Les Referts," E. Sauzet 1978	E
2	Gewürztraminer, Hacienda 1981	C		Germany	
2	Sauvignon Blanc, Brander 1981	C	1	Mosel-Saar-Ruwer, Molz-Laurentiushof, Trittenheimer Felsenkopf Milz-Laurentiushof Auslese 1978	E
	France				
3	Albert Lucas, NV	A	2	Mosel-Saar-Ruwer, Vereinigte Hospitien, Wiltinger-Braune Kupp, Spätlese 1979	C
1	Burgundy, Bourgogne Hautes-Côtes-de-Nuits, Geisweiler 1979	C		**CHAMPAGNE/SPARKLING WINE**	
1	Burgundy, Pinot Gris Reserve, Timbach 1979	C	1	Laurent Perrier Brut NV	E
1	Chablis, Domaine de la Tour Vaubourg 1980	C	1	Veuve Clicquot Brut NV	E
	Germany				
1	Mosel-Saar-Ruwer, Whelener Sonnenuhr Prüm Kabinett 1981	C			
	Italy				
2	Bianco Della Lega, Olivieri 1979	B			
	APÉRITIF/DESSERT WINE				
1	Graham's Royal Consort Port, NV	C			
	CHAMPAGNE/SPARKLING WINE				
2	Venegazzu, Brut 1977	C			

HENNESSY'S WINES & SPIRITS San Francisco, CA

"If I were starting out today to learn about wines, one thing I would always do when I went out to eat, or even when I was dining at home, would be to drink half bottles instead of fifths. You get to sample more wines, and it doesn't cost you any significant amount."

—Leslie Hennessy, Retailer

$250 Wine List

Qty.	REDS	Cost	Qty.	WHITES	Cost
	California			California	
2	Cabernet Sauvignon, Château Montelena	D	1	Chardonnay, Stag's Leap	D
2	Cabernet Sauvignon, Clos du Val	D	1	Chardonnay, Vichon	D
1	Pinot Noir, Acacia	D	1	Gewürztraminer, Joseph Phelps	C
2	Zinfandel, Ridge	C	1	Riesling, Trefethen	C
	France		1	Sauvignon Blanc, Brander	C
2	Bordeaux, Château Lynch-Bages	E	1	Sauvignon Blanc, Château St. Jean	C
2	Burgundy, Volnay Santenay	D		France	
2	Côtes-du-Rhône	B	1	Burgundy, Meursault Antonin Rodet	E
	Italy		1	Loire, Muscadet di Sevre et Maine	C
1	Chianti Classico, Castelli	C		Germany	
	Spain		1	Mosel-Saar-Ruwer, Mainzer Domherr Spätlese	C
1	Rioja, Olarra	C			

DRAPER & ESQUIN WINE MERCHANTS   San Francisco, CA

"Never assume that because you're a beginner, you don't have a right to opinions. Learn to trust your own palate early on, and don't base your evaluations purely on the reputation of a wine or comments of "experts." It's a good idea to read as much as you can about wine, but the only true way to become knowledgeable is to drink as many different kinds as possible."

—Stephen Gilbertson, Wine Manager

$250 Wine List

Qty.	REDS	Cost
	California	
2	Cabernet Sauvignon, Jordan Winery 1978	E
3	Zinfandel, BeauVal 1980	B
	France	
1	Bordeaux, Château La Lagune 1970	E
1	Bordeaux, Château Lussac 1979	C
2	Burgundy, Groffier 1978	D
3	Côtes-du-Rhône, E. Guigal 1978	C
	Italy	
3	Monte Antico Rosso, Castel di Monte 1978	A
	Spain	
2	Rioja, Olarra, 1973	A

Qty.	WHITES	Cost
	California	
1	Chardonnay, Château Montelena 1979	D
3	Eshcol White, Trefethen	B
1	Pinot Noir Blanc, Schramsberg	D
2	Sauvignon Blanc, Frogs Leap	C
	France	
1	Barsac, Château Climens 1975	E
1	Côtes de Beaune, Mersault, Dufouleur Frères 1978	D
1	Graves, Château Redon Blanc, 1980	
	Germany	
2	Mosel-Saar-Ruwer, Wehlener Klosterbert, M. Prüm	B
	Italy	
3	Chardonnay Bollini	A

Qty.	APÉRITIF/DESSERT WINE	
1	Tawny Port, Dow	C
1	Tio Paco Amontillado, Manuel Cortina	D

Qty.	CHAMPAGNE/SPARKLING WINE	
1	NV Paillard Brut, Rheims	D

$600 Wine List

Qty.	REDS	Cost
	California	
3	Cabernet, Alexander Valley Vineyards 1979	C
3	Cabernet, Charles Woods 1978	D
2	Merlot, Rutherford Hill 1979	C
2	Zinfandel, Silver Mountain 1979	B
	France	
2	Bordeaux, Château Léoville-Las-Cases 1978	E
2	Bordeaux, Château Pichon-Lalande 1970	E
3	Burgundy, Corton, Charles Vienot 1978	E
6	Côtes-du-Rhône, Rasteau	B
2	Rhône, Côte Rôtie, Guigal 1978	E
	Italy	
3	Gattinara, Dessilini 1978	C
2	Barolo, Marcarini 1974	D
	Spain	
2	Rioja, Cabernet, Jean Leon	D

Qty.	WHITES	Cost
	France	
3	Alsace, Gewürztraminer, Bott Frères 1979	C
3	Burgundy, Meursault, Clos de la Barre, Lafon 1978	D
3	Burgundy, St. Aubin Thomas 1980	C
	Italy	
3	Soave Calvarino, Pieropan	B

Qty.	APÉRITIF/DESSERT WINE	
1	Fino Montesa Sherry, Manuel Cortina	B
1	Oporto, Grahams 1970	E
1	Pedro Ximénez Cream Sherry, Manuel Cortina	C
1	Tawny Porto, Dow	B

THE WINE SHOP San Francisco, CA

"A cellar should include a variety of bottles from the most important wine regions of the world. Today people are drinking more white wine than red and eating lighter meals, so you must also make a cellar selection for lighter dishes."

—Richard Schenone, Retailer

$250 Wine List

Qty.	REDS	Cost	Qty.	France	Cost
	California		1	Burgundy, Mâcon Blanc Le Chazzles	B
1	Cabernet Sauvignon, Rutherford Ranch	C	1	Burgundy, Pouilly-Fuissé, Boissett	B
1	Cabernet Sauvignon, William Hill	E		**Italy**	
1	Gamy Beaujolais, Charles Shaw	B	1	Soave, Pieropan	B
1	Petite Sirah, Stag's Leap	C	1	Lombardy, Visconti Lugana	B
1	Zinfandel, Fetzer	B		**ROSÉ**	
1	Zinfandel, Sutter Home	B	1	Petite Rosé, Mirassou	B
	France			**APÉRITIF/DESSERT WINE**	
1	Beaujolais, Louis Latour	B	1	Apéritif, San Rafael	C
1	Bordeaux, Château Pichon-Lalande Pauillac	E	1	Jubilee Cream Sherry, Gonzales Byass	B
1	Bordeaux, Château Senejac Haut-Médoc	C	1	Manzanilla Sherry, Romate	B
1	Côtes-du-Rhône, Boissett	A	1	Tawny Port, Croft Distinction	C
	WHITES			**CHAMPAGNE/SPARKLING WINE**	
	California		1	Domaine Chandon, Brut	D
1	Chardonnay, Iron Horse	C	1	Mirassou au Naturel	D
1	Chardonnay, Spring Mountain	D			
1	Chenin Blanc, Fetzer	B			
1	Chenin Blanc, Kenwood	B			
1	Chenin Blanc, Parducci	B			
1	Fumé Blanc, Château St. Jean	C			
1	Fumé Blanc, Robert Mondavi	C			
1	Gewürztraminer, Hacienda	C			
1	Gewürztraminer, Joseph Phelps	C			
1	Johannisberg Riesling, Jekel	C			
1	Johannisberg Riesling, Obester	C			
1	Sauvignon Blanc, Preston	C			
1	White Burgundy, Mirassou	B			

WINE & CHEESE CENTER San Francisco, CA

"What I recommend for people who are starting to collect wine is to put together as varied a selection as possible—a lot of different wines with different brands. The idea is to get impressions of different styles of wines and different winemakers."

—Paul Moser, Wine Manager

$250 Wine List

Qty.	REDS	Cost	Qty.	France	Cost
	California		6	Bordeaux, Château Bonnet 1980	A
3	Cabernet Sauvignon, Duckhorn 1978	D	3	Burgundy, Duc de Magenta 1979	D
3	Eshcol Red, Trefethen	B		**German**	
3	Zinfandel, Sausal 1976	B	3	Mosel-Saar-Ruwer Wiltinger Scharzberg	B
	France			Max Erben QbA 1979	
3	Beaudet Rouge, NV Vin Ordinaire	A		**APÉRITIF/DESSERT WINE**	
3	Côtes-du-Rhône, E. Guigal 1978	B	1	Fine Crusted Port, Smith-Woodhouse	D
	WHITES			**CHAMPAGNE/SPARKLING WINE**	
	California		3	Sparkling Penedes, Paul Chaeneau (Spain)	B
3	Chardonnay, Alexander Valley	C	1	Veuve Clicquot Brut NV	E
6	Colombard, Sausal 1980	A			
3	Sauvignon Blanc, Brander 1980	D			

CENTURY WINES & LIQUORS Denver, CO

"It's tough to get any true sense of a wine on the basis of a single tasting. So don't be in too much of a hurry to become an "expert." Get to know good wines a little at a time, but really get to know them."

—Steve Heinz, Wine Manager

$250 Wine List

Qty.		Cost
	REDS	
	California	
1	Cabernet Sauvignon, Pine Ridge 1978	C
1	Merlot, Sterling 1978	C
1	Napa Gamay, Charles Shaw 1981	B
1	Zinfandel, Robert Mondavi 1979	C
	France	
1	Bordeaux, B&G Médoc 1978	D
1	Bordeaux, Château Olivier 1978	
1	Burgundy, Faiveley Passe-Toui-Grains 1978	B
1	Burgundy, George Deboeuf St. Amour 1981	D
	Italy	
1	Bardolino, Bolla 1980	B
1	Chianti Classico, Ruffino 1977	C
	Argentina	
1	Cabernet Sauvignon, Concha y Toro 1976	B
	Spain	
1	Gran Corona Riserva, Torres 1973	D
	WHITES	
	California	
1	Chardonnay, Clos du Bois, 1980	C
1	Chenin Blanc, Robert Mondavi 1981	C
1	Fumé Blanc, Dry Creek 1980	C
1	Johannisberg Riesling, Jekel 1980	C
	France	
1	Burgundy, Mâcon Blanc Drouhin 1978	C
1	Burgundy, Valbon 1979	A
1	Burgundy, Pouilly-Fuissé Jadot 1978	D
1	Vouvray, Wildman 1974	C
	Germany	
1	Mosel-Saar-Ruwer, Piesporter Michelsberg Kreush 1980	CQ
1	Mosel-Saar-Ruwer, Bernkastel Meyer Bereich 1979	B
1	Mosel-Saar-Ruwer, Sonnenhur, Meyer Wehlener 1979	C
	Italy	
1	Frascati, Fontana Candida 1980	B
1	Soave, Bolla 1980	B
	Spain	
1	Gran Vina Sol "Green Label," Torres 1978	B
	ROSÉS	
1	Gamay Rosé, Robert Mondavi	B
1	Rosé of Cabernet, Simi	B
	APÉRITIF/DESSERT WINES	
1	Cream Sherry, Beaulieu	B
1	Muscat d'Andrea, Robert Pecota	C
1	Panache, Domaine Chandon	B
	CHAMPAGNE/SPARKLING WINE	
1	Brut, Domaine Chandon	D
1	Brut, Korbel	C

$600 Wine List

Qty.		Cost
	REDS	
	California	
1	Cabernet "Boshé," Freemark Abbey 1978	D
1	Cabernet Reserve, Robert Mondavi 1976	E
1	Cabernet Sauvignon, Beaulieu 1974	E
1	Cabernet Sauvignon, Jordan 1978	D
1	Pinot Noir, Chalone 1978	D
	France	
1	Bordeaux, Château Mouton-Rothschild 1976	E
1	Bordeaux, Château Kirwan 1976	E
1	Burgundy, Echézeaux 1974	E
1	Burgundy, Savigny-lès-Beaune, Villamont 1974	D
1	Châteauneuf-du-Pape, Mommessin 1974	D
	Italy	
1	Amarone, Santa Sofia 1971	C
1	Chianti Classico, Ruffino	D
	Spain	
1	Gran Coronas "Black Label," Torres	D
	WHITES	
	California	
1	Chardonnay, Grgich Hills 1978	E
1	Chardonnay, Château Montelena 1978	E
1	Fumé Blanc Reserve, Robert Mondavi 1978	D
1	Johannisberg Riesling "Late Harvest," Chappallett 1978	D
1	Beaujolais, Puligny-Montrachet, Jadot 1979	E
1	Burgundy, Mommessin Chablis 1979	
1	Burgundy Mersault, Drouhin 1979	E
1	Graves, Château Olivier 1980	D
1	Sauternes, Château Volgny 1975	D
	Germany	
1	Mosel-Saar-Ruwer, Piesporter Goldtröpfchen Auslese 1971	E
1	Mosel-Saar-Ruwer, Prüm Graacher Himmelreich Kabinett 1976	D
1	Mosel-Saar-Ruwer, Bernkastler Doktor Auslese 1976	E
	Australia	
1	Chardonnay, Seppelt 1979	D
	ROSÉS	
1	Tavel 1980	B
	APÉRITIF/DESSERT WINE	
1	Port, Ficklin	D
1	Port, Quady	D
1	Sherry, Setubal	E
	CHAMPAGNE/SPARKLING WINE	
1	Blanc de Blanc, Schramsberg	E
1	Dom Perignon 1973	E

THE WINE SHOP Denver, CO

"Don't make the mistake of thinking of only France and California when you're setting up an initial collection. A lot of wines from Italy, Spain, and Portugal represent some of the best buys on the market. Don't overlook the wines from Australia, Chile, and Argentina, either."

—Peter McLaughlin

$250 Wine List

Qty.		Cost
	REDS	
	California	
2	Cabernet Sauvignon, Clos du Val 1978	D
2	Cabernet Sauvignon, Sterling 1977	C
2	Zinfandel, Ridge, Early Harvest 1978	D
	France	
1	Beaujolais, Morgon 1978	C
1	Beaujolais, Moulin-à-Vent 1978	C
1	Bordeaux, Château Lanessan 1975	C
4	Bordeaux, Château Pédesclaux, St.-Emilion 1975	D
1	Côtes-du-Rhône 1978	B
	Italy	
2	Chianti Classico Nozzole 1977	B
	Spain	
3	Catalonia, Gran Coronas, Torres 1975	C
2	Rioja, Vino Tinto, Olarra 1975	B
	Australia	
3	Cabernet Sauvignon, Brown Brothers 1977	B
2	Shiraz, Brown Brothers 1976	C
	WHITES	
	California	
1	Chardonnay, Beringer 1980	C
1	Vouvray, Jacques Scott 1980	B
	Italy	
1	Soave, Bolla 1980	B
	Spain	
1	Catalonia, Gran Vina Sol, Torres 1980	B
	APÈRITIF/DESSERT WINE	
1	Sherry, Pedro Domecq	B
1	Port, Quady 1978	C

$600 Wine List

Qty.		Cost
	REDS	
	California	
2	Cabernet Sauvignon, Clos du Val 1978	D
3	Cabernet Sauvignon, Jordan 1978	D
2	Cabernet Sauvignon, Sterling 1977	C
2	Merlot, Clos du Val 1977	C
2	Zinfandel, Ridge, Early Harvest 1978	D
	France	
1	Beaujolais, Moulin-à-Vent 1980	C
1	Morgon-Beaujolais 1980	C
2	Bordeaux, Château Gloria 1978	C
2	Bordeaux, Château Lanessan 1975	C
3	Bordeaux, Château Larose-Trintaudon 1978	D
4	Bordeaux, Château Pédesclaux, St.-Emilion 1975	D
2	Burgundy, Côte de Beaune-Villages Jadot 1976	D
1	Côtes-du-Rhône 1980	C
3	Lescours, Abbaye Reserve 1978	C
	Italy	
2	Borgogno, Barolo 1970	C
2	Chianti Classico, Nozzole 1977	B
2	Gattinara, Trovaglini 1974	D
	Spain	
3	Catalonia, Gran Coronas, Torres 1975	C
4	Rioja, Cune Imperial Reserva 1970	D
2	Rioja, Vino Tinto, Olarra 1975	B
	Australia	
3	Cabernet Sauvignon, Brown Brothers 1977	B
3	Cabernet Sauvignon, Penfold's 1977	C
2	Shiraz, Brown Brothers 1976	B
	WHITES	
	California	
1	Chardonnay, Beringer 1980	C
1	Chardonnay, Chalone 1979	E
1	Gewürztraminer, Joseph Phelps 1979	C
	France	
1	Burgundy, Joseph Drouhin 1975	E
1	Vouvray, Jacques Scott 1980	B
	Germany	
1	Mosel-Saar-Ruwer, Piesporter Goldtröpfchen 1980	C
	Italy	
1	Soave, Bolla 1980	B
1	Catalonia, Gran Vina Sol, Torres 1980	B
	APÉRITIF/DESSERT WINE	
1	Port, Quady 1978	D
2	Sherry, Hartley & Gibson Dry	C
1	Sherry, Pedro Domecq	B
	CHAMPAGNE/SPARKLING WINE	
1	Cordoniu	C
2	Domaine Chandon	E
2	Seaview NV	C
2	Sparkling White, Great Western Imperial Brut	D

WEST SIDE WINES & SPIRITS   West Hartford, CT

"My feeling is that plenty of good table wine is always available for current consumption. Even at the beginning level, other than having a few bottles each of red and white wines for spontaneous drinking, I would invest in young red wines that promise to develop charm and complexity with time. For the most part, whites don't age well and should not tie up dollars better invested in reds that do."

—David Levin, Retailer

$250 Wine List

Qty.	REDS	Cost
	California	
2	Eshcol Red, Trefethen	B
2	Merlot, Clos du Val 1979	D
1	Zinfandel, Joseph Phelps 1977	B
	France	
2	Beaujolais-Villages, Georges Duboeuf 1981	B
2	Bordeaux, Château LaClare 1979	C
2	Bordeaux, Château Phelon-Segur	D
2	Bordeaux, Château Prieuré-Lichine 1979	D
2	Bordeaux, Troplong Mondot St. Emilion 1979	D
1	Rhône, Château Beaucastle Châteauneuf-du-Pape 1978	D
1	Rhône, Gigondas 1978	C
	Italy	
1	Gaja, Dolcetto d'Alba 1979	C
	Spain	
2	Bodegas Olarra Cerro, Anon Riserva	B

Qty.	WHITES	Cost
	California	
1	Chardonnay, Dry Creek 1979	D
1	Eschol, Trefethen	C
1	Sauvignon Blanc, Sterling 1980	D
	France	
2	Burgundy, Labouré-Rio Mâcon-Villages 1979	C
	Germany	
1	Mosel-Saar-Ruwer, Wehlener Sonnenuhr Dr. Thanisch Kabinett	C
	Italy	
1	Pinot Grigio, Cavit 1980	A
	CHAMPAGNE/SPARKLING WINE	
1	Blanc de Blanc, Schramsberg	E

SCHAGRIN'S WINE AND SPIRITS   Fort Lauderdale, FL

"Keep an open mind. A lot of people get married to a particular brand, unaware that the same varietal grape—a Chadonnay, for instance—comes in a number of varieties, each with its own character."

—Joseph Schagrin, Retailer

$250 Wine List

Qty.	REDS	Cost
	California	
4	Cabernet Sauvignon, Willow Creek 1978	B
4	Zinfandel, Willow Creek 1978	A
	France	
4	Côtes-du-Rhône, Chemin des Mulets 1980	A
4	Bordeaux, Médoc-Cuvée de la Commanderie du Bontemps 1979	B
4	Beaujolais Villages, Maison Frères 1979	B
	Italy	
4	The Abruzzi, Montepulciano di Abruzzi, Illuminati 1978	B

Qty.	WHITES	Cost
	California	
4	Chardonnay, Willow Creek Limited Release 1980	C
4	Fumé Blanc, Willow Creek 1978	B
	France	
4	Burgundy, St-Véran Du Boeuf 1979	C
	Germany	
4	Mosel-Saar-Ruwer, Piesporter Michelsberg Kabinett 1981	B
	Italy	
4	The Abruzzi, Trebbiano di Abruzzo, Illuminati 1979	A
	APÉRITIF/DESSERT WINE	
4	Vin Blanc Cassis, Maison Frères	B

SUNSET CORNERS, INC. Miami, FL

"The biggest mistake you can make when you start collecting wine is to start out with only famous glamorous names. There are two things wrong with this approach. One, "glamour" doesn't always translate into value; two, you can't appreciate a really fine wine, like Château La Lagune, until you become familiar with the everyday middle-of-the-road wines."

—Chip Cassidy, Wine Consultant

$250 Wine List

Qty.		Cost	Qty.		Cost
	REDS			**France**	
	California		2	Alsace, Riesling Timbach 1979	B
2	Cabernet Sauvignon, Beaulieu Vineyard Beau Tour 1978	B	2	Burgundy, Patriarche Père et Fils Blanc de Blancs	A
2	Merlot, Souverain 1978	B		Germany	
2	Zinfandel, Pedroncelli 1977	B	2	Mosel-Saar-Ruwer, Bernkastler Kurfürstlay Müller QbA 1979	B
	France		2	Rheinhessen Niersteiner Gutes Domtal Ludwig Kabinett 1981	B
2	Bordeaux, Château Greysac 1978	B		Spain	
2	Côtes-du-Rhône, Paul Jaboulet 1978	C	2	Codorniu Blanc de Blanc	C
	Spain			Argentina	
2	Coronas, Torres 1978	A	2	Chardonnay, Andean 1978	A
2	Pinot Noir, Torres 1976	C		**APÉRITIF/DESSERT WINE**	
	Chile		1	Port, Dow Ruby #1	B
2	Cabernet Sauvignon, Concha y Toro 1976	A	1	Sherry, Tio Lola Fino	B
	WHITES			**CHAMPAGNE/SPARKLING WINE**	
	California		2	St. Germain Blanc de Blancs Brut	C
2	Chardonnay, Parducci 1980	C	2	Louis Roederer Brut NV	D
2	Fumé Blanc, Diamond Oak 1979	C			
1	Johannisberg Riesling, Robert Mondavi 1980	C			
2	Vin Blanc, Château St. Jean 1980	B			

Hawaii

VINTAGE WINE CELLAR Honolulu, HI

"The warmer the climate, the more important it is that a wine merchant stores wine correctly. The storage temperature should be constant. If there are variations, the wines on sale won't age predictably and the consumer may end up holding on to a wine for four or five years and then being disappointed when the time comes to open it."

—Allen Y. Kam, Retailer

$250 Wine List

Qty.		Cost	Qty.		Cost
	REDS		2	Fumé Blanc, Robert Mondavi	C
	California		2	Johannisberg Riesling, Firestone 1979	C
5	Cabernet Sauvignon, Beaulieu 1978	C		France	
2	Cabernet Sauvignon, L. Martini 1978	B	2	Burgundy, Mâcon-Villages, Rodet 1979	B
2	Zinfandel, Montevina Special Selection 1979	C	2	Burgundy, Pouilly-Fuissé, Rodet 1979	C
	France		2	Graves, Chevalier de Vedrine	B
4	Bordeaux, Château La Tour de By 1978	C		Germany	
1	Bordeaux, Château Léoville-Lascases 1978	E	2	Mosel-Saar-Ruwer, Piesporter Goldtröpfchen Kabinett 1981	B
2	Burgundy, Savigny-lès-Beaune 1978	D	2	Rheingau, Steinberger Kabinett 1981	C
	Italy			Italy	
2	Chianti Classico 1975	A	2	Chardonnay, Cavit 1980	B
	WHITES		4	Soave 1980	A
	California				
2	Chenin Blanc, Hoffman Mountain Ranch 1980	B			

ARMANETTI INC. Chicago, IL

"A wine collector's best friend is a retailer he can talk to and trust—somebody who doesn't just sell wine, but has a real interest in it and can give good advice."

—Len Armanetti, Retailer

$250 Wine List

Qty.	REDS	Cost
	California	
1	Cabernet Sauvignon, Beaulieu Vineyard Reserve 1974	E
1	Cabernet Sauvignon, Jordan 1977	E
	France	
1	Bordeaux, Château Cos d'Estournel 1978	E
1	Bordeaux, Château Mouton-Rothschild 1976	E
1	Côtes-du-Rhône, Chapoutier, Côte-Rôtie 1979	D
	Italy	
1	Brunello di Montalcino, Poggie alle Mura 1971	E

Qty.	WHITES	Cost
	California	
1	Chardonnay, Napa Valley Acadia, NV	D
1	Chardonnay, Schramsberg Blanc de Blancs	E
	France	
1	Barsac, Château Coutet 1973	D
	Germany	
1	Mosel-Saar-Ruwer, J. J. Prüm Wehlener Sonnenuhr Auslese 1978	D

Qty.	CHAMPAGNE/SPARKLING WINE	Cost
1	Laurent Perrier Brut NV	E

$600 Wine List

Qty.	REDS	Cost
	California	
1	Cabernet Sauvignon Cask, Inglenook 1969	E
1	Cabernet Sauvignon, Robert Mondavi Private Reserve, 1975	E
	France	
1	Bordeaux, Château Lafite-Rothschild 1970	E
1	Bordeaux, Château Latour 1971	E
	Italy	
1	Brunello di Montalcino, Poggie Alle Mura 1971	E

Qty.	WHITES	Cost
	California	
1	Chardonnay, Grgich Hills 1978	E
	France	
1	Bordeaux, Château Carbonnieux Blanc 1978	E
1	Bordeaux, Château Cheval Blanc 1978	E
1	Bordeaux, Château d'Yquem 1970	E
1	Burgundy, Moillard Corton-Charlemagne 1978	E
	Germany	
1	Mosel-Saar-Ruwer Riesling, Bernkasteler Dr. Thanisch Auslese 1975	E

Qty.	CHAMPAGNE/SPARKLING WINE	Cost
1	Louis Roederer Cristal Brut	E

ALBANY LIQUORS Beech Grove, IN

"When you go to a wine merchant, make sure you tell him what your motives are. Do you want to learn about wine? Do you just want good wines to enjoy? Do you want wines you can keep for a few years? The more you let the merchant know about what you're looking for, the better your chances are of getting a list that's tailored to your situation."

—Tom Steinkampf, Retailer

$250 Wine List

Qty.	REDS	Cost
	California	
2	Burgundy Jug Wine, Parducci	A
1	Cabernet Sauvignon, Sebastiani Private Reserve	C
3	Cabernet Sauvignon, Simi	C
1	Vintage Red Jug Wine, Parducci	B
1	Zinfandel, Ridge, Amador	C
1	Zinfandel, Simi	C
	France	
2	Beaujolais-Villages, Louis Jadot	C
3	Bordeaux, Graysac	C
3	Bordeaux, Petit Château André Corbin	C
	Italy	
2	Chianti Classico Riserva, Ruffino	C

Qty.	WHITES	Cost
	California	
2	Chablis Jug Wine, Parducci	A
2	Chardonnay, Iron Horse	D
2	Chardonnay, Simi	C
2	Chenin Blanc, Parducci	B
2	Vintage White, Parducci	B
	France	
2	Burgundy, Mâcon-Villages, Louis Jadot	C
2	Burgundy, Pouilly-Fuissé, Nicolas	C
	Germany	
2	Rheingau, Riesling Steinberger Kabinett	C

Qty.	APÉRITIF/DESSERT WINE	Cost
1	Amontillado, Cockburn	C
1	Port, Cockburn Special Reserve	C
2	Ste. Croix du Mont	B

Qty.	CHAMPAGNE/SPARKLING WINE	Cost
1	Domaine Chandon Brut NV	C
1	Lanson Père et Fils Brut NV	D

KINGS CELLAR   South Bend, IN

"The smaller the cellar, the more important value becomes. I'd rather see a $250 wine cellar with 40 to 50 wines than one with only 30 wines, even though the 30 wines might be "better." The idea in any cellar is to optimize the aging potential of your wines, and you can't do this unless you have enough wines to keep you happy on a day-to-day basis."

—Steve Haskins, Wine Manager

$250 Wine List

Qty.		Cost
	REDS	
	California	
12	Burgundy, Beaulieu	A
3	Cabernet Sauvignon, Stag's Leap Wine Cellars 1977	D
1	Chablis, Summit	C
6	Classic California Red, Monterey 1978	A
	France	
12	Burgundy, Père Patriarche	
	WHITES	
	California	
12	Chablis, Beaulieu	A
1	Chablis, Geyser Peak	C
	France	
3	Burgundy, Mâcon-Lugny Les Charmes 1978	C
12	Burgundy, Père Patriarche	A

$600 Wine List These wines should be added to the $250 list.

Qty.		Cost
	REDS	
	California	
6	Cabernet, Clos du Val 1976	D
	France	
6	Bordeaux, Château Haut-Beycheville-Gloria 1978	D
2	Bordeaux, Château Lafite-Rothschild	E
	WHITES	
	California	
6	Chardonnay, Iron Horse 1979	D
3	Chardonnay, Lambert Bridge 1979	D
	France	
1	Burgundy, Puligny-Montrachet 1978	E
	Germany	
3	Mosel-Saar-Ruwer, Wehlener Sonnenuhr Auslese 1976	C

G. B. RUSSO & SON, LTD. Grand Rapids, MI

"Before you invest money in a collection, join a wine club. After a number of tastings, you'll have enough of a foundation so that you can get together with a wine merchant and set up a collection that will satisfy your particular objectives."

—John Russo, Retailer

$250 Wine List

Qty.		Cost	Qty.		Cost
	REDS			**Michigan**	
	California		1	Aurora, Leelanau Limited	A
1	Barbera, Sebastiani	B	1	Chablis, St. Julian	A
1	Cabernet Sauvignon, Louis Martini	C	1	White, Riesling, Fenn Valley	B
1	Petite Sirah, Concannon	C		**Washington State**	
1	Zinfandel, Mirassou	B	1	Johannisberg Riesling, Chateau St. Michelle	C
	France				
1	Beaujolais, Sichel	B		**ROSÉ**	
1	Bordeaux, Château Lartigue, St.-Estèphe	C	1	Petite Rosé Mirassou (California)	B
	Italy		1	Rose Gewürztraminer, Sebastiani (California)	B
1	Barolo, Vietti	E	1	Zinfandel Rosé, Concannon (California)	B
1	Emilia-Romagna, Vivano Lambrusco	A		**APÉRITIF/DESSERT WINE**	
1	Piedmont, Beccaro Pinot Noir	B	1	Marsala, Fici Siciliano Rosso	B
1	Sicily, Corvo Rosso	C	1	Moscato Amabile, Beccaro	A
	Spain		1	Port, Bronte-Hartford Light	B
1	Catalonia, Torres Sangre de Toro	B	1	Sherry, Perez Cream	B
	WHITES		1	Sherry, Perez Dry Cocktail	B
	California			**CHAMPAGNE/SPARKLING WINE**	
1	Chablis, Mirassou, Dry	B	1	Dellapierre Brut (Spain)	B
1	Chardonnay, Pedroncelli	C	1	Spumante Americano, Gina Russo	B
1	Chenin Blanc, Concannon	B	1	Veuve Galien, Nicolas	D
1	Fumé Blanc, Chateau St. Jean	D			
1	Green Hungarian, Sebastiani	B			
1	Riesling, Parducci	B			

GOODRICH'S SPARTAN SHOP RITE, INC. East Lansing, MI

"Make up your mind right from the start: are you setting up a cellar for drinking or for laying down wine? Your buying strategy should reflect that decision."

—Steven Scheffel, Wine Manager

$250 Wine List

Qty.		Cost	Qty.		Cost
	REDS			**France**	
	California		3	Bordeaux Blanc, Chevalier de Védrines 1979	B
2	Classic Red, Monterey 1978	B	2	Burgundy, Bourgogne du Chapitre Blanc 1980	C
	France		2	Graves, Château le Merle 1978	C
2	Bordeaux, Château D'Agassac 1976	C	1	Sauternes, Château Rayne-Vigneau 1976	
2	Burgundy, Bouchard Père et Fils 1978	B		**Germany**	
2	Burgundy, Bourgogne du Chapitre 1979	C	2	Rheingau, Geisenheimer Kilzberg 1978	B
4	Côtes-de-Bourg, Château Sauman 1979	C	2	Rheingau, Steinberger Kabinett 1979	C
	Italy		1	Mosel-Saar-Ruwer, Agler Kupp Auslese 1978	C
2	Chianti Classico Castello di Uzzano 1978	C		**Spain**	
2	Piedmont, Dessilani Spanna 1978	A	2	Tarragona, Torres Viva Sol 1978	B
	Spain			**ROSÉ**	
2	Rioja, Vega 1975	A	2	Rosé d'Anjou, Lichine NV	B
	WHITES			**CHAMPAGNE/SPARKLING WINE**	
	California		2	Philipponnat NV Brut	E
2	Chardonnay, Conn Creek 1980	B			
2	Classic White, Monterey 1979	B			

CHESHIRE CELLARS St. Louis, MO

"Do as much reading as you can. There are a lot of very good basic wine books. The more you can learn from these books, the more you're in a position to put together an intelligent wine list, not just one that is filled with impressive labels."

—Russell Raney, Retailer

Qty.	REDS	Cost	Qty.		Cost
	California			**France**	
1	Cabernet Sauvignon, Boeger 1978	C	1	Alsace, Gewürztraminer "Mandelberg" Preiss-	
1	Cabernet Sauvignon, Burgess 1978	C		Henny 1976	C
1	Pinot Noir, Pedroncelli 1978	A	1	Chablis, Valmur-Moreau 1978	D
1	Zinfandel, Dehlinger 1978	C	1	Burgundy, Chassagne-Montrachet "Morgeot,"	
	France			Ramonet 1978	D
1	Beaujolais-Villages, Georges Duboeuf 1981	B	1	Loire Valley, Muscadet, Marquis de Goulaine	
1	Bordeaux, Château La Pointe 1978	D		1979	B
1	Bordeaux, Château La Tour Blanc 1978	C		**Italy**	
1	Côte de Beaune, Beaune Cent-Vignes-		1	Chardonnay, Barone de Cles 1981	C
	Remoissenet 1971	E		**Germany**	
1	Côtes-du-Rhône, Gigondas, Paul Jaboulet 1980	C	1	Mosel-Saar-Ruwer, Ayer Kupp, Auslese	
1	Rhône, Hermitage, E. Guigal 1978	D		A. Rheinhart 1976	C
	Germany		1	Nahe, Schloss Böckelheimer Kupfergrube	
1	Mosel-Saar-Ruwer, Brauneberger Juffer Auslese,			Kabinett 1979	C
	F. Haag 1979	D		**Spain**	
1	Rheingau, Schloss Johannisberg Kabinett 1979	C	1	Rioja, Cumbrero Blanco, Bodegas Montecillo 1978	C
	Spain			ROSÉS	
1	Bodegas Montecillo 1978	B	1	Tavel, Domaine de Longval 1979	C
	WHITES			APÉRITIF/DESSERT WINE	
	California		1	Fino Sherry, La Riva "Tres Palmas"	D
1	Chardonnay, Napa Cellars 1979	D	1	Port, Warre 1966	D
1	White Riesling, Trefethen 1981	C		CHAMPAGNE/SPARKLING WINE	
			1	Deutz Brut	E

THE CELLAR Lincoln, NE

"Saving labels is a good idea. Soak the label off and paste it in a book with comments. By the way, save the labels of even the wines you don't like. That way, you won't make the same mistake twice."

—Robert Mueller, Retailer

$250 Wine List

Qty.	REDS	Cost	Qty.	WHITES	Cost
	California			**Italy**	
1	Cabernet Sauvignon, Jordan	D	1	Frascati, Fontana Candida	B
2	Cabernet Sauvignon, Paul Masson	B		**Germany**	
1	Pinot Noir, Clos du Bois	B	2	Mosel-Saar-Ruwer, Piersporter Goldtröpfchen,	
2	Zinfandel, San Luis Ridge	C		Jacques Scott	C
	France		3	Rheinhessen Liebfraümilch, P. J. Valckenberg	B
3	Beaujolais-Village, Louis Jadot	C		ROSÉS	
	Italy		2	Rosé d'Anjou, Alexis Lichine	B
1	Valpolicella, Bolla	B	3	Taylor California Cellars	B
	WHITES			CHAMPAGNE/SPARKLING WINE	
	California		2	Asti Spumante, Zonin	B
3	Chablis, Colony Classic	B	1	Korbel Natural	D
3	Chablis, Heitz	B			
2	Chenin Blanc, Parducci	B			
2	French Colombard, Lawrence	B			

WINE & SPIRIT WORLD   Hohokus, NJ

"Although some of the wines might improve slightly in the bottle, this is basically a working cellar with a variety of wines that represent all the nuances that go with food and wine. As you taste a wine, place judgment on it; see what it goes well with."

—Carlo Russo, Retailer

$250 Wine List

Qty.		Cost	Qty.		Cost
	REDS			**France**	
	California		2	Alsace, Pinot Gris, Klug 1979–80	B
2	Cabernet Sauvignon, McDowell 1979	D	2	Bordeaux, Entre-Deux-Mers 1980–81	A
4	Monterey, Classic Red 1978–79	B		Magnum Bordeaux, La Fleur Blanc	B
2	Zinfandel, Montevina 1979	B	2	Burgundy, Mâcon Vire 1980–81	B
	France			Italy	
4	Beaujolais-Villages, Georges Duboeuf 1981	B	4	Chardonnay, Plozner 1980–81	B
4	Bordeaux, Château du Castena 1979	B	4	Tuscany, Frescobaldi Romino 1980–81	B
4	Côtes-du-Rhône 1979	A	4	Veneto, Torresella Piṅot 1980–81	B
	Italy			**APÉRITIF/DESSERT WINE**	
2	Campania, Aglianico del Vulture Riserva, D'Angelo 1975	B	1	Alvear Fino	B
	Portugal		1	Amontillado	B
4	Serradayres	B	1	Cream Sherry	B
	Spain			**CHAMPAGNE/SPARKLING WINE**	
4	Rioja Vega or Rioja Olarra	A	1	Domaine Chandon	D
	WHITES		1	Paul Cheneau	B
	California				
2	Chardonnay, Beringer 1980	C			
2	French Colombard or Sauvignon Blanc, McDowell	B			

GOLD STAR   Forest Hills, NY

"Working with a good wine merchant is a must if you're new to collecting. But if I were just starting out, I'd read as much as I could on my own before looking around for a merchant. That way, I'd be in a much stronger position to make a good choice."

—Lou Iacucci, Retailer

$250 Wine List

Qty.		Cost	Qty.		Cost
	REDS		1	Cabernet Sauvignon, Vasse Felix, Margaret River	D
	California			**WHITES**	
1	Cabernet Sauvignon, Mt. Veeder Winery, Bernstein Vineyard	E		California	
1	Zinfandel, Sutter Home Winery	B	1	Chardonnay, Far Niente Winery	E
	France			France	
1	Beaujolais, Fleurie Trenel Fils Les Moriers	B	1	Bordeaux, Domaine de la Tourmaline Muscadet de Sèvre-et-Maine	B
1	Bordeaux, Château Ducru-Beaucaillou	E	1	Burgundy, Meursault A. Grivault Clos des Perrieres	E
1	Bordeaux, Château Pichon-Longueville	C	1	Sauvignon Blanc, Château du Cros	A
1	Côtes-du-Rhône, Sablet	B	1	Vouvray Moelleux, Le Mont	D
	Italy			Germany	
1	Barolo Riserva, Prunotto Bussia di Monforte	E	1	Mosel-Saar-Ruwer, J.J. Prüm Wehlener Sonṇenuhr Spätlese	C
1	Chianti Classico, Monte Vertine	C		Italy	
1	Lombardy, Monsupello Oltrepo Pavese	B	1	Soave Classico, Pieropan	B
1	Piedmont, Castello di Gabiano Riserva	B	1	Piedmont, Gavi La Giustiniana	B
1	Rosso Piceno Superiore, Vallone	A		Australia	
1	Vecchio Chianti, Villa La Selve	A	1	Pinot Noir, Yerinberg	
	Spain			**CHAMPAGNE/SPARKLING WINE**	
1	Catalonia, Torres Viña Sol	A	1	Veneto, Venegazzu Brut, Italy	D
	Argentina				
1	Cabernet Sauvignon, Toso	B			
	Australia				
1	Cabernet Sauvignon, Lake's Folly, Hunter Valley	D			

CORK & BOTTLE, LTD. New York, NY

"You need a certain amount of diversity—to support the learning process. Having an opportunity to compare by having a second bottle to come back to gives you an opportunity to learn and grow. That's what it's all about. After all, we're not drinking wine just for the alcoholic effect. It's a lifestyle—it's a fun thing, and people want to learn more about it."

—Harold Baron, Retailer

$250 Wine List

Qty.	REDS	Cost
	California	
2	Cabernet Sauvignon, Beaulieu Beau Tour 1979	C
2	Cabernet Sauvignon, Rutherford Hill 1976	D
1	Merlot, Carneros Creek 1977	C
	French	
6	Bordeaux, Château d'Agassac, Ludon-Médoc 1976	C
6	Bordeaux, Château de la Grave, Côtes-de-Bourg, 1978	B
3	Côtes-du-Rhône, Domaine Gerin, Côte Rôtie 1974	B
	Italian	
1	Piedmont, Spanna Traversagna, Vallana 1967	D
	Spanish	
3	Cataluna, Coronas Torres 1979	A

Qty.	WHITES	Cost
	California	
2	Chardonnay, Jekel 1979	D
	France	
6	Bordeaux, Château de Hartes, Entre-Deux-Mers, 1980	A
2	Bordeaux, Château Le Tuquet, Gravee 1979	B
	Italy	
6	Soave, Pasqua 1979	A
	German	
2	Mosel-Saar-Ruwer, Ockfener Bockstein, 1977	A
	APÉRITIF/DESSERT WINE	
1	Dow Vintage Port 1977	E
	CHAMPAGNE/SPARKLING WINE	
3	Brut Champenoise, Paul Cheneau NV	B

MORRELL & COMPANY New York, NY

"Variety. Variety. Variety. The point of any wine cellar—regardless of how big or small it is—is to have a variety of wines at your immediate disposal. With a smaller cellar ($250), you spend more money because you can't buy by the case, but the added variety you get puts you ahead of the game."

—Peter Morrell, Retailer

$250 Wine List

Qty.	REDS	Cost
	California	
3	Cabernet Sauvignon, Calistoga 1979	B
	France	
3	Beaujolais, Morgan Domaine de Lathevalle 1981	B
3	Bordeaux, Château Les Ormes-de-Pez, St. Estèphe 1976	D
3	Bordeaux Château Grand-Jour Côtes-de-Bourg, 1979	A
3	Bordeaux Supérieure, Château Gobert 1976	B
3	Burgundy, Pinot Noir Quillardet 1972	B
	WHITES	
	California	
3	Chardonnay, Calistoga 1981	B
3	Fumé Blanc, San Martin 1980	B
	France	
3	Bordeaux, Château de Grand Moueys 1980	B
3	Burgundy, Mâcon-Villages Cuvée l'Etoile 1979	A
3	Loire Valley, Muscadet de Sèvre 1981	B
	Germany	
3	Mosel-Saar-Ruwer, Wiltinger Schlossberg Kabinett 1979	A
	Italy	
3	Tuscany, Bianco di Carobbio 1980	A
3	Tuscany, Vernaccia NV	A
	CHAMPAGNE/SPARKLING WINE	
½	Perrier Jouet Brut NV	E
1	Philipponat Vintage Brut 1975	C

$600 Wine List

Qty.	REDS	Cost
	California	
3	Merlot, Duckhorn 1980	E
	France	
3	Bordeaux, Château Lascombes, Margaux 1978	D
3	Bordeaux, Château Les Ormes-de-Pez, St. Estèphe 1978	D
3	Bordeaux, Château Lynch-Bages Pauillac 1978	E
2	Bordeaux, Château Mouton-Rothschild Pauillac 1979	E
3	Burgundy, Les Monts Battois Cauvard 1978	C
3	Burgundy, Monthélie Domaine Bouzerand 1978	D
3	Burgundy, Pommard Epenots Domaine Parent 1978	E
	Italy	
3	Montalbano Spanna 1969	C
	WHITES	
	California	
3	Chardonnay, St. Francis 1979	D
	France	
3	Alsace, Gewürztraminer Clos St. Landelin 1978	D
3	Burgundy, Auxey-Duresses Domaine Xavier Bouzerand 1979	D
3	Chablis, Les Clos A. Gourland 1979	D

SHERRY-LEHMANN, INC., New York, NY

"The key to a good $250 wine cellar is plenty of inexpensive wines of good quality. Never buy just one bottle of a wine—always at least two, because you're frequently going to be serving four people and one bottle will not be enough. If you find a wine you like, get into the habit of buying it in case lots. Remember, wine is an agricultural product. It comes from a grape grown on a vine in a specific plot of land and each year is different. There's only so much made and when the supply is gone, you can't go back for more."

—Michael Aaron, Vice-President
Sherry-Lehmann, Inc.

$250 Wine List

Qty.	REDS	Cost
	California	
3	Gamay Beaujolais, Hultgren & Samperton	B
	France	
6	Beaujolais, Brouilly, Château de la Chaise 1981	B
6	Graves, Château de Chautegrive 1976	B
6	Sherry-Lehmann Maison Rouge	A
	Italy	
3	Chianti Rufina, Frescobaldi 1980	A
	WHITES	
	California	
6	Eschol White, Trefethen	B
	France	
3	Burgundy, Mâcon Blanc Georges Duboeuf 1980	B
6	Cler' Blanc	A
3	Alsace, Riesling Hansi 1979	B
	Germany	
6	Mosel-Saar-Ruwer, Ockfener Bockstein 1980	A
	Italy	
6	Pinot Grigio, Plozner 1981	B

$600 Wine List

Qty.	REDS	Cost
	California	
3	Cabernet Sauvignon, Hultgren & Samperton 1979	D
3	Cabernet Sauvignon, Jordan 1978	E
	France	
6	Beaujolais, Fleurie, Georges Duboeuf 1981	C
6	Bordeaux, Château de Mouchac 1976	A
2	Bordeaux, Château Lafite 1979	E
2	Bordeaux, Château Prieuré-Lichine 1978	D
2	Burgundy Le Chambertin, Domaine Trapet 1976	E
2	Burgundy, Morey-St.-Denis, R. Goulet 1964	E
	Italy	
2	Amarone, Speri 1974	C
2	Barolo Riserva, Prunotto 1974	D
6	Dolcetto, Einaudi 1979	B
	WHITES	
	California	
3	Chardonnay, Conn Creek 1979	D
	France	
3	Burgundy, Puligny-Montrachet, Sauzet 1980	D
3	Chablis, Louis Michel 1980	B
6	Loire, Muscadet, Château de Cleray 1981	B
	Germany	
1	Mosel-Saar-Ruwer, Drum Whelener Sonneberg Beernaulsese 1976	E
1	Rheingau, Hattenheimer Nussbrunnen, von Simmern	E
	Italy	
3	Gavi dei Gavi, La Scolca 1980	D

67 WINE & SPIRITS MERCHANTS New York, NY

This list represents a $250 wine cellar purchased in single bottles. All are excellent wines, but, based on individual tastes, they may or may not be repeated as the cellar begins to concentrate and reflect its owner more and more.

—Jack Lang, Retailer

$250 Wine List

Qty.	REDS	Cost
	California	
1	Merlot, Souverain 1978	C
1	Zinfandel, Château Montelena 1979	C
	France	
1	Bordeaux, Château Haut-Bages Pauillac 1978	D
1	Bordeaux, Château Latour-Bicheau, Graves, 1979	C
1	Bordeaux, Château Lezongars,Côtes du Bordeaux 1978	B
1	Bordeaux, Château Lynch-Bages, Pauillac 1977	C
1	Bordeaux, Château Sigognac, Médoc 1979	B
1	Burgundy, Clos St. Denis, G. Lignier 1976	E
1	Burgundy, Côte de Beaune-Villages, G. Prieur 1978	D
1	Burgundy, Pernand Vergelesses, R. Radit 1979	D
1	Cahors, Clos Triguedina 1978	C
1	Rhône Valley, Châteauneuf du Pape, Comte de Lauze 1976	D
1	Rhône Valley, Gigondas, R. Combe 1979	C
1	Rhône Valley, Vacqueyras, R. Combe 1979	C
	Italy	
1	Cabernet Trentino, Leonardo 1979	B
1	Merlot, Donati 1979	B
1	San Leonardo 1979	B
1	Terodigo, Donati 1979	B

Qty.	WHITES	Cost
	California	
1	Chardonnay, Rutherford Hill 1981	B
1	French Colombard, Beringer 1981	B
	France	
1	Bordeaux, Château Latour-Bichen, Graves 1980	C
1	Bordeaux, Sauvignon St. Foy 1980	A
1	Burgundy, Bourgogne Aligote, R, Monnier 1979	B
1	Burgundy, Chablis "Vaillons," S. Collet 1979	C
1	Burgundy, Mâcon-Villages, S. Bedin 1979	B
1	Burgundy, Rully, Ropiteau Frères 1978	C
1	Loire Valley, Muscadet Sur-Lie, Domaine de la Grange 1980	B
1	Sancerre, Domaine de Garennes 1980	C
1	Pouilly-Fumé, J. Pabiot 1979	C
	Italy	
1	Cantina Porto Russo, Gavi 1980	B
1	Pinot Bianco, Donati 1980	B

Oregon

THE WINE RACK Salem, OR

"Strive for balance. At least 70 percent of whatever you buy you should plan to keep for at least four or five years. But make sure you have enough interesting wines on hand to serve on the spur of the moment. Stick with Chardonnays and Cabernets for the long haul, and Rieslings, Chenin Blancs, and other light wines for the short term."

—Nathan E. Allen, Retailer

$250 Wine List

Qty.	REDS	Cost
	California	
1	Cabernet Savignon, Jekel 1979	C
1	Zinfandel, Clos du Val 1978	D
1	Zinfandel, Ridge	C
	Northwest U.S.A.	
1	Pinot Noir, Eyrie 1979	C
1	Pinot Noir, Hidden Springs 1980	C
	France	
1	Beaujolais, Robert Drouhin 1978	C
1	Bordeaux, Pichon Comtesse de Lalande 1976	E
1	Bordeaux, Château Gloria 1978	E
1	Bordeaux, Château La Cardonne 1978	C
1	Bordeaux, Château Larose-Trintaudon 1976	C
	Italy	
1	Chianti Classico, Nozzole 1974	C
1	Barolo, Prunotto	D

Qty.	WHITES	Cost
	California	
1	Chardonnay, Pedroncelli 1980	C
1	Chardonnay, Trefethen 1980	D
1	Chenin Blanc, Robert Mondavi	C
1	Johannisberg Riesling, Trefethen	C

$600 Wine List

Qty.	WHITES	Cost
	Northwest U.S.A.	
1	Chardonnay, Eyrie 1980 (Oregon)	D
1	Chardonnay, Ste. Chapelle 1980 (Idaho)	D
1	Riesling, Sokol Blosser	C
	France	
1	Burgundy, La Forêt, Mâcon-Villages	C
	Germany	
1	Mosel-Saar-Ruwer Bernkasteler Badstube, Dr. Thanisch	C
	Italy	
1	Orvieto, Barbelani	B
1	Soave, Pieropan	B
	Australia	
1	Johannisberg Riesling, Kaiser-Stuhl	A
	APÉRITIF/DESSERT WINE	
1	Dry Vermouth, Lillet	C
1	Ruby Port, Dow	C
	CHAMPAGNE/SPARKLING WINE	
1	Blanc de Blancs, Schramsberg	D
1	Asti Spumante, Bonardi	C
1	Carta Nevada, Frexinet	B
1	Kornell, Brut	C

MENDENHALL SQUARE LIQUORS Memphis, TN

"Analyze your own tastes. What things do you buy at a butcher shop? What do you buy at the fish store? Consider your own particular likes in terms of meals. Be willing to experiment a little bit and find wines that are appropriate to your tastes as far as the food is concerned."

—Sam Ward, Retailer

$250 Wine List

Qty.	REDS	Cost	Qty.	WHITES	Cost
	California			**California**	
1	Cabernet Sauvignon, Beaulieu Vineyard Reserve 1974	D	1	Chardonnay, Clos du Val 1980	C
1	Cabernet Sauvignon, Clos du Bois 1974	D	1	Fumé Blanc, Robert Mondavi Reserve 1980	C
1	Cabernet Sauvignon, Freemark Abbey 1974	D	1	Johannisberg, Riesling, Chateau St. Jean Selected Late Harvest 1980	C
1	Cabernet Sauvignon, Robert Mondavi Reserve 1974	E		**France**	
1	Cabernet Sauvignon, Sterling Vineyards 1974	D	1	Bordeaux, Château Carbonnieux 1971	D
	France		1	Burgundy, Chassagne-Montrachet 1974	D
1	Bordeaux, Château Beychevelle 1975	D	1	Burgundy, Meursault 1973	D
1	Bordeaux, Château Langoa-Barton 1975	D	1	Sauternes, Château Boigny 1969	D
1	Bordeaux, Château Palmer 1975	D		**Germany**	
1	Bordeaux, Château-Triatadon 1975	D	1	Mosel-Saar-Ruwer, Scharzhofberger Estate-bottled Kabinett 1976	D
1	Burgundy, Chambolle Musigny 1973	D	1	Rheingau, Schloss Vollrads 1976	D
1	Burgundy, Clos de Vougeot 1971	D		**ROSÉ**	
1	Burgundy, Gevrey-Chambertin 1976	D	1	Rosé of Cabernet Souvignon, Simi	C
1	Burgundy, Nuits-St-Georges 1973	D			
1	Côtes-du-Rhône Châteauneuf-du-Pape, Louis Latour 1976	C			
1	Côtes-du-Rhône, Kreusch 1979	B			

SIGEL'S, THE WINE MERCHANTS Dallas, TX

"If you're serious about learning about wine, get together with another couple whenever you're tasting a new wine. Better still, open two bottles and have six people do the tasting. Make the two wines similar —not necessarily in price, but in color and type. Compare, for instance, a French wine with a California wine. Don't let yourself get hooked on any one wine. As soon as you get a favorite wine, you are liable to stop experimenting, and the minute you stop tasting new wines, you stop learning."

—Victor Wdowiak, Retailer

$250 Wine List

Qty.	REDS	Cost	Qty.	WHITES	Cost
	California			**France**	
3	Cabernet Sauvignon, Fetzer Estate-bottled	C	3	Burgundy, Rodet Mâcon-Villages	B
3	Gamay Beaujolais, Stag's Leap	B	3	Fleuredor, Vin Ordinaire	B
	France		3	Vouvray, Châtelaine Desjacques	A
3	Beaujolais, Beaudet Moulin-à-Vent	B		**Italy**	
3	Bordeaux, Château Grand Maserolles	C	3	Orvieto Secco, Carpineto	A
3	Côtes-du-Rhône, La Vieille Ferme Côtes du Ventoux	B		**Germany**	
	Italy		3	Mosel-Saar-Ruwer, Nicolay Ayler Kupp Kabinett	B
3	Corvo di Salaparuta	B	3	Rheingau, Binger St. Rochus Kapelle Spätlese	B
	Spain			**APÉRITIF/DESSERT WINE**	
3	Rioja, Marqués de Cáceres	A	1	Tawny Port, Sandeman	B
	WHITES			**CHAMPAGNE/SPARKLING WINE**	
	California		1	Cordon Negro, Frexinet	B
3	Chablis Blanc, Gallo	B			
3	Chardonnay, Paul Masson Pinnacles	B			
3	Johannisberg Riesling, Conn Creek	B			

CAPITOL HILL WINE & CHEESE Washington, DC

"Developing a sophisticated palate is a gradual process. You can't rush it. If you've been drinking inexpensive wines most of your life, you shouldn't jump immediately into the expensive category. Take it gradually. What I do with customers who tell me that they like "light" red wines is to steer them toward a Côtes-du-Rhône or a Beaujolais, but with the idea that I'll eventually move them toward the fuller-bodied wines."

—John A. Rusnak, Retailer

$250 Wine List

Qty.		Cost	Qty.		Cost
	REDS				
	California		2	Gewürztraminer, Simi 1978	C
2	Cabernet Sauvignon, Trefethen 1977	D	2	Pinot Chardonnay, Simi 1977	C
2	Cabernet Sauvignon, Beaulieu Beau Tour 1978	C	2	Pinot Chardonnay, Taylor NV	D
2	Cabernet Sauvignon, Taylor NV	B	2	Riesling, Soft, Monterey	C
2	Pinot Noir, Husch 1976	C		France	
2	Zinfandel, Fetzer 1976	B	2	Bordeaux, Château Lescours 1978	B
2	Zinfandel, Monterey 1976	B	2	Burgundy, Pouilly Fumé-Michael Redde 1979	D
	France		2	Graves, Château de Chantegrive 1978	D
2	Bordeaux, Château Greysac 1976	C		Germany	
2	Bordeaux, La Cour Pavillon	B	2	Mosel-Saar-Ruwer, Piesporter Michelsberg 1977	B
	WHITES		2	Rheingau, Schloss Vollrads 1978	C
	California				
2	Chenin Blanc, Krug NV	C			

SIEGEL'S WINE CELLAR Milwaukee, WI

"The standard ratio of "future" wines to "daily" wines is at least 60 percent future to 40 percent daily, and I like to see more red wines than white."

—Norman Siegel, Retailer

$250 Wine List			$600 Wine List Add two bottles of each of the following wines to the $250 list above.		
Qty.		Cost	Qty.		Cost
	REDS			**REDS**	
	California			California	
3	Cabernet Sauvignon, Beaulieu Beau Tour 1979	B	2	Cabernet Sauvignon, Beaulieu Beau Tour 1975	E
3	Petite Sirah, R. J. Cook 1979	B	2	Cabernet Sauvignon, Carneros Creek 1978	D
3	Zinfandel, Rutherford Ranch	C	2	Petite Sirah, Stag's Leap 1977	D
	France		2	Zinfandel, Clos du Val 1978	C
3	Beaujolais-Villages, Georges Duboeuf 1981	B		France	
3	Bordeaux, La Cour Pavillon	B	2	Bordeaux, Château Coutet, Barsac 1975	E
	Italy		2	Bordeaux, Château Pichon-Lonqueville, Baron Pauillac 1978	E
3	Corvo 1979	C	2	Côte de Beaune, Bichot Meursault 1978	D
3	Rubesco, Lungarotti	C		Italy	
	Spain		2	Amarone, Bolla 1971	D
3	Rioja, Marqués de Cáceres, 1975	B	2	Barolo, Borgogno 1970	C
	Hungary				
3	Egri Bikaver 1979	B		**WHITES**	
				California	
	WHITES		2	Chardonnay, Chateau St. Jean, Robert Young	E
	California		2	Chardonnay, Freemark Abbey 1978	D
3	Chardonnay, Bel Arbres 1979	B	2	Fumé Blanc, Robert Stemmler 1978	C
3	Chenin Blanc, Fetzer 1981	B	2	Johannisberg Riesling, Joseph Phelps, Selected Late Harvest	E
3	Gewürztraminer, Fetzer 1979	C		France	
3	Sauvignon Blanc, Beaulieu 1981	C	2	Bordeaux, Château Bouscaut, Graves 1978	D
	France				
3	Bordeaux, Château La Tour de Bonnet, Entre-Deux-Mers	B			
3	Burgundy, Mâcon Blanc-Villages, Georges Duboeuf 1980	B			
	Germany				
3	Mosel-Saar-Ruwer, Eitelsbacher Marienholz Weingut St. Georg-Hof, Kabinett 1979	B			
	Italy				
3	Orvieto, Villa Banfi Classico Secco 1980	B			
	APÉRITIF/DESSERT WINE				
2	Montilla, Cortina Pedro Ximénez	B			

A Personal Wine Library

The books, magazines, and newsletters listed here represent only a small part of the publishing explosion that has accompanied the increase of interest in wine and wine-drinking. Some excellent writing has been done on the subject. These books and periodicals are well worth considering for your personal library.

GENERAL READING

Fireside Book of Wine, by Alexis Bespaloff. New York: Simon & Schuster, 1977, 445 pages.

Noted wine authority Bespaloff has selected literature, poems, epigrams, essays, stories, journals, diaries, and letters from the world's wine lovers. Over 400 writers are represented in this unique collection.

The Foods and Wines of Spain, by Penelope Casas, introduction by Craig Claiborne. New York: Alfred A. Knopf, Inc., 1982, 416 pages.

An attempt to bring Spain the recognition it deserves for both its food and wines. Contains recipes for Spanish dishes and a comprehensive and extremely informative section on Spain's wines.

Frank Schoonmaker's Encyclopedia of Wine, by Frank Schoonmaker. Revised 7th edition edited by Julius Wile. New York: Hastings House, 1978, 473 pages.

Offers information on the wines of California, France, Germany, Italy, and other wine-producing countries. This reference book contains over 2,000 definitions arranged in alphabetical order. Julius Wile, a noted wine authority, has updated Mr. Schoonmaker's classic book.

Grossman's Guide to Wines, Beers and Spirits, by Harold J. Grossman. Revised by Harriet Lembeck. New York: Charles Scribner's Sons, 1977, 634 pages.

For over 30 years, this book has been acclaimed by people in the alcoholic beverage industry. Of value to the general reader, it has also been used as a textbook in wine appreciation and beverage management courses. It offers comprehensive and detailed information about the origins, production, and characteristics of wine from all over the world.

The Insider's Guide to Wine Basics, by Lucio Sorre and James Wagenvoord. New York: Western Publishing, 1983, 144 pages.

Lucio Sorre, one of the nation's leading winetasters, and wine author James Wagenvoord offer insight on all aspects of wine from the world's wine experts. Tasting and buying tips from over 14 wine-producing countries are included.

Joys of Wine, by Clifton Fadiman and Sam Aaron. Edited by Darlene Geis. New York: Harry N. Abrams, Inc., 1975, 450 pages.

This large, informative volume includes maps of the major wine regions; photographs, paintings, and lithographs; information on understanding wine labels; counsel on wine and food, with menus and recipes; and a treasury of wine-related verses and stories.

New Encyclopedia of Wines and Spirits, by Alexis Lichine. New York: Alfred A. Knopf, Inc., 1978, 716 pages.

Recognized as the most comprehensive book in its field. This work contains hundreds of entries on the wines, spirits, and vineyards of the world.

New Signet Book of Wine, by Alexis Bespaloff. New York: New American Library, 1980, 293 pages.

An outstanding guide to the wines of the world. The book includes information on buying, storing, and serving wine; reading wine labels, and statistics on drinking habits in various countries.

New York Times Book of Wine, by Terry Robards. New York: Times Books, 1976, 467 pages.

The first part of this book tells how wine is made, discusses its enjoyment, and offers suggested wine lists. Part two is an encyclopedia of major vineyards, wines, and winemaking processes.

Winemaking in California, by Ruth Teiser and Catherine Harroun. New York: McGraw-Hill, 1983, 256 pages.

This volume, with a foreword by Leon D. Adams, details the entire history of California's winemaking history in text and photographs.

Wines & Spirits, by Alec Waugh and the Time-Life editors. New York: Time-Life, Inc., 1968, 208 pages.

This extensively illustrated volume contains a wealth of information on wine cultivation, production, and customs throughout the world.

Wines of America, by Leon D. Adams. New York: McGraw-Hill, 1978, 623 pages.

Leon Adams travels across North America, tasting the current vintages, telling the stories of the people who make wine, and researching a 400-year span of American viticulture. There are informative chapters on the wines of Canada and Mexico, kosher wines and winemakers, maps of principal wine districts, and a glossary of wine terms.

World Atlas of Wine: A Complete Guide to the Wines and Spirits of the World, by Hugh Johnson. New York: Simon & Schuster, 1978, 288 pages.

This book, which has been a best-seller in nine languages, features the major vineyards of the world, with descriptions and full-color maps.

RATING THE WINES

Alexis Lichine's Guide to the Wines and Vineyards of France, by Alexis Lichine. Fifth revised edition, New York: Alfred A. Knopf, Inc., 1979, 210 pages.

Regarded as the classic book on French wines, this revised edition embodies Lichine's reexamination of French wine châteaux and vineyards. He rates all the wines from 1929 through 1973, describing the personalities of the winemakers and various wines they produce.

California Wine Label Album, by Terry Robards. New York: Workman Publishing, 1981, 176 pages.

Terry Robards provides his tasting notes about a variety of California wines, accompanied by reproductions of the labels from the wineries mentioned. Space is provided for the reader's notes on the wines as well. Robards is the wine writer for the New York *Times*.

Drinking Wine: A Complete Guide with Ratings, by David Peppercorn, et al. New York: Louis J. Martin & Associates, Inc., 1979, 256 pages.

This is a visual reference guide to the wines that people drink—the tempting, and frequently bewildering, array of bottles available in stores. David Peppercorn is a well-known wine consultant.

Great Vintage Wine Book, by Michael Broadbent. New York: Alfred A. Knopf, Inc., 1980. 432 pages.

This book offers information for both the novice and the connoisseur. It discusses, in detail, good and bad vintages from 1945 to the present, exploring the reasons why they vary. It also contains a color guide that identifies and differentiates between particular wines.

"I rather like bad wine,"
said Mr. Mountchesney;
"one gets so bored with
good wine."
—Benjamin Disraeli,
                Sybil

Pocket Guide to Wine, by Barbara Ensrud. New York: G. P. Putnam's Sons, 1980, 144 pages.

Over 1,500 wines, representing 20 wine regions, are rated in this volume, including mention of essential quality factors, wine laws and history.

Vintage Wine Book, by William S. Leedom. Revised edition. New York: Random House, 1975, 264 pages.

A reference for experienced wine drinkers, and a guide to wines at moderate prices for beginners. Wines of the world are listed and discussed in detail.

Whole-World Wine Catalog, by William I. Kaufman. New York: Penguin Books, 1978, 224 pages.

A reference guide to the world of wines, wine labels, and tastings. This book includes pictures and detailed explanations of 2,500 wine labels from several wine-producing countries, as well as descriptions of the wines they represent.

Wine Buyer's Guide, by Clifton Fadiman and Sam Aaron. New York: Harry N. Abrams, Inc., 1977, 168 pages.

This guide describes the wines of significant American vineyards and the important vine-growing districts of France, Germany, Italy, Spain, and Portugal, and recommends specific wines.

WINE TOURS

The Great Wine Châteaux of Bordeaux, edited by Pamela V. Price and Philip Seldon. New York: Hastings House, 1975, 199 pages.

This guide includes details of wine production techniques, output, personalities, and history in addition to anecdotes, architecture, and a description of the tastes of the wines themselves. Over 80 châteaux are profiled, with color illustrations and reproductions of labels.

Guide to the Wines of the United States, by Dominick Abel. New York: Simon & Schuster, 1979, 160 pages.

Author and former wine columnist Dominick Abel discusses the history and backgrounds of wines and vineyards in the United States. The book includes information on where the wines and grapes originated, and on the types of wine produced in each region of the country.

Pocket Encyclopedia of California Wines, by Bob Thompson. New York: Simon & Schuster, 1980, 128 pages.

An A to Z listing of California wines, vineyards, grapes, labels, and towns. There is a section on wine and food, plus instructions for understanding wine labels and detailed maps of wine regions.

Traveller's Guide to the Vineyards of North America, by William I. Kaufman. New York: Penguin Books, 1980, 203 pages.

This detailed guide to visiting vineyards from New York to California includes information about tours, wine-tasting, and retail sales. Recommendations for visitors include local points of historic, cultural, and scenic interest.

Vino, by Burton Anderson. Boston: Atlantic Monthly Press, Inc., 1980, 568 pages.

Vino is an introduction, a guide, and an homage to Italian vintages and winemakers of Italy's 20 wine-producing regions, with illustrations and maps. Fully indexed.

Wines of California, by Robert Lawrence Balzer. New York: Harry N. Abrams, Inc., 1978, 271 pages.

This book provides information about 128 California vineyards, including history, present owners, and advice about wine in general. It is organized according to the five California wine regions, with detailed maps and color photographs.

Winetaster's Guide to Europe, by Anthony Hogg. New York: E. P. Dutton, Inc., 1980, 256 pages.

For over 20 years, the wine writer Anthony Hogg has played a major role in opening up Continental vineyards to English-speaking visitors. The book lists over 300 vineyards, cellars, and distilleries throughout Europe, briefly discusses their histories, and provides information for visiting them.

COOKING WITH WINE

Entertaining with Wine, by Ruth Ellen Church. Chicago: Rand McNally & Company, 1976, 176 pages.

A cookbook for wine lovers, with 200 recipes, menus for all occasions, and a guide for choosing, serving, and enjoying wine. Also included are color illustrations and an informal section on the wines of the world.

The Wine Book, by James Wagenvoord. New York: Quick Fox, Inc., 1980, 128 pages.

Cut in the shape of a bottle, this guide to major wines of the world includes information on serving and storing wines, recipes for wine-based drinks, hints for choosing the most appropriate wine for any meal, and recipes and tips for cooking with wine.

INDIVIDUAL WINES

Port, by George Robertson. London: Faber and Faber, Ltd., 1978, 188 pages.

This is the first book on port wine in many years, by an author who has spent a lifetime in the trade. It includes a brief history of the wine, how the land, soil, and climate of Portugal make Port possible, how it is made, and advice on serving and drinking Port.

Sherry, by Manual M. Gonzalez. London: Cassell and Company, Ltd., 1972, 237 pages.

A noted authority on Sherry discusses a range of topics, including the chemical change that occurs when grape juice becomes wine, the complex ritual of the *solera*, and the history of the trade. Includes maps and historical photographs of the tools, people, and places involved in Sherry production.

White Wines of the World, by Sheldon and Pauline Wasserman. New York: Stein & Day, 1980, 251 pages.

In dictionary format, white wines are described and classified by taste categories, with advice on serving and drinking. Nearly 1,000 individual entries and cross-references list countries and grape varieties. The Wassermans cover the major wine-producing areas in Europe and the United States.

Wine Diary, by James Wagenvoord. New York: Bobbs-Merrill Company, Inc., 1979, 159 pages.

This book is designed as a fingertip reference to the reader's own tastes. The main section of the book consists of diary pages on which to record the complete history of wine purchases, including tax records for business entertaining, and a record of wine investments.

MAGAZINES, NEWSLETTERS, PUBLICATIONS

Bacchus Data Services
P. O. Box 5973–193
Sherman Oaks, CA 91493
This informed enophile newsletter, published ten times a year, features up-to-date wine-tasting information presented in a unique "Wines at a Glance" format.

A bottle of good wine, like a good act, shines ever in the retrospect.
—Robert Louis Stevenson

California Wine Wonderland
California Wine Institute
165 Post Street
San Francisco, CA 94108
This publication provides a comprehensive listing of California's winery tours.

California Wineletter
P. O. Box 70
Mill Valley, CA 94941
This wineletter is published 23 times a year and contains the latest news on every aspect of the California wine industry, including announcements of wine-related events and updates on grape growth.

Eastern Grape Grower & Wine News
Box 329
Watkins Glen, NY 14891
A news and technical features periodical about winegrowing and winemaking styles and techniques, pertinent east of the Rocky Mountains. There are bimonthly issues and one annual directory of the industry.

Enjoy Wine
111 Bubbling Spring Road
St. Clairsville, OH 43950
A bimonthly newsletter containing consumer-oriented tasting reports from the major wine-producing areas of the world that export wine to the American market; a supermarket wine survey of best buys; and a rating of wines according to their current drinkability.

The Friends of Wine Magazine
2302 Perkins Place
Silver Spring, MD 20910
(301) 588-0980
Les Amis du Vin's popular bimonthly magazine of wine and food has been in existence for 15 years. It contains information on many aspects of the wine world and is a current source of wine news. This leading wine society has about 160 chapters in towns throughout America and arranges some of the best wine tours available in the United States and other wine-producing countries.

Impact Wine & Spirits Newsletter
c/o M. Shanken Communications, Inc.
305 East 53rd Street
New York, NY 10022
This bimonthly newsletter provides marketing, financial, and economic news for the wine and spirits executive.

The Impact Annual Wine Market Review and Forecast
c/o M. Shanken Communications, Inc.
305 East 53rd Street
New York, NY 10022
An inside look at the U.S. wine market, this publication gives an analysis of the significant trends in the marketplace with projections of future sales.

Market Watch
c/o M. Shanken Communications, Inc.
305 East 53rd Street
New York, NY 10022
A monthly publication that analyzes the wine and spirits industry trends and market developments, primarily for marketing and sales personnel.

Moody's Wine Review
6134 Inwood Drive
Houston, TX 77057
This quarterly wine newsletter contains a digest of recent wine books, publications, and articles, and tips on best wine buys.

Robert Finigan's Private Guide to Wines
100 Bush Street
San Francisco, CA 94104
This publication, founded in 1972, includes recommendations and opinions about 250 wines tasted and evaluated by Robert Finigan. Each eight-page issue has advice and information on particular wines, sherries, liquors, cordials, beers, and their regions of origin.

Valley Guide
P. O. Box 655
Pengrove, CA 94951
A biannual catalogue of the Napa Valley with extensive restaurant information featuring complete menus, recreational activities in the area, lodging, shopping, and sightseeing information. Also included is a listing of all Napa vineyards with tour days, locations, and hours.

It's a naïve domestic Burgundy without any breeding, but I think you'll be amused by its presumption.
—James Thurber

Wines and Vines
703 Market Street
San Francisco, CA 94103
A widely read monthly wine magazine containing the current news of the people, places, and happenings in the wine industry. It features an overseas report and import news monthly statistics.

The Wine Register
P. O. Box 6031
San Mateo, CA 94403
A comprehensive up-to-date monthly wine guide focusing on about 2,000 currently available California wines. The information is in a convenient pocket-sized booklet.

The Wine Spectator
TASCO Publishing Corp.
305 East 53rd Street
New York, NY 10022
America's only national wine consumer newspaper is published bimonthly. Up to the minute news on the wine world that includes tasting results, festivals and auctions, investing and collecting new wine releases, as well as tips on serving wine, storing wine, and cooking with wine.

Wine Tour Guide to the East, Midwest, South and Southwest
Association of American Vintners
Box 84G
Watkins Glen, NY 14891
This guidebook lists more than 260 American wineries that are open to the public.

Wines of the World
P. O. Box 530425
Miami, FL 33153
This newsletter is primarily for the wine consumer who wants to learn more about wines, but many people in the trade also subscribe. It features a question-and-answer section.

Index

MASSON LIGHT™

Premium California
LIGHT CHABLIS

A light, white wine. Perfect before, during, and after dinner.
Serve well chilled.

MADE & BOTTLED BY PAUL MASSON
ALCOHOL 7.1% BY VOLUME

CROFT

VINTAGE
CHARACTER
PORT

The
Monterey
Vineyard®

BORDEAUX
750 ml

B&G
FONDÉE EN 1725

RED WINE
ALC. 11% TO 14%
BY VOLUME

1978
SAINT-ÉMILION
APPELLATION SAINT-ÉMILION CONTRÔLÉE

BOTTLED BY
BARTON & GUESTIER
PRODUCE OF FRANCE

AU CHÂTEAU DU DEHEZ
GIRONDE – FRANCE

MEURSAULT
PORUZOT

PRODUCT OF FRANCE

APPELLATION MEURSAULT 1er CRU CONTRÔLÉE
1979
Domaine René Manuel,
Récoltant à Meursault, (Côte-d'Or)

Mis en bouteille et distribué par
BOURÉ-ROI, Négociant-Éleveur à Nuits-Saint-Georges (Côte-d'Or)
BURGUNDY   ALCOHOL 13% BY

GRGICH HILLS

Harvest

Napa Va
JOHANNISBER
1977

Grapes 25% Sugar by Weight · Wine

PRODUCED AND BOTTLED BY GRG
RUTHERFORD, CALIFORNIA ALCOHO

SAUTERNES-APPELLATION CONTRÔLÉE

Château d'Yquem
Lur-Saluces
· 1949 ·
MIS EN BOUTEILLE AU CHÂTEAU

P. GRANDAU 87

Parducci

DOCINO COUNTY

MIS EN BOUTEILLE AU CHATEAU

1er Cru
Classé
en 1855

CHATEAU
RAUSAN-SÉGLA
GRAND CRU CLASSÉ
1976
MARGAUX
APPELLATION MARGAUX CONTRÔLÉE

HOLT FRÈRES & FILS, PROPRIÉTAIRES A MARGAUX (GIRONDE)
DISTRIBUTEUR EXCLUSIF LOUIS ESCHENAUER S.A.
BORDEAUX (GIRONDE)
MARQUE ET BOUTEILLE DÉPOSÉES   PRODUIT DE FRANCE

RED BORDEAUX WINE
Contents: 1 Pint 8.5 Fl. Ozs   Alcohol: 11 % to 12 % by vol.
Shipped by: Paul RIBOU - BORDEAUX, France
Imported by: AUSTIN NICHOLS & Cie Inc. - NEW YORK, N.Y.

1975

DAVID BRUCE
Santa Cruz, California
PINOT NOIR

CHÂTEAU PICHON LONGUEV
LALANDE

SHIPPED AND BOTTLED BY THE CAFÉ

Mirassou
Fleuri

Produced
Jose, C

La Tour Roya
GRAVES

Shipped and Bottled by
CAFÉ ROYAL
LONDON.W.1.
Produce of France

IMBOTTIGLIATO ALL'ORIGINE
NELLE CANTINE DI

MARCA DEPOR
FUORI SANS FINE

DALLA C.V.B. RICASOLI S.p.A.
GAIOLE IN CHIANTI

BROLIO
CHIANTI CLASSICO
DENOMINAZIONE DI ORIGINE CONTROLLATA
RISERVA

CASA VINICOLA
BARONE RICASOLI
FIRENZE - ITALIA
750 ML. (25.4 FL. OZ.)   ALCOHOL 12.7 %E

IMPORTED BY BROWNE VINTNERS CO
NEW YORK, N.Y. - S.F. CA.
SOLE DISTRIBUTORS IN THE U.S.A.

J. PEDRONCELL
SONOMA COUNTY
ENCH COLOMBARD
ALCOHOL 12% BY VOLUME
1978

PRODUCED AND BOTTLED BY
EDRONCELLI WINERY
SONOMA COUNTY, CALIF. ★ BONDED WINERY

Louis M. Martin

ALMADÉN
SAN BENITO

LAMBERTI

FL. 8 FL. OZ.   ALCOHOL 12% BY

SOAVE
DENOMINAZIONE DI ORIGINE CONTROLLATA
CLASSICO · SUPERIORE
DRY WHITE WINE

PRODUCED AND BOTTLED IN ITALY BY CANTINE DI PASTRENGO
LAMBERTI s.p.a.
LAZISE (VERONA) ITALY

VERBAND DEUTSCHER
PRÄDIKATSWEIN-
VERSTEIGERER

Unsere Mitglieder besitzen
Lagen von Weltruf!

V
D P
P

VEREINIGUNG
RHEINGAUER
WEINGÜTER E.V.
Erzeugerabfüllung
A. P. Nr.

Qualitatswein mit Pradikat

1976er SPÄTLESE rosagold
SCHLOSS VOLLRADS

1974
PETRVS
POMEROL
Grand Vin

Mme L P LACOSTE-LOUBAT
PROPRIÉTAIRE A POMEROL (GIRONDE)
MIS EN BOUTEILLES AU CHÂTEAU

APPELLATION POMEROL CONTRÔLÉE